Remaking Chinese Cinema

Critical Interventions
Sheldon H. Lu, general editor

Cinema, Space, and Polylocality in a Globalizing China
Yingjin Zhang

Children of Marx and Coca-Cola: Chinese Avant-garde Art and Independent Cinema
Xiaoping Lin

Uneven Modernity: Literature, Film, and Intellectual Discourse in Postsocialist China
Haomin Gong

Remaking Chinese Cinema: Through the Prism of Shanghai, Hong Kong, and Hollywood
Yiman Wang

CRITICAL INTERVENTIONS

Remaking Chinese Cinema

Through the Prism of Shanghai, Hong Kong, and Hollywood

Yiman Wang

University of Hawai'i Press
Honolulu

Printed in the United States of America
Paperback edition 2014

19 18 17 16 15 14 6 5 4 3 2 1

Critical Interventions
Sheldon H. Lu, general editor

Critical Interventions consists of innovative, cutting-edge works with a focus on Asia or the presence of Asia in other continents and regions. Series titles explore a wide range of issues and topics in the modern and contemporary periods, especially those dealing with literature, cinema, art, theater, media, cultural theory, and intellectual history as well as subjects that cross disciplinary boundaries. The series encourages scholarship that combines solid research with an imaginative approach, theoretical sophistication, and stylistic lucidity.

Library of Congress Cataloging-in-Publication Data

Wang, Yiman, 1972–
Remaking Chinese cinema : through the prism of Shanghai, Hong Kong, and Hollywood / Yiman Wang.
p. cm. — (Critical interventions)
Includes bibliographical references and index.
ISBN 978-0-8248-3607-8 (cloth : alk. paper)
1. Motion pictures—China—History—20th century. 2. Film remakes—China—History and criticism. I. Title. II. Series: Critical interventions (Honolulu, Hawaii)
PN1993.5.C4W278 2013
791.430951—dc23

2012023411

ISBN 978-0-8248-5107-1 (pbk.)

University of Hawai'i Press books are printed on acid-free paper and meet the guidelines for permanence and durability of the Council on Library Resources.

Designed by University of Hawai'i Production Department
Printed by Sheridan Books, Inc.

This book is dedicated to my parents,
who enabled me to explore across the Pacific

We deeply feel that shadow play [or movie, *yingxi* 影戏] is the basic vehicle of social education, the supreme art form, the memoir of modern civilization, and the most effective tool for bridging variant nationalities and dissipating their misunderstanding. . . . We esteem shadow play as the vehicle that delivers the masses from miseries to the happy land [*letu* 乐土].

—Gu Kenfu, "Fakan ci," 1924

Contents

Acknowledgments

> It is the very darkness of memory that allows visual images to come loose from their contexts, forming new combinations, superimposing themselves on each other or finding hidden similarities.
>
> —Mikhail Iampolski, *The Memory of Tiresias*

The conception of this book started with surprise glimpses of points of resemblance, affinity, and dialog between China-made films and Western cinema throughout the twentieth century. These moments of connection inspired me to explore the ways in which such interactions have contributed to the formation and transformation of Chinese-language cinema. Thus, the phenomenon of border-crossing film remakes emerged as the core of my study. To underscore the dialogic relationship both between China and the West *and* between different Chinese-language regions, I evoke a filmic triangle composed of the Hollywood, Shanghai, and Hong Kong film industries. Based on wide historical and geopolitical coverage and extensive research in various archives, this book brings into focus some not so apparent border-crossing connections and constellations that gradually percolated through film history and formed the foundation of a multiaccented Chinese-language cinema.

From its inception to the current book form, this project has undergone continuous "remaking" and indeed is poised to spawn its own "sequels"—triggered by Hollywood's increasing attention to East Asian commercial cinema in the new millennium. Throughout the entire process, Chris Berry has been the guiding spirit who has nourished my intellectual growth with unfailing faith and scintillating suggestions. Yomi Braester and Yingjin Zhang have witnessed every stage of my academic life in America with great care and support. Zhiwei Xiao has tirelessly responded to my queries regarding specific Hollywood films' exhibition and reception in Republican Shanghai.

Indeed, my thinking and writing have benefited tremendously from all my intellectual interlocutors. I am permanently indebted to those who enabled me to launch this project: Jane Gaines inspired me with thought-provoking questions and rigorous feedback. Jing Wang and Ralph Litzinger helped me anchor my work in the thick, messy, and volatile Chinese context. Stan Abe encouraged me to indulge in the reverie of cinematic art. Thomas Lahusen enlightened me with his comparative perspective. Fredric Jameson significantly shaped my argument through his teaching and writing on film, allegory, and utopia.

At Haverford College, my participation in the translation workshop as Andrew Mellon postdoctoral fellow usefully enhanced my understanding of translation in border-crossing film remakes. At UCLA, my graduate seminar on border-crossing film remakes turned out to be a productive crucible where my students and I brainstormed, posed questions, and tested various hypotheses. At the Department of Film and Digital Media of the University of California, Santa Cruz, I received the wisest shepherding from my colleagues Amelie Hastie, Shelley Stamp, Peter Limbrick, Warren Sack, and L. S. Kim, who, in their different capacities, have steered me through times of hesitation, stagnation, and anxiety, not to mention the most suspenseful biannual personnel reviews. I must also thank Lisa Rofel for keeping me focused on the first book (instead of fantasizing about future books) and getting me jumpstarted for the rewriting process. My gratitude also goes to Paul Pickowicz, who generously shared his precious pre-1949 film knowledge as well as materials with me.

For being able to bring out a book predicated on my encounter with firsthand audio-visual and print materials, I must thank my archivist friends. I remember the feel of the crispy pages from nearly a century ago crumbling between my fingers, making me wonder how long they would remain accessible. I also remember the despair of facing a U-matic tape that refused to play in the steaming Beijing summer and having to return a year later to try my luck again. There were occasions of a scrapbook disappearing from the archive when I came back to recheck it and of seeing microfilm racing across the screen, and yet I was not allowed to print the desired pages without a special permit from the collection copyright owner. Fortunately, my archivist friends came to the rescue, helping me secure the ever-receding traces. They made me truly understand the power of collaboration and persistence. To all of you (Yang Yuanying at the Beijing Film Academy, Ainling Wong at the Hong Kong Film Archive, and Erin Lee at Cathay Organization) I owe the material basis of this book. Additionally, I owe my first viewing of *The Sister Flowers from the South* (1939, Hong Kong) (a key film in Chapter 2) to the generous staff at Udine Far East Film Festival in Italy.

Portions of Chapters 3 and 4 were published in *Journal of Chinese Cinemas* 2.1 (2008): 9–21, and *Quarterly Review of Film and Video* 21.4 (2003): 317–326, under the titles "The 'Transnational' as Methodology: Transnationalizing Chinese Film Studies through the Example of *The Love Parade* and Its Chinese Remakes" and "The Phantom Strikes Back—Triangulating Shanghai, Hong Kong and

Hollywood." I thank the publishers for allowing me to use some of the material and to expand it into book chapters.

This book could not have been completed without indispensable support offered by various funding organizations. This includes multiple faculty major grants and research grants from the Arts Research Institute and Committee on Research at UC Santa Cruz; as well as a postgraduate award from University of Hong Kong, which enabled my first trip to the Hong Kong Film Archive; and several International Research Travel Grants from Duke University.

My developmental editor, Anitra Grisales, offered invaluable help in keeping me on track and seeing me through the revision process. In the final stage of book revision, I was fortunate to enlist Sheldon Lu's enthusiastic support. His recommendation of my book to Patricia Crosby at the University of Hawai'i Press was crucial. Working with Ms. Crosby has been a thoroughly enjoyable experience. Her professionalism and unparalleled efficiency have ensured the manuscript's speedy review and the book's timely appearance. I am also grateful to the two readers whose insightful suggestions and positive feedback helped me to strengthen my book and improve its readability. Copy editor Susan Stone and indexer Mary Mortensen put final touches on this book with so much care and patience that I can happily move on to my next project.

Finally, this book congeals a persistent labor of love from my family and friends. My parents from across the Pacific have kept me buoyant with their indefatigable faith. My mother spent half a year in Santa Cruz with me, picking wild berries to make my days of writing "fruitful." Lili Hsieh, Qi Wang, Benjamin Huang, Ai-ru Cheng, Huibing Yan, and Jialing Li came to my rescue when life took an ominous turn. Yike Liu offered godsend superior kitty care when I needed to be away for research. Francis Steen injected lyrical laughter into my life as well as brainstormed with me on the book title. Last but not least, Kitty Flo (aka Maomao)—the little comedian in my life—has kept me entertained and inspired me to look beyond the present toward future projects.

NOTE ON ROMANIZATION

All Chinese proper names are romanized based on Mandarin Chinese pronunciation except where spelling based on Cantonese is established and conventionalized (e.g., Dr. Sun Yat-sen).

Introduction

> Every film is always the bearer of another, a secret film . . . the strong points [of the implicit film] are found in the weak points of the apparent one.
>
> —Raúl Ruiz, *Poetics of Cinema*[1]

In June 2008, DreamWorks' freshly minted animated comedy *Kung Fu Panda 1* opened in multiple countries and regions, including the United States, China, and Hong Kong. By juxtaposing two quintessential icons of "Chineseness"—kung fu and a panda—this animation embodies Hollywood's new trend of chinoiserie characterized by self-conscious appropriation and expropriation of "Chinese elements" (*Zhongguo yuansu* 中国元素). This version of chionoiserie, developed under the aegis of twenty-first-century globalization, simultaneously wowed the Chinese mass audience[2] and alarmed Chinese filmmakers and commentators, who were left excited, inspired, and/or befuddled by, even indignant with, Hollywood's ability to out-Chinese the Chinese with a "China-born, US-raised" (*tusheng yangzhang* 土生洋长) cross-bred film.[3] Interestingly, such anxiety voiced by Chinese critics evaporated at the 2011 release of *Kung Fu Panda 2,* a 3-D sequel that was applauded as "a Chinese animation film made by the United States" (*Meiguo zhizao de Zhongguo donghuapian* 美国制造的中国动画片)."[4]

The confounding authorship surrounding these two animation films signals a major development in border-crossing film culture in cinema's second centennial, namely, Hollywood's increasing investment in commercializing and cinematizing East Asian elements, and East Asia's active engagement with "global Hollywood."[5] Other than appropriating iconic Chineseness (as illustrated in *Kung Fu Panda*), Hollywood has also taken an increasing interest in buying the remake rights of East Asian hit films and producing English versions.[6] This practice has been maligned as yet another instance of Hollywood's hegemony that vampirizes and destroys peripheral film industries. Such criticism is concerned with preserving the authenticity of peripheral cinemas as sites of resistance to global Hollywoodization. However, these critics fail to consider the historical complexity of the practice of film remaking. Indeed, remaking started with film's inception at the end of the nineteenth century and has historically been practiced in peripheral as well as dominant film industries, with a range of ramifications.

This book focuses on an under-studied strain of peripheral and subaltern remaking: namely, Shanghai and Hong Kong remakes of certain Hollywood genre films, and Hong Kong remakes of Shanghai and Hollywood films. I contend that film remaking should not be dismissed as derivative imitation; rather it should be studied as a situation-dependent strategy of negotiation with a cultural and political Other. By tracing the trajectories of cross-Pacific film remaking between Hollywood, Shanghai, and Hong Kong from the 1920s to the present day—encompassing the eras of colonialism, nationalism, postwar socialism, Cold War politics, and, finally, postcolonialism, postsocialism, and globalization—I analyze the ways in which filmic representation inscribes, intersects with, and reconfigures sociopolitical circumstances. I examine how a remake at a different historical conjuncture in a different geopolitical context can begin to anticipate (without necessarily accomplishing) a definitive, new regional or national cinema; analogously, the remake may facilitate the emergence (but does not guarantee the accomplishment) of a collective, location-specific subject positioning. By teasing out the mutual constitution of three domains—film remaking, the border-crossing construction of Chinese national or regional cinema, and the (re)formation of location-specific collective consciousness—this book offers a new framework for reconsidering national cinema and collective subjectivity through the lens of cross-Pacific film remaking.

I use the phrase "location-specific collective consciousness" to designate a sense of subjectivity that evolves on the basis of shared experiences and sentiments associated with a specific location and its translocal geopolitics. Here I follow Yingjin Zhang's emphasis on the translocal and the polylocal in order to problematize the "national" and to rethink the "scale relations" between global, regional, national, provincial, and local "as a set of 'translocal' processes" that involve "multiple places of attachment experienced by highly mobile people."[7] In this spirit, the kind of "collective" I have in mind may include or intersect with the "national," yet it also goes against, beyond, or below it, forming such dimensions as the transnational, the regional, the subnational, the paranational, the supranational, and the antinational, if not all together the postnational.[8] Furthermore, I use "consciousness," "subjectivity," or "subject position(ing)" instead of "identity" in order to highlight the oftentimes inchoate, fluid, and performative nature of the becoming-collective, as opposed to the prescribed, reified, and teleological collective. Such location-specific collective consciousness resists a priori reification and constantly reconfigures itself in response to shifting experiential circumstances.

One key venue for practicing and enacting such location-specific collective consciousness is filmmaking and movie going. More specifically, cross-Pacific film remaking offers a privileged site for examining these issues because it stages ways of becoming different through repetition across a wide spatial and temporal span. It illustrates the intricate dialectic relationship between continuity and divergence, the local Self and the foreign Other, past history and the present response. As such, it helps to shape and reshape location-specific collective consciousness.

In film remaking, production, exhibition, and reception are dynamically conjoined, forming a loop pattern in which reception feeds into and generates new production. Hence, film viewers become filmmakers through active appropriation and re-creation. Furthermore, film remaking scrambles temporality by fusing the past and the future, memory and projection. Such play with temporality telescopes and intertwines different film traditions and practices into an overlayered nodal point of convergence and cinematic *mise en abîme*. Mobilizing the most recent technology and working with different casts, audiences, and settings, cross-Pacific film remaking stages continuous reenactments and renewal in accordance with the shifting and expanding temporal-spatiality throughout cinematic history. The difference that emerges from such reenactments fuels the gestation of location-specific collective positioning.

Remaking Film, Rebirthing Utopia

To understand how film remaking discursively produces localized collective subject positioning, I focus on one central operation: the processes through which a vision or utopia in one film is refigured in its remake(s) and the ways in which such refiguration contributes to projecting a new national/regional cinema and location-specific collective consciousness. My premise here is that film remaking, the construction of national or regional cinema, and the formation of collective self-positioning are fundamentally connected, and that they are structurally analogous with utopia.

As parallel venues, they facilitate each other in the processes of negotiating the Self-Other, center-periphery relationship. This is especially important given the global colonial system and the attendant worldwide power inequity. Within this system, non-Western geopolitical sites (such as Shanghai and Hong Kong) are subjected to layers of marginalization, while their relative positioning also constantly shifts.

Furthermore, these parallel venues share the underlying compulsion of repetition driven by the desire for reinvention and reconfiguration. Compulsion of repetition in psychoanalysis has been associated with trauma that simultaneously demands working through and annuls any definitive resolution. When trauma unfolds as a collective experience, it becomes a collective historical "wound" that reopens and recovers repetitively. The historical "wound" in this current context is associated with the semicolonization of Shanghai and the colonization of Hong Kong. Encountering economic and political subjugation yet enchanted by modern media technology that was simultaneously entertaining and didactic, the early Shanghai and Hong Kong film viewers (some of them assistants to Western filmmakers and exhibitors) gradually embarked upon indigenous filmmaking. In the process of appropriating a Western media technology for the Chinese audience while responding to evolving anticolonial discourses, some of these filmmakers (along with commentators) started to emphasize the importance of building a distinct Chinese cinema (*guopian* 国片) geared toward the Chinese market.

However, local filmmakers and critics disagreed on what constituted national traits, especially with regard to the new medium, and they also had different understandings of the Western impact on Chinese culture and identity. Consequently, their projection of national cinema and national identity necessarily followed what I call an asymptotic curve. That is, even as it strived toward a posited "national" position, this position remained elusive and unreachable owing to the inherent difficulty of defining this position. Such asymptotic approximation without fulfillment fueled the repeated drive to (re)construct a national/regional cinema and (re)formulate collective positioning. Both of these were mediated through the act of film remaking. Overdetermined by the colonial/semicolonial experience and the underlying compulsion of repetition, film remaking, national or regional cinema formation, and collective subject positioning became structurally analogous and mutually constitutive.

The (re)figuration of utopia in the remakes follows a similar asymptotic curve. Etymologically, utopia refers to a place that is nowhere and nonexistent, an unrealizable dream. Its virtuality makes it simultaneously alluring and unattainable. Transliterated into *wutuo bang* (乌托邦) in Chinese, this term has come to be associated with a vacuous pipe dream since the 1990s owing to the loss of social vision following the bankruptcy of communist ideology in China. While Utopia as a philosophical or ideological concept has become deflated in a post-1990s China increasingly saturated by pragmatic materialism and global capitalism, utopia in its vernacular implications remains useful for understanding film remaking in relation to modern China's formation of a collective consciousness.

My use of utopia draws on Ernst Bloch's "hope,"[9] Fredric Jameson's "Utopia,"[10] and Peter Brooks' "as-if proposition" in melodrama.[11] Despite their different agendas and methodologies, all these critics use utopia to designate an anticipatory and projective vision formulated in provisionary terms. Bloch relates utopia to hope, or the "intellectual surplus that went beyond the status quo."[12] In my analysis, I link utopia with the intent to resolve the social contradiction that drives the narrative of the films and their remakes, an intent that brings about a provisionary conclusion and a vision of positive change. What makes the vision alluring is that the exact form and ramifications of the future remain open ended. In other words, the projected utopia necessarily remains elusive, undetermined, and provisionary. As such, it operates as another asymptotic curve, approaching without ever reaching the projected destination. Or, more exactly, the projected destination itself is constantly changing, thus making its accomplishment impossible.

The persistent distance from the vision debunks the notion of teleological history and foregrounds the sociopolitical conditions that circumscribe each utopic attempt. In the Shanghai and Hong Kong contexts, these conditions include the colonial power structure in the first half of the twentieth century and post–Cold War ideology, postcolonialism, and globalization in the latter part of the century up to the present day. Among these ideological structures, China's pre-1949 semicolonial status was reified during the Cold War era to legitimate the communist Chinese government. During the postsocialist era, the emphasis on semicolonialsim has been jettisoned as a symptom of Cold War era panpoliticization. Meanwhile, little attention has been paid to the discourses on semicolonialism in early-twentieth-century China. In this book, I argue that the notions of semicolonialism and colonialism need to be reexamined and reactivated since they are crucial for our understanding of the cultural politics of film remaking between Hollywood, Shanghai, and Hong Kong throughout the twentieth century.

Peripheral Subaltern Film Remaking through the Semicolonial Lens

China between 1842 and 1949 has conventionally been described as a "semicolonial" (*ban zhimindi* 半殖民地) society. In 1842 the British Empire defeated the Qing dynasty in the first Opium War, leading to the Treaty of Nanking—the first unequal treaty between China and the West. This treaty stipulated that Shanghai, along with four other cities, be designated as treaty ports for British merchants and that Hong Kong Island be ceded to Britain as a colony. Nearly a century later, in December 1941, the International Settlement in Shanghai, comprising British and American concessions, came to an abrupt end owing to the eruption of Pacific War and Japan's complete occupation of Shanghai. In 1945, with the defeat of Japan in World War II, the International Settlement was returned to Chinese rule. This situation contrasts with Hong Kong's colonial condition, which began in 1842 and lasted until 1997, when Hong Kong was returned to the mainland Chinese government. During the Cold War era in socialist China, the categories of the "colonial" and the "semicolonial" were ossified, leading to the reductive and dogmatic politicization in all domains of life. Cheng Jihua et al.'s *The History of Chinese Cinema,* published in 1963, exemplifies such a panpolitical approach by disparaging most pre-1949 films for their parasitic nature and slavish imitation of Western capitalist cinema.[13] The exceptions, which were also canonized by the socialist ideology, were films produced under leftist auspices and with leftist participation in the early to mid-1930s and the realistic films made between 1945 and 1949, mostly dealing with the miseries and struggles of the lower classes during and immediately after World War II.

Since the 1980s, critics and historians have been challenging such leftist dogmatism,[14] and beginning in the 1990s, four main interventions have contributed to a revised view of twentieth-century Chinese cinema: (1) reexamining early- to mid-1930s leftist cinema; (2) shifting the terrain of pre-1949 Chinese cinema studies by including nonleftist films; (3) exploring various dimensions of pre-1949 cinema, including gender, urban modernity, connections with other forms of visual culture, literary and theatrical practices, and the wartime reconfiguration of film culture; and, finally, (4) diversifying methodologies by incorporating cultural studies, gender studies, cultural history, and in-depth archival research.[15]

Central to all these efforts is the critique of the communist government's whole-scale repudiation of Western capitalism and the attendant reductive political determinism in treating cultural issues during the Cold War era. To better describe the complex urban culture (including the culture of cinema) in Republican Shanghai (1911–1949), these works tend to veer away from the issue of "semicolonialism" toward concepts such as "cosmopolitanism" and "vernacular modernism."[16] This critical move develops in tandem with the post-1990s postsocialist cultural politics, which has ostensibly replaced the previous revolutionary and anticolonial ideology. Yet, this revisionist turn elides the fundamental question of how exactly Republican cinema (as well as Shanghai's urban culture in general) developed through negotiating (rather than bypassing) the power inequity dictated by global coloniality. Short-circuiting this question would risk depoliticization and missing the opportunity to explore the ways in which material and discursive conditions of semicolonialism shaped Republican Chinese film culture, especially through cross-Pacific film remaking.[17]

To redress this elision, I reexamine the pre-1949 debate on China's semicolonialism as the political and discursive condition under which specific strategies of film production and consumption were developed. Unlike the dogmatic political label ordained by the postrevolutionary Chinese government, "semicolonialism" started as a much debated and multivalent notion. In 1924, Dr. Sun Yat-sen (1870–1925), the founder of the Republic of China, called for a distinction between subcolonialism and semicolonialism. "Subcolony," or *ci zhimindi* (次殖民地), a word coined by Sun, signaled China's subordination by multiple Western countries. According to Sun, China's subcolonial situation was even worse than that of Korea (exclusively colonized by Japan) or Vietnam (exclusively colonized by France) because a subcolony was enslaved by multiple countries without the benefit of being cared for by a full-time master in a time of crisis. Because of this, Sun argues, to call China a "semicolony" would be self-delusive.[18] Sun's term, "subcolony," was soon adopted by vernacular social and cultural discourses. In 1926, Lu Mengshu, an important Shanghai film critic, described China as an "oppressed subcolony" (*ci zhimindi*), and he urged the Chinese filmmakers to give up the "static" or "quiescent" (*jing* 静) attitude that had become a national trait and instead to deploy proactive "neoheroism" (*xin yingxiong zhuyi* 新英雄主义).[19]

By the 1930s, however, Sun's argument was turned upside down when the term "semicolonial" (*ban zhimindi*) became a more common diagnosis of the subjugation of Shanghai (and China in general). Denoting a lesser degree of colonization, "semicolonial" allowed China-centered critics to privilege Shanghai over complete colonies, such as Hong Kong, India, and the Southeast Asian regions. This constructed hierarchy precipitated long-standing contentions between Shanghai and Hong Kong in cultural, economic, and sociopolitical domains. The prefix "semi" also served to position China at a crucial forking point where it could either lose sovereignty and slip into total colonization or regain independence and ascend to the status of an independent modern nation-state.

The debate on subcolonialism versus semicolonialism suggests that semicolonialism did not start as a homogenous ideology, but rather as a tentative diagnosis driven by a political agenda that was subjected to constant reevaluation. These discourses significantly shaped filmmakers' and reviewers' understanding of film's sociopolitical functions and the directions of local filmmaking. It is therefore important that we reenergize the political valences of subcolonial and semicolonial discourses for the study of cross-Pacific film remaking. Only by so doing can we fully grasp the power inequity that subtended Chinese cinematic "modernity" or "cosmopolitanism" in the early twentieth century. This power inequity continues into our contemporary era of globalization and becomes a "power geometry," which means that global movements and interconnections affect different social groups and individuals in different ways.[20] Thus, the differential experiences of modernity and globalization based on one's class, gender, racial, ideological, and geopolitical positions in the power structure are significant not only in studying twentieth-century Chinese remakes of Hollywood, but also for understanding twenty-first-century Hollywood remakes of East Asian cinema.

The underlying power inequity not only necessitates and enables cross-Pacific film remaking, but also shapes the strategies of remaking. The strategies of film remaking in subcolonial or semicolonial China and in colonial Hong Kong constitute what I describe as a mode of "subaltern" articulation. For Antonio Gramsci and Gayatri Spivak, the "subaltern" refers to classes that are not only physically but also mentally subordinated by hegemony. The subaltern have "limited or no access to . . . cultural imperialism," occupy "a space of difference," and cannot speak, since the voice of the subaltern is destined to be muted or displaced in the available dialogic field.[21]

In my context, the subaltern includes filmmakers in semicolonial Shanghai and colonial Hong Kong who started as audiences of dominant cinemas, through which they constantly negotiated their peripheral positioning. Instead of affirming their subordinate mentality in the colonial system, however, my analysis demonstrates their efforts and capacity to develop strategies of filmmaking and remaking. My intention is not to romanticize the subaltern position, but rather to explore heterogeneous strategies of negotiation developed from the subaltern position in response to specific geopolitical and filmic situations. I consider the subaltern to be a position occupied by a social collective, or, more precisely, a becoming-collective, that is partially or completely denied sovereignty and agency yet strives to constitute itself through practices such as film (re)making. To the extent that the coming-into-being of the collective is circumscribed by its sociopolitical subjugation, such subjugation becomes the very condition for developing "situated agency" in the power hierarchy. By "situated agency," I emphasize two things. First, I affirm the desire and necessity of achieving a collective subjectivity from a subaltern position. Second, I argue that such agency is antithetical to the liberal notion of individual will, choice, and freedom, for it is emphatically contingent upon the specific situation and derived from constant negotiation and strategization vis-à-vis the power hierarchy.[22]

It is important to note that Shanghai and Hong Kong filmmakers have historically occupied the subaltern position in different ways. In the first part of the twentieth century, semicolonial Shanghai was subaltern vis-à-vis the imperialist West and Japan, while colonial Hong Kong was perceived as inferior (thereby rendered subaltern) in relation to both Shanghai and the West by China-centered critics. According to Wong Wang-chi, a contemporary Hong Kong cultural critic, pre-1949 Shanghai writers and critics tended to see Hong Kong as the colonized margin without realizing their own marginalized position as a treaty port.[23] In other words, even though Western-educated Chinese intellectuals saw Shanghai cinema as artistically primitive in comparison to Western cinema, they still considered it a notch higher than Hong Kong cinema, which was deemed ideologically conservative and artistically crude.

Nevertheless, this pecking order experienced a dramatic reversal in the second half of the twentieth century. During the Cold War, Mao's People's Republic of China became the political rival of the capitalist bloc, whereas Hong Kong was developing into Britain's crown colony and one of Euro-America's last Asian posts. As China largely confined its filmic interactions to socialist countries, Hong Kong film companies (Shaw Brothers and Cathay in particular) actively continued and expanded their connections with Europe, America, Japan, and Southeast Asia.[24] Consequently, Hong Kong developed into a major film kingdom in Asia. The late 1970s ushered in another twist when China's economic reform launched by Deng Xiaoping eventually led Shanghai to reclaim its pre-1949 glamor and resume its "kinship" as well as its rivalry with Hong Kong. The realignment between Shanghai and Hong Kong was further complicated by Hong Kong's handover to China in 1997. Whereas some critics see Hong Kong as being sandwiched between and repressed by two colonial powers (Britain and China) (*jiafeng lun* 夹缝论),[25] others, especially those based in Hong Kong, critique what they see as Hong Kong's capitalist fantasy of northward colonization (*beijin xiangxiang* 北进想象). They are concerned with Hong Kong's exploitation of mainland China's cheap labor and market even as its sovereignty was apparently annexed to the Chinese government in 1997.[26]

All of these circumstances have contributed to the reversal of the early-twentieth-century order of subalternity. In filmmaking, the contemporary Hong Kong industry, boasting cutting-edge technology, ample financing, and greater creative latitude, has increasingly turned to China for actors, location shots, and an expanded market.[27] Consequently, contemporary Chinese commercial cinema and pop culture have been significantly reshaped by Hong Kong's commercial practices. Furthermore, Hong Kong gangster, action, and horror genres have become so popular that American filmmakers have increasingly appropriated selected Hong Kong elements[28] in addition to remaking box office hits such as *Infernal Affairs* (dir. Wai-keung Lau, Siu Fai Mak, 2002) and *The Eye* (dir. Oxide Pang, Danny Pang, 2002).

The constant reshuffling of the order of subalternity underscores its historical contingency, which further complicates the Shanghai and Hong Kong filmmakers and remakers' situated agency. By studying subaltern remaking as a situation-dependent practice, my study departs from current scholarship that emphasizes film remaking as a postmodern game.[29] Such scholarship has primarily focused on Hollywood remakes of French and other European cinemas, with little attention to the cross-Pacific filmic transposition.[30] Its agenda is, in Mazdon's words, to replace the "original"/"copy" binary with "circles of intertextuality and hybridity."[31] My task is not just to debunk the binary of the original and the copy, the high and the low, but, more importantly, to explore the cultural and political ramifications of the subaltern copy per se. Evoking Michel de Certeau's notion of "textual poaching,"[32] which emphasizes readers' or viewers' active interpretation and resignification of a media text (independent of the text's intended meaning), I understand subaltern remaking not just as a manifestation of de facto power (as Hollywood remakes tend to imply) or a postmodern game of transformation and intertextuality, but also as a vehicle for appropriating power and reshuffling the power geometry, even if it simultaneously borrows from, depends on, and partakes in the existing power structure.

Politics of Allegorical Representation

To discuss the political efficacy of subaltern film remaking, we need to address two questions. First, what exactly is the relationship between the realm of representation (or remaking in the current context) and the sociopolitical conditions under which a remake is produced? And, second, in what ways might the figural representations acquire political efficacy (such as the capacity to constitute alternative collective subject positioning)? The key to these questions is not only to acknowledge that a text (or film) is inevitably imprinted by its time and space, but also to scrutinize the extent to which a film may in turn reconfigure the sociopolitical structure.

I describe this dual direction of imprinting in terms of allegory as it pertains to modern technologies of reproduction (of which filmmaking and remaking are perfect examples). In his seminal treatise on modern artistic work, Walter Benjamin points out the lack of authenticity and aura in reproductions, for "[e]ven the most perfect reproduction of a work of art is lacking in one element: its presence in time and space, its unique existence at the place where it happens to be."[33] Yet, he does admit that a photograph, enabled by none other than technologies of reproduction, is "seared" by its immediate context (the Here and Now).[34] It is the "the tiny spark of contingency, of the Here and Now," or reality-on-the-spot, in short, that inextricably stitches the photograph into a unique, present time and space. The act of searing (or what I call imprinting) may literally result from the physical process of light being reflected from an object, penetrating the camera obscura, burning the emulsion on the negative, and then being rendered into a positive image through chemical processes. Yet "searing" also offers a trope for conceptualizing the interlocked, even potentially violent manners in which the contingent geopolitical conjuncture impinges upon the filmic form (as well as content). If a photograph or a film inevitably results from being "seared" by the "the tiny spark of contingency, of the Here and Now," then to decrypt the film's "expressive contingency" in relation to "social-historical dynamics" entails a "forensic" or an "archeological" reading, as Paul Willemen argues.[35]

Different from Willemen's formulation that implies a cryptic and potentially violent relationship between an artistic work and its historical and geopolitical circumstances (the artistic work seen as akin to the remains of a crime), Fredric Jameson and Ismail Xavier deploy the concept of allegory to highlight the political subtext inherent in the imprinting process. In his study of Third World literature as national allegory, Jameson describes allegory as crystallizing "a specifically political resonance" of a cultural work.[36] Ismail Xavier goes further to argue that a film is allegorically related to its geopolitical circumstances and is "situated in its own time" rife with "ambiguities and contradictions."[37] A film's allegorical relationship with its time and geopolitics, therefore, is manifested in the ways it registers the latter's ambiguities and contradictions. To the extent that the film serves as a textual attempt to address geopolitical and ideological "ambiguities and contradictions," the filmic representation also foregrounds a "crisis of representation," thus calling into question the possibility of representation.[38] In other words, a film does not simply re-present or mirror geopolitics in the mimetic manner; rather, it must engage with existing representational conventions and generate specific strategies of representation (or figuration) in order to address and allegorize its geopolitical ambiguities. Thus, the resulting film is imprinted or (violently) "seared" by its geopolitics in an allegorical manner.

Conversely, the film, mobilizing specific strategies of representation, also helps to generate new geopolitical and discursive coordinates that conduce to different modes of subject positioning. In so doing, the film acquires political efficacy. Using the heterogeneous makeup of Chinese cinema as an example, Chris Berry spells out precisely the discursively *constitutive* power of cinematic representation.[39] Instead of assuming an a priori national agency that produces an easily recognizable national cinema, Berry argues that the national is discursively reiterated and pluralized through region-specific filmmaking practices that both intersect and conflict with each other. I extend Berry's study and argue that filmmaking and remaking lead not only to national agency, but also to other collective subject positions such as the regional, the antinational, the subnational, the supranational, and the paranational.

Furthermore, film remaking is not only imprinted by and constitutive of extrafilmic and geopolitical circumstances, but also explicitly engages with one or more predecessor film text(s) on the formal, technical as well as thematic levels. As such, film remaking self-consciously explores the relationship between the representational form and geopolitics, thus offering an ideal platform for studying the cultural-political efficacy of forms of (re)presentation.

In this book, I focus on one specific (re)presentational form as a means of structuring my study of cross-Pacific remakes: genre. A film genre is inherently conducive to remaking to the extent that it turns on a relatively consistent yet constantly mutating representational formula that governs the entire feedback loop of production, exhibition, reception, and reproduction. Additionally, my selection of genre as the basis of remaking is inspired by Jameson's understanding of genre not simply as a given coded representation (or as representational codes), but more as a form that is "apprehended as content."[40] As Jameson explains, the generic form necessarily inscribes and manifests politics (or content) because it embodies "*a formal conjuncture* through which the 'conjuncture' of coexisting modes of production at a given historical moment can be *detected and allegorically articulated.*"[41] The coexisting modes of production are indicative of social contradictions, or what Xavier calls social ambiguities.

As a form "apprehended as content," the genre constantly develops specific representational strategies for the purpose of managing and resolving social contradictions and ambiguities. This becomes more obvious when a genre travels from one geopolitical context to another, registering and addressing different social contradictions. Encountering the "crisis of representation" caused by the traveling process, genre necessarily becomes destabilized, hybridized, and reformulated.

In my study, I see genre not only as related to forms of representation, but also as speaking to and cultivating modes of reception (or viewing habits). It functions as an interactive map that guides us to anticipate, discern, and comprehend the specific filmic mediation of various vectors of geopolitical contradictions and resolutions. Since genre-specific representational strategies arise from staging and managing specific social contradictions (according to Jameson), to remake a genre film means to innovate new strategies in order to register shifting geopolitics and actively reconfigure it. This process in turn fosters a new horizon of reception and its attendant collective subject positioning.

Structure: Melodrama, Singsong Drama, Operetta Film, and Horror

I focus on four broadly defined genres, each genre consisting of a Western formula and a comparable Chinese counterpart. They are melodramas (and family ethics drama, or *jiating lunli ju* 家庭伦理剧), musicals (and singsong drama, or *gechang pian* 歌唱片), operetta films (and Western-costume Cantonese opera film, or *xizhuang ju* 西装剧), and horror films (*kongbu pian* 恐怖片). Each genre remake revolves around a major social issue or contradiction that seeks a resolution in the form of a utopic vision. My concern is not just how each issue is represented in a genre, but how a genre and its remakes make the issue representable in different ways, or how the issue gets obscured or foregrounded through different strategies of representation. My guiding questions are: What strategies of representation emerge in the process of border-crossing remaking? With what utopic implications? And how does the utopic thrust suggest an emerging collective subject positioning?

By comparing the utopic visions in remakes with those in their predecessors, all drawn from the above four broadly defined genres, I critically contextualize and politicize the transtemporal and transspatial filmic trajectories. My goal is not simply to compare and contrast the utopic visions, to blur the high and the low, or to rehearse the argument of postmodern simulacrum. Rather, I am more interested in uncovering geopolitical politics at the spatial level and the politics of memory (and reenactment) at the temporal level. Both the spatial and the temporal dimensions are inherent in cross-Pacific film remaking, where the reception of films from different times and spaces generates new communities of spectators, precipitating new rounds of reception and production.

I understand the continuous transspatial and transtemporal practices in terms of *Nachleben* (afterlife) and *Urgeschichte* (prehistory), offered by Walter Benjamin. Taking the cue from Benjamin, I suggest that the predecessor films do not simply elicit the anxiety of influence for the remakes; rather, they embody an *Urgeschichte* that needs to be rewritten and fulfilled through remakes (or *Nachleben*).[42] Importantly, the afterlife fulfills its predecessor not by mimicking it, but rather by intersecting with and reorienting it, thereby developing and fulfilling what Raúl Ruiz calls the "secret film" embedded in it.[43] To put it more strongly, by reworking or even reversing the predecessor film, and denaturalizing its strategies of representation, the remake not only *bears* and brings forth a secret film embedded in its predecessor, but also potentially *bares* and undermines the predecessor's ideological premise and structural principle.

To remake a film is therefore to critically engage in dialog with that film, with the goal of producing a new vision through reversioning. To quote Walter Benjamin again, "To articulate the past historically does not mean to recognize it 'the way it really was.' It means to *seize hold of memory as it flashes up at a moment of danger.*"[44] In my context, it means that a film remake does not restore the predecessor film as it was, but rather repurposes it for emerging and emergency situations, or moments of danger. Such moments of danger have permeated the colonial, Cold War, and postcolonial eras throughout the twentieth century in Chinese-language regions. By striving to seize hold of and reset (or respatialize) a re-membered film, the peripheral and subaltern Chinese remakes reconfigure the previous utopic projection, thereby contributing to fostering alternative, situated collective subject positions.[45] I map out these complicated processes and strategies in four chapters, each dealing with a genre and its cross-Pacific remaking.

I start with three maternal melodramas: *Stella Dallas* (dir. Henry King, 1925), *The Goddess* (*Shennü*) (dir. Wu Yonggang, 1934, Shanghai), and *Rouge Tears* (*Yanzhi lei*) (dir. Wu Yonggang, Chen Pi, 1938, Shanghai/Hong Kong). They all narrate the ultimate disappearance of a lower-class mother who sacrifices her own interests and relinquishes her child to the more respectable patriarchal figure. Simultaneously virtuous (embodying selfless maternal love) and abject (being a woman of bad taste or an illegal streetwalker), the lower-class mother poses a representational dilemma. That is, how can maternal melodrama—a genre that privileges virtuous femininity and normalizes the middle-class, nuclear home space—portray a mother who is inextricably mired in moral decrepitude and illicit female sexuality and desire? This representational dilemma is key to understanding Shanghai and Hong Kong remakes in the mid- to the late 1930s, when social problems and Chinese national politics tended to be coded in terms of gender politics.

A major factor that precipitated the prioritization of Chinese nationalism during this period was the escalating Japanese invasion. Indeed, not only Chinese politics but also the Chinese film industry were significantly reshaped by this event. It experienced decentralization from an increasingly Japan-occupied Shanghai to other regions, including Hong Kong and hinterland China. Meanwhile, the industry was also undergoing the difficult transition from silent to sound technology. The rapidly shifting geopolitics and filmmaking conditions led the Shanghai and Hong Kong remakes to adopt opposite strategies of representation, namely, elliptical sketch in *The Goddess* and elaboration (or what I call "excessive mimesis") in *Rouge Tears*. These strategies resulted in divergent utopic visions in the two films, which reveal different ways of treating the core sociopolitical issue, that is, the gendered experiences of urban colonial modernity and nationalism. The juxtaposition of the Shanghai and Hong Kong remakes also raises the issue of Hong Kong's locality, which is implicated though not narrativized or thematized in the Hong Kong–made remake. Relatedly, it invites us to consider the emerging southern Chinese cinema (*Hua'nan dianying*) vis-à-vis the more dominant Shanghai cinema at this historical conjuncture of political and filmic reconfiguration.

Chapter 2 continues to study the interregional production of the location-specific Chinese-language cinemas by examining a set of singsong "sisterhood" films—a highly popular genre that hybridizes musical and melodrama, thereby appealing to its audience on the acoustic as well as dramatic level. To examine the remaking of this genre, I interweave gender and class issues, as dramatized in four films: *Sister Flowers* (*Zimei hua*) (dir. Zheng Zhengqiu, 1933, Shanghai), *The Sister Flowers from the South* (*Nanguo zimei hua*) (dir. Li Bin, Liang Chen, 1939, Hong Kong), *The Happy Reunion* (*Xin zimei hua*) (dir. Hu Peng, 1962, Hong Kong), and *Stage Sisters* (*Wutai jiemei*) (dir. Xie Jin, 1964, Shanghai). The first three films center on twin sisters, whereas the last replaces the biological bond with symbolic sisterhood as a sociopolitical relationship. All four films deploy the sisters' separation and reunion as a vehicle for staging domestic and social contradictions and structural shifts. In the four sisterhood films, gender is consistently foregrounded, while the issue of class conflict is alternately obscured or highlighted. The different strategies of managing the two issues in each film suggest the films' radically different political positions, which are in turn determined by 1930s (semi)colonial and 1960s Cold War geopolitics in Shanghai and Hong Kong. By projecting divergent visions of domestic reunion and social reconfiguration, these films become imprinted by their specific geopolitics and strive to articulate situated collective subject positions at different historical conjunctures. Each remake reworks and repurposes its predecessor film(s) through what I call the act of "re-version."

Chapter 3 takes on a fantasy genre, the operetta film (or Western-costume Cantonese opera film), and examines the significant ways in which the exotic "foreign" Other constructs the local Self in the 1930s and the 1950s. The films I analyze are *The Love Parade* (dir. Ernst Lubitsch, 1929, Paramount), its 1930s Shanghai operatic and film adaptations, and the 1957 Hong Kong Cantonese opera film *My Kingdom for a Husband* (*Xuangong yanshi*, lit. Romance in the Jade Palace). The 1957 Hong Kong film version was directed by Zuo Ji, Hong Kong's veteran Cantonese film director who also remade *Scaramouche* (dir. George Sidney, 1952) and *Love Me or Leave Me* (dir. Charles Vidor, 1955). In this chapter, I examine how Lubitsch's "internal foreigner" perspective (along with the use of exotic, fantastic mise-en-scène) is translated for 1930s and 1950s Cantonese-speaking audiences. The remakes' privileging of the exotic foreign Other has an important implication. It posits a strategy of remaking that is antithetical to pure domestication and instead explores self-foreignization. This furnishes a new perspective for our understanding of cross-Pacific film remaking, national/regional cinema construction, and situation-based subaltern positioning. It demonstrates that the (re)formation of the local Self hinges on what Lawrence Venuti would call the "foreignizing translation,"[46] which entails violent and awkward encounter and juxtaposition between incommensurable elements that resist assimilation and simple hybridization.

In the last chapter, I switch from the spatial Other to the temporal Other by studying the remaking of the horror genre. I analyze the (dis)figuration of traumatic past history and the ways in which it impacts and shapes the present. The films in question are *The Phantom of the Opera* (dir. Rupert Julian, 1925, Universal Pictures), *Song at Midnight* (*Yeban gesheng*) (dir. Maxu Weibang, 1937, Shanghai), and *The Phantom Lover* (*Xin yeban gesheng*) (dir. Ronny Yu, 1995, Hong Kong). The traumatic history in these films is crystallized in the image of horror: the disfigured phantom who emerges from the past and whose disembodied voice both inspires and haunts his disciple in the present. The phantom's voice is significant in two ways. On the literal level, it reflects the different sound recording techniques available at diverse historical moments. On the allegorical level, it registers semicolonial and prepostcolonial tensions in Shanghai and Hong Kong respectively. The tension between the phantom teacher's ventriloquism and the disciple's (coerced) vocal mimesis allegorizes a twofold subaltern negotiation: the negotiation of the present with the historical past and the Self's negotiation with the Other.

The meanings of the "past" and the "Other" vary significantly from late-1930s Shanghai to mid-1990s Hong Kong. In the process of grappling with the past to achieve a utopic vision of the future, the Shanghai remake, released on the eve of the Second Sino-Japanese War, redresses historical trauma by affirming history's mandate over the present. For its part, the 1995 Hong Kong remake, made in the midst of the pre-1997 collective anxiety, emphatically asserts the present's independence (as embodied by the defiant disciple), yet in the meantime acknowledges the present's inevitable intertwining and reconciliation with the past. From the phantom teacher's ventriloquism of the disciple in the Shanghai remake to the disciple's reverse-ventriloquism and mimesis of the teacher in the Hong Kong remake, we witness a subtle power shift from the past to the present, and from the historical "Other" to the present "Self." The two remakes' different figurations of history speak to the complexities of Shanghai's semicolonial and Hong Kong's prepostcolonial identity politics.

To conclude the book, I turn to the recent and unfolding phenomenon of Hollywood's remaking of East Asian popular genres, including horror, romance, and gangster movies from Japan, South Korea, and Hong Kong. Does this new trend complete the circle, bringing cross-Pacific film remaking from the margin back to the center, thus suspending Hollywood's hegemony through its unprecedented acknowledgement of East Asian cinema? Or does this entail yet another round of Hollywood colonization in the form of misreading, usurping, and high-handed, unfair competition with East Asian cinema, as many critics and East Asian cinema fans have worried? On the one hand, the full-circle account suggests illusory confidence in East Asia's soft power, failing to recognize that such apparent empowerment is ultimately buttressed by Hollywood patronage and authority, and is allowed only to the extent that East Asian films abide by Hollywood's rules. On the other hand, the unnuanced discourse of Hollywood colonialism betrays a misplaced desire for pure, locally grown films originating from East Asian countries, a desire that denies the latter's participation in producing global commercial cinema. It also fails to acknowledge the new roles that East Asian filmmakers and artists are carving out through the creative/critical interventions they have introduced into global flows. Both accounts therefore miss the opportunity to use this recent development to understand the intricate strategies and cultural politics of cross-Pacific film/media interactions that are unfolding under globalization.

Instead of seeing Hollywood as either the mecca of globalization or the nemesis of East Asian local/regional film cultures, I emphasize the situation-based comparative approach, which guides this entire book. This approach is sensitive to the shifting border politics and politics of memory inherent in translational and transfilmic practices. Given the expanding interactions between ever-dominant Hollywood and increasingly important East Asian cinemas, cross-Pacific film remaking leads to a complex repertoire of negotiation strategies characterized by the interplay of domestication and foreignization. Since contemporary Hollywood remakes tend to appear at the heels of their East Asian predecessors (contrary to some of the case studies in the first several chapters, which often span several decades), the relationship between "prehistory" and "afterlife" is not so much temporal continuation as coeval cross-referencing. Thus, the positions from which the films are made and remade do not replace each other, as the new for the old, the advanced for the backward, or even simply neocolonial globalization replacing subaltern localism.

Rather, the almost simultaneous availability of the films and their remakes combined with proliferating portable interactive medium formats such as DVD and Blu-ray restructures global film reception, complicating the circuit of competition and dialog. Within this circuit, postcolonial politics, critical cosmopolitanism, and the global capitalist economy intertwine with each other to produce flexible viewing positions that exceed national confines and the attendant Self-Other, local-foreign binary structure. To understand the cultural politics of contemporary Hollywood remaking of East Asian popular cinema and cross-Pacific filmic flows in general, one must trace the shifting positions of production, reception, and intervention in order to examine the ways in which these positions have reinforced or transformed the power structures in the global film culture since the early twentieth century.

To accomplish this task, we must place the recent Hollywood remaking of East Asian popular cinema in the context of twentieth-century cross-Pacific remaking, which has produced positions of production and reception that are hierarchical without being necessarily oppositional, dialogical without being necessarily equal. Such cross-Pacific remaking begins with early- to mid-twentieth-century East Asian borrowings from Western cinemas (especially Hollywood), which give rise to a spectrum of strategies of border-crossing translation and remediation. These strategies have played a crucial role in (re)fashioning national and regional cinemas, and (re)configuring location-specific collective subject positions. The same issues continue to drive and galvanize important cultural and political debates in our era of globalization, as epitomized by discourses on contemporary Hollywood remaking. With this, let us rewind to the early twentieth century, when the history of cross-Pacific remaking began to unfold, with far-reaching ramifications.

CHAPTER 1

The Goddess

Tracking the "Unknown Woman" from Hollywood through Shanghai to Hong Kong

Maternal melodramas featuring self-sacrificial mothers abound in the history of world cinema. From classic Hollywood women's films to Lars von Trier's new-millennium musical drama *Dancer in the Dark* (2000), the mother figure works tirelessly for her child only to eventually withdraw herself from the child's life in order to secure a prosperous future for him or her.[1] In this chapter, I trace the Shanghai and Hong Kong remaking of an exemplary Hollywood maternal melodrama, *Stella Dallas,* in the 1930s. Instead of rehashing the feminist critique of the mother figure's marginalization, I explore why the very attempt to present virtuous, self-effacing motherhood in melodrama entails a crisis of representation. I describe the strategies of representation that emerge from the Shanghai and Hong Kong remakes' negotiation with this crisis of representation and how these strategies of representation allegorize the remakes' respective historical and geopolitical circumstances while enabling certain utopic visions of a different social structure. Furthermore, this chapter traces the transnational/transregional constitution of local cinema, including Cantonese cinema (*Yueyu dianying* 粤语电影) and southern Chinese cinema (*Hua'nan dianying* 华南电影), before they became what we know as Hong Kong cinema today.

Stella Dallas (dir. Henry King, 1925), a melodrama that has been remade several times in America (the most famous being King Vidor's 1937 sound remake), features a lower-class mother in a small town in post–World War I Massachusetts who gives her daughter up to her former husband—a well-respected man living in New York and now married to a refined upper-class lady. By relinquishing her daughter, the mother hopes to secure the daughter's marriage into the upper class, which means upward social mobility. At the end of the film, the mother stands outside a well-lit window on a rainy night, watching her daughter's wedding ceremony. She then turns around and walks toward the audience with an ecstatic smile.

In 1927, the Shanghai film magazine *Yin xing* (The Movie Guide) listed this film, its title translated as *Yanzhi lei* (Rouge Tears), as one of the top ten Hollywood movies of 1926.[2] Over ten years later, in 1938, *Yanzhi lei* appeared again as the title of a film made in Hong Kong by Wu Yonggang (Mandarin Chinese version) and Chen Pi (Cantonese version). This film's resonance with Henry King's *Stella Dallas* and even with King Vidor's 1937 remake was subtle yet undeniable. The ending similarly shows a mother (this time a 1930s Chinese streetwalker recently released from prison) witnessing her child's (this time her son's) engagement party from outside a window on a snowy day before she disappears into the white void.

Rouge Tears is also an explicit remake of Wu Yonggang's 1934 directorial debut, *The Goddess* (*Shennü*). Unlike the American mother Stella Dallas, whose stigma has to do with her working-class background, the mother in Wu's two films is not just a worker, but also an illegal sex worker (or *an chang* in Chinese), euphemistically known as a *shennü*, or "goddess." In *The Goddess*, the prostitute-mother's plan is to provide her son with a modern education so that he can have a respectable life. This plan is thwarted by the communal discrimination against her, which leads to the son being expelled from school. Her second plan, to relocate with her son and start from scratch, also fails, when a local thug steals all her savings (her son's education funds) (a narrative twist that is uncannily echoed in *Dancer in the Dark*). In a fit of despair and anger, she confronts the thug and accidentally kills him, for which she is sentenced to twelve years in prison. While imprisoned, she entrusts her son to the righteous male school principal, who promises to provide her son with a good education and to tell him that his biological mother is "dead." Having relinquished her son to a respectable father figure, the mother imagines her son happy and then contentedly closes her eyes to the camera (and the audience), bringing the film to a close.

Wu's self-remake, *Rouge Tears* (1938), shot in Hong Kong four years later, when the Second Sino-Japanese War had recently broken out in China, largely reprises the narrative of *The Goddess*, yet also adds a "sequel" section. Twelve years later, the now-aged mother is released from jail on a snowy day and has the opportunity to witness her son's engagement party through the window of the school principal's house. Reassured of her son's good prospects, the mother leaves contented. Her self-sacrifice for her son's interests embodies traditional gender-sexual politics that privileges male-centered education while also dovetailing with the early-twentieth-century discursive call for a new generation of citizens. This new generation shoulders the task of rejuvenating semicolonial China; its interests are aligned with those of the nation-state. To achieve the nation-strengthening project, it is necessary to produce a new citizenry (often gendered male) through modern education. Thus, a traditional familial-social emphasis on male-centered education acquires new urgency and justification in modern China's struggle to transcend its economic and political subjugation by the West and Japan.

Despite the narrative similarity between *The Goddess* and *Rouge Tears,* the latter has been largely obscured or occasionally mentioned only to be dismissed as Wu's minor work. The silent predecessor, *The Goddess,* in contrast, has been canonized as a leftist milestone and unanimously praised for its artistic accomplishments. Considered exemplary of Chinese silent cinema that emerged from the early- to mid-1930s golden era, *The Goddess* has been released on DVD with English subtitles and a new score by the San Francisco Silent Film Festival in 2004 and by University of Hong Kong Press in 2005. The film is also available for high-quality streaming at archive.org.[3] Together these factors have made *The Goddess* the most popular Chinese silent film with international art house and academic viewers and its leading star, Ruan Lingyu (1915–1935), the best-known silent-era Chinese actress for Western film scholars.

Indeed, Ruan Lingyu's depiction of the tragic mother in this film has been universally celebrated as the soul of the film. Additionally, her suicide on March 8, 1935, in the prime of her life, which uncannily mirrored the fate of many of her screen personae, precipitated heated debate that has since fueled public speculation, nostalgia, and legendification of the 1930s Chinese tragedy queen. Meanwhile, the film has been considered a leftist masterpiece owing to its perceived direct depiction of social oppression. Nevertheless, no attention has been paid to the film's allegorical relationship with its geopolitical context. To recontextualize the film's hypervisible aesthetics and pathos, and to decipher the ways in which it allegorizes its historical, political circumstances, I triangulate *The Goddess* with its Hollywood "before" (i.e., *Stella Dallas*) and its Hong Kong "after" (i.e., *Rouge Tears*), and compare their strategies of representation, especially with regard to their figuration of the gendered experience of urban modernity in post–World War I New England and the pre–World War II Shanghai.

The connections between the three films were historically overdetermined rather than accidental, given China's saturation by Western cinema—a situation caused and reinforced by Western subjugation of China in the first half of the twentieth century.[4] The fundamental connection is the genealogy between the Western genre of melodrama and the Chinese genre commonly known as the family ethics drama (*jiating lunli ju* 家庭伦理剧), which was first developed by Shanghai's Star Film Studio (Mingxing Dianying Gongsi 明星电影公司) in the mid- to late 1920s. Both genres privilege the domestic space associated with a female/mother figure. Yet, contrary to *Stella Dallas*' single-minded focus on the domestic space, Wu's two films show how the mother's domestic space is increasingly threatened and eventually obliterated by the negative social space occupied by the prostitute (the other side of the "goddess") and the thug.

The vying spaces (home versus urban street) and the corresponding schizophrenic mother-prostitute figure symbolize China's semicolonial sociopolitical contradictions. Her abject sexuality contradicts and threatens her maternal virtue, just as the urban street encroaches on the home, foregrounding China's gender and class inequality. These conditions are further complicated (even aggravated) by China's semicolonial state and the attendant exploitative relationship in the economic, cultural, and political realms. In other words, the mother-prostitute's relationship with the diegetic domestic and social space parallels lower-class women's gendered experience with the urban space on the extradiegetic level; both are circumscribed by gender, class, and subaltern politics inherent in urban modernity, on the one hand, and semicoloniality, on the other.

To unpack exactly how China's semicolonial circumstances imprint Wu's remaking of *Stella Dallas* and, conversely, how his remakes envision a more desirable, utopic future, I compare Wu's different strategies of representing abject female sexuality in *The Goddess* and *Rouge Tears*. These strategies are not just formal devices, but are allegorical of ideological conditions that endured from 1934 Shanghai to 1938 Hong Kong, accompanied by shifting sociopolitics and technologies of film production. French critic Pierre Macherey describes these conditions as the "unconscious of the work," which precedes and circumscribes the production of the work and is figured into the work through an "effort of expression."[5] My term, "strategy of representation/figuration," underscores precisely such an "effort of expression" as an overdetermined process of negotiating the crisis of representing the abject. This negotiation, started in *The Goddess* and rehearsed in its remake, *Rouge Tears*, was undertaken by a male humanist filmmaker whose utopic vision of a better society both foregrounded the gender issue in semicolonial China and left the issue glaringly irresolvable.

In the pages that follow, I argue that *Rouge Tears*, instead of being the inferior remake of *The Goddess*, actually offers a perspective to politicize the aesthetics of *The Goddess* (including Ruan Lingyu's performance). Furthermore, the fact that *Rouge Tears* was made in Hong Kong in Cantonese as well as Mandarin Chinese calls attention to the locality of southern China, especially its role in constructing a southern Chinese regional cinema vis-à-vis Chinese national cinema. This also has significant ramifications for the interactions between the regional and the national subject positions. On this basis, I suggest that *Rouge Tears* adumbrates southern Chinese regional consciousness despite its reenactment of the Shanghai-centered narrative.[6]

Beginning with the Ending: An "Unknown Woman's" Quest for "Feminine Difference"

Western film scholarship on *Stella Dallas* has so far focused on King Vidor's 1937 sound remake for MGM. Given the close resemblance between the endings of the 1925 silent version and the 1937 sound version, arguments stimulated by the latter largely pertain to the former as well. In my analysis, I emphasize the silent version because it was referenced by the Shanghai film magazine *Yin xing* as one of the top ten Hollywood movies in 1926;[7] thus, it was likely to have contributed to Wu's conception of *The Goddess* (which predated Vidor's sound version) as well as *Rouge Tears* (which followed the Chinese title of the silent *Stella Dallas*).

In both versions of *Stella Dallas,* the ending shows the lower-class mother, having witnessed her daughter's successful marriage into the upper class through a large window of a mansion, turning away from the scene and walking toward the camera (and the audience) with an ecstatic smile on her face. While feminist critics agree on the mother's self-abnegation, they disagree on how the (female) audience relates to the disappearing (albeit happy-looking) lower-class mother figure. For E. Ann Kaplan, the ending implicates the spectator "in this process of rejection [of Stella as good mother]," thereby clinching "Stella's position as absent Mother."[8] Linda Williams, on the contrary, describes the female spectator as being "divided," capable of experiencing empathy for Stella's sacrifice, while at the same time recognizing the ideological contradictions that lead to the character's predicament.[9] Teresa de Lauretis further underscores the "doubled vision" of the feminist critic (a special type of spectator), as both Woman and women, as both female and feminist. The "twofold pull" constitutes their simultaneous pleasure and displeasure at inclusion and exclusion by dominant discourses.[10] All these positions revolve around the feminist critique of the classic Hollywood film apparatus for its inscription of patriarchal ideology. Williams and de Lauretis complicate the critique by acknowledging the spectator's ambivalent position vis-à-vis the gender-biased film apparatus.

Stanley Cavell, in contrast, disregards the ideological implications of the classic Hollywood film apparatus and reads Stella's walking away as a self-affirming gesture that suggests "the woman's demand for a voice, for a language, for attention to, and the power to enforce attention to, her own subjectivity, say to her *difference of existence*."[11] Cavell forcefully defines Stella's achievement of individual difference as one that entails self-exclusion from the mainstream community. This reading leads to a reversal of the order; it is the woman that gains freedom and subjectivity by exiling herself from the domestic space, whereas the wealthy family in the mansion remains trapped in an illusion. "In fancying Stella walking away as one continuation of Nora walking out, there is the additional moment to consider of her *walking toward us*. Again, a house is turned away from, one that for a woman contains (self-)destructive illusion, or a way of illusory perception she had taken as reality, a way allegorized as a perception of the film screen."[12] Stella's "pain of individuation" is predicated on loss, or what the American transcendentalists (such as Emerson and Thoreau) describe as the "mourning as grieving." Just as "mourning as grieving" may become "morning as dawning or ecstasy,"[13] the loss also makes possible the "difference of existence." Stella's walking away thus exemplifies the possibility for the "unknown woman" to achieve happiness outside the marriage bond and the maternal role.

Cavell's reading goes against the feminist critique and affirms Stella's individual agency. Yet to pursue such a transcendentalist thesis, Cavell needs not only to ignore the ideological implications of the film apparatus (which do exist, even if nontotalizable), but also to disregard the post–World War I American sociopolitical conditions that shape Stella's working-class origins and limit her options.

For an attempt to empower female characters without complete decontextualization, we can turn to Miriam Hansen. Drawing upon the Habermasian "public sphere," Hansen's argument focuses on women's empowerment by modernity. It applauds the emergence of "vernacular modernism" for offering "a sensory-reflexive horizon for the experience of modernization and modernity."[14] This new sensory-reflexive horizon in turn gives rise to the female flaneur, or the female figure who derives pleasure and agency from navigating the modern urban space while defying the pathologizing gaze at her as a prostitute.[15] The emphasis on women's enhanced visibility, mobility, and empowerment in the modern urban space seeks to describe women's multifaceted vernacular experiences with urban modernity as a new mode of production, consumption, and existence. However, such an understanding of modernity tends to evade colonial and subaltern politics, and thereby risks short-circuiting the entrenched gender, class, and colonial power hierarchies.

The Goddess and *Rouge Tears* foreground precisely such power hierarchies that underpinned colonial modernity in 1930s China. Colonial modernity, as Tani Barlow defines it, means that modernity in colonies and the so-called semicolonized Shanghai and China is inextricably bound up with global coloniality.[16] Overlaid upon the preexisting gender and class hierarchies, colonial modernity deepens the difficulty of representing abject female sexuality in the modern urban space. Wu's films register precisely his negotiation with the crisis of representation as manifested in (1) the films' "effort of expression" in order to mediate gender, class, and colonial politics in 1930s China into the film space, or the diegetic "scenography" (à la David Bordwell);[17] and (2) the films' utopic projections of a different future that correspond with their respective strategy of representation.

To address the dialectic relationship between the film and its geopolitical background, I begin with its in-film analogy, that is, the relationship between the figure and the ground within the scenography. Here the figure refers to the mother at home, and the ground refers to the prostitute on the street. The home's invasion and contamination by the street is analogous with the film's imprinting or searing by semicolonial China's geopolitical conditions.

Beyond the Limits of Epistemology: Recognizing the "Unknown Woman"

In 1980, Wu Yonggang recalled that in the 1920s he used to commute daily between the art school he was attending and Unique (Tianyi 天一) Film Production, where he worked as an art designer.[18] From the tram, he caught sight of clusters of young women, with painted faces and forced smiles, roaming the night streets of Shanghai. After repeated encounters with this nightscape, he finally realized that these young women were *an chang*, or illegal prostitutes. Realizing his feebleness as "a weak petty bourgeois intellectual," which prevented him from making a direct social intervention, he decided to express social criticism via an oil painting. This imaginary painting would depict "a dim street lamp, under which stands a woman with her face covered with lipstick, rouge, and misery." She would emblematize "people's miseries" in the "dark society."[19] Although the painting was never realized, Wu eventually translated this imaginary still image into moving images on the screen in *The Goddess* (1934), his directorial debut produced by United China Photoplay and Publishing Service (Lianhua Yingye Yinshua Gongsi 联华影业印刷公司).

Two details of Wu's account demand further examination. The first has to do with the difficulty of recognizing and identifying the illegal streetwalker from the background—Shanghai's night streets. The fact that the women were perceived as hardly distinguishable from the street had to do with Wu's surprise encounter with them through a single glance. The beam of light from the passing tram rendered his glance akin to a long shot, with everything happening in the background. To be able to make the distinction between the women and the street and to comprehend the economic and social positioning of these painted streetside women demanded the filmmaker's persistent inquiry, which pushed beyond his habitual epistemological frame defined by his class and gender role. Aside from his epistemological limits, Wu's account also brings up issues regarding the efficacy of artistic representation (in contrast with social action) and the specificity of the film medium (as compared to oil painting). Writing in 1980, Wu described his selection of artistic representation as an inferior stand-in for the more desirable social activism, which he was not capable of owing to his status as "a weak petty bourgeois intellectual."

If Wu voluntarily performed self-criticism in 1980 (to demonstrate his compliance with the post-1949 ultraleftist revolutionary ideology) in privileging social activism over artistic representation, he simultaneously affirmed artistic representation as an indispensable vehicle for comprehending a street scene that he initially failed to make sense of. Interestingly, his first vision, an oil painting, depicting a solitary woman with a painted face under a dim, solitary street lamp, would be textured, mimetic, yet decontextualized from the messy and befuddling night scene he actually encountered. Both the streetwalker and the street would become visual icons, which would serve to produce an exposé of China's semifeudal, semicolonial condition. When this mental image was ultimately transcoded and remediated into moving images in 1934, Wu deployed the strategy of *xieyi* 写意, or sketch, as a strategy of representing abject female sexuality. In 1938, when Wu remade the film as *Rouge Tears, xieyi* was replaced by *gongbi* 工笔, or detailed elaboration. Both strategies of representation stemmed from Wu's negotiation with the problematic of figuring abject female sexuality in combination with specific film technologies in the context of China's colonial modernity.

Having been subjugated by Western forces since 1842 (when China was defeated by the British Empire in the First Opium War), China further suffered Japan's repeated incursions from 1894 on, culminating in the outbreak of the Second Sino-Japanese War in 1937. When Japan invaded China on September 18, 1931, occupying northeast China, and then bombing Shanghai on January 28, 1932, nationalism came to the fore, triggering leftist participation in filmmaking and criticism, which precipitated the emergence of leftist cinema in the early to mid-1930s. When the full-scale Second Sino-Japanese War broke out on July 7, 1937, followed by another round of Shanghai bombing on August 13, China's film industry was completely reconfigured. Major film studios in Shanghai like Star and United China Photoplay and Publishing Service folded. Large numbers of film and theater workers migrated from Shanghai to Hong Kong and inland China, directly boosting film and theatrical activities in those areas. The massive migration also led to more collaborations between Shanghai and southwest China, on the one hand, and Hong Kong, on the other, as exemplified by *Rouge Tears.*

Meanwhile, on the technological side, Chinese cinema completed the transition from the silent to the talkie era.[20] This transition combined with the governing Nationalist Party's (Guomindang) banning of the use of Cantonese in talkies made within China led to the flourishing of the Cantonese film industry in Hong Kong, the British colony.[21] It was precisely under such tumultuous and constantly shifting sociopolitical and technological circumstances that Wu made his two film attempts (*The Goddess* and *Rouge Tears*) to deliver a humanist social exposé through the trope of an illegal prostitute roaming Shanghai's night streets.

Figuring the "Unknown Woman": Mother in the Sweet Home or Prostitute on the Joyless Street?

In Wu Yonggang's projects, the attempt to embody the illegal prostitute crystallizes the fundamental problematic of representation. The need for a euphemism, *shennü* (goddess), for the low-class, illegal streetwalker suggests her unfigurability. This difficulty is further complicated by Wu's lack of understanding (as a male intellectual-artist) of the reality of low-class prostitution,which is indicated in his initial cryptic image of the "painted woman" (a mute image in the distance), an image that defies his cognitive and epistemological comprehension. In other words, whereas Wu's social conscience leads him to articulate social criticism, he cannot automatically relate or have access to the existential conditions of the subaltern, low-class streetwalker.

In his 1934 essay written shortly after the release of *The Goddess,* Wu reflected on his lack of "living knowledge," which circumscribed his strategy of representation:

> When starting to write the script, I wanted to focus more on [the prostitutes'] actual life experiences. But *my circumstances* made this impossible. To hide this weakness, I *shifted to maternal love while consigning prostitution to the background* by depicting an illegal prostitute struggling between two lives for the sake of her child. I used an exploitative thug to propel the plot. I also put words of justice into the mouth of an upright school headmaster, letting him expose the social cause of prostitution. I did not offer a solution to the problem. *My circumstances* only allowed me to cry out for sympathy and justice. I recognize my cowardice, which led to a humble attempt.[22]

This apologia offers a glimpse into Wu's representational strategy of deflecting from prostitution to motherhood, which creates a melodramatic, Manichean plot structure polarized between virtue and vice—a contradiction that meets no resolution at the end. This strategy is necessitated by the hampering "circumstances" that Wu refers to twice without any clarification. One could speculate that such circumstances had to do with at least two factors: his lack of "living knowledge" and the Nationalist government's censorship of explicit depictions of the sex trade.

By refocusing from prostitution to motherhood, Wu does not so much resolve the representational problem as complicate it, since he now brings into being a schizophrenic female protagonist—the mother-cum-prostitute (as opposed to a one-dimensional character). This schizophrenic figure is manifested in three formats: the verbal text (i.e., intertitles), the still image (i.e., the background image of the title cards), and, most important of all, the moving images (i.e., the film's scenography). In the verbal text, the opening title describes the schizophrenic mother-prostitute in these terms: "The prostitute struggles in the whirlpool of life. In the streets of the night, she is a lowly prostitute. When she holds her child up, she is a saintly mother. Between these two lives, she has shown her formidable character."[23] This is visualized in the still image on which the titles are superimposed. The image is a relief depicting a nude woman with her arms tied behind her back as she struggles to bend down to nurse her baby.[24] If the intertitle, being verbal, bypasses the difficulty of visualization, the relief short-circuits the difficulty of visualizing prostitution by transcoding it to the generic, symbolic image of captivity and enslavement. In both cases, the act of prostitution is distanciated (if not totally disavowed) through metaphors ("struggling in the whirlpool of life" and kneeling with her hands tied behind her back), while the mother figure (holding up and nursing the child) is directly visualized up close.

The same bifurcation characterizes the film's scenography, including the narrative, mise-en-scène, and cinematography. As a family ethics drama that shares Western melodrama's emphasis on the sanctified home space, *The Goddess* presents a Manichean structure of the home (with the mother, the son, and the school headmaster as the good father figure), on the one hand, and the night street (the prostitute and the thug as the bad father figure), on the other. Revolving around the Manichean structure, *The Goddess* vacillates between the foreground (i.e., the home and the mother) and the background (i.e., the street, prostitution, and the local thug). Given the importance of the street scenes, I describe the illegal streetwalker's experience of the urban space as "street modernity"—a concept partially derived from Patrice Petro's study of Weimar era "street film."[25]

The "street" in *The Goddess* is neon-lit, showcasing modernity and commercial attractions along with their exploitative underbelly. This "street's" real-life model could be Nanjing Road and its vicinity, which could also be where Wu first caught sight of the roaming illegal streetwalkers during his nightly commute. Running westward from the Bund, cutting through the east part of the International Settlement,[26] Nanjing Road emerged as Shanghai's commercial center in the 1930s, lined with international landmarks and three major modern department stores: Sincere (Xianshi), Wing On (Yong'an), and Sun Sun (Xinxin). These stores were launched in Hong Kong by overseas Chinese businessmen and then expanded to Shanghai. The neon lights of the store names writ large in the night sky appear frequently in 1930s films set in Shanghai, including *The Goddess.* As such, they constitute a major visual spectacle in pre-1949 Shanghai cinema.[27]

However, the spectacularly cosmopolitan Nanjing Road and its vicinity coexisted with low-class prostitution, fueled by an expanding number of urban poor that partially resulted from the influx of rural women escaping the deteriorating economy in the countryside.[28] On the surface, the gendered moral degeneration in the city resembles Petro's exemplary "street film," *The Joyless Street* (1925). However, China's subaltern position and colonial modernity determine that the female characters' urban experiences depicted in Chinese films must be understood as emblematic of the global colonial political economy.

To the extent that Shanghai's social exposé films oftentimes feature the urban street as the site of pedestrian and underclass experiences as well as dramatic twists (especially in the female character's fate),[29] I use "street modernity" to characterize these films' depiction of the impact of colonial modernity on the urban poor who depend on the street for their means of living. The notion of "street modernity" is specifically geared for understanding gender- and class-specific experiences in a Chinese treaty port, which, significantly, echoes what Mary L. Pratt calls the "contact zone." This zone is characterized by "copresence, interactions, interlocking understandings and practices, often within radically asymmetrical relations of power."[30] Given its concern with and critique of the "asymmetrical relations of power," *The Goddess,* unsurprisingly, portrays the prostitute as a victim and Shanghai's night street as a site of urban commerce traversed by systemic exploitation and violence. Modernity in this context is thus inherently ambivalent, mirroring the schizophrenic character of the mother-prostitute.

As an apt visual embodiment of the ambivalent "street modernity," the schizophrenic mother-prostitute figure also registers the unrepresentability of abject female sexuality in the contact zone of Shanghai. As Wu admits, the mother figure is foregrounded as the positive and unproblematic image precisely in order to circumvent the difficulty of representing prostitution. Furthermore, prostitution, as manifested in the streetwalking sequences, is not depicted directly, but rather suggested through oblique and elliptical camera work. Wu describes this strategy of representation as *xieyi* (sketch), an aesthetic tradition drawn from a style of classical Chinese brush painting. It literally means "expressing the intent," "abstract[ing] the elements of graphic discourse in order to represent a meaning which transcended form."[31] Trained as a set designer, Wu uses *xieyi* to emphasize the suggestive and evocative effect. He sees the setting as being truthful to reality but not mimetic. It should be adapted to "narrative need and aesthetic choice." The principle of *anshi* (suggestiveness) should precede and determine the tone of color and the mise-en-scène.[32] Both *xieyi* and *anshi* seek to "convey a meaning subtly through *simple composition* . . . not embellishments."[33] Wu's conception of *xieyi* and suggestive evocation characterizes the three highly acclaimed aesthetic moments in *The Goddess,* which all occur in the streetwalking sequences.

The first scene begins with the hustle and bustle of the neon-lit Shanghai street. Then the camera identifies the prostitute walking up from the background, loitering on the street. A man is shown following her. She looks back and down, as the camera tilts down her flashy, close-fitting *qipao* dress (a tell-tale sign of her job), pauses, then cuts to the sunrise of the following morning, when she walks out of a hotel in a long shot, tidying her hair.

The second instance begins with the prostitute leaving home, walking into the background as the gossipy neighbor women point their fingers. The shot of her back is suddenly lit up, then lap-dissolves into a close-up shot of the lower train of her *qipao* (with the lace lining showing at the side slit), her foot tapping on the streetside pavement. The camera holds on this detail, while capturing other feet passing by in the background, until a pair of shining male leather shoes approach to her right, her feet turning toward his and pausing. The camera then tracks the four feet walking screen right in sync, the lace lining revealed in luminous lighting,[34] while gradually dissolving into an interior shot, showing domestic objects including a dresser mirror and laundry on a clothesline (Figure 1.1). When the

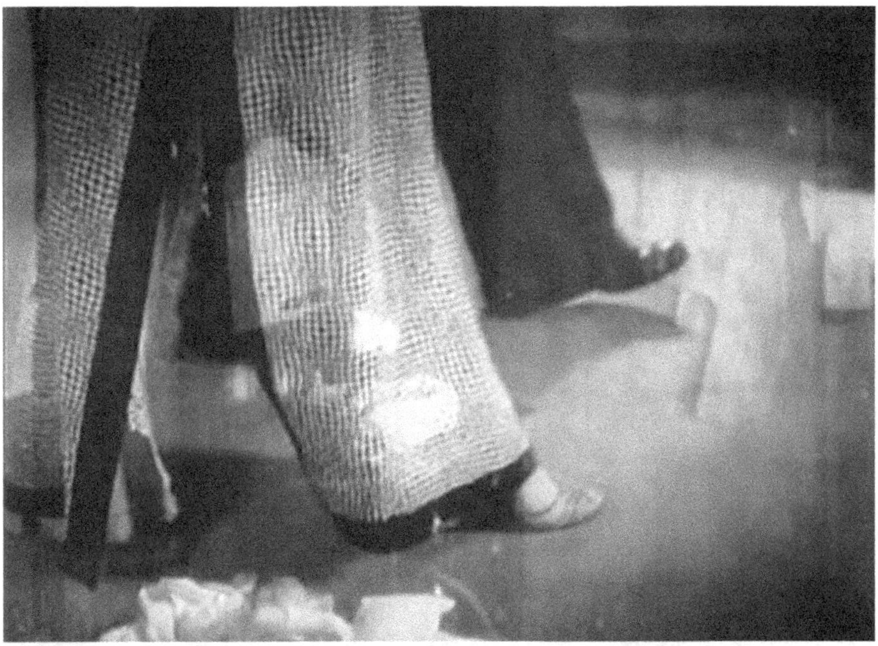

Figure 1.1 A tracking shot showing four feet walking screen right while dissolving into the interior scene in the mother-prostitute's home in *The Goddess*

dissolve ends, we see the prostitute pushing open a door and back in her own home, her image reflected in the dresser mirror right next to the door. The only sign of her nocturnal transaction is a medium shot of the stash of bills she takes out of her purse.

The last instance of streetwalking is even more elliptical. One single overhead shot from an unauthored perspective captures a woman standing under a street lamp, a suited man walking up, she nodding, and both walking out of the frame, fading out.[35]

All three streetwalking sequences privilege the aesthetics of suggestive evocation (or *xieyi*) through unusual camera angles, luminous lighting, and elliptical editing. The focus on the anonymous feet evokes Lotte Eisner's observation that the urban street "cannot be evoked by faces and bodies, only by the movements of legs and feet."[36] The feet-street symbiosis forms the substratum of street life—the pedestrian energy that animates the neon-lit urban nightscape and the vibrant urban display culture. It is also counterpoised to the interior shots that emphasize the mother's face. When the mother appears at home, the camera work largely adopts the style of Hollywood glamor shots, focusing on her luminously lit face, emphasizing the aura effect and her tranced look into the distant space. These glamor shots elevate the mother to saintly ethereality (Figure 1.2).

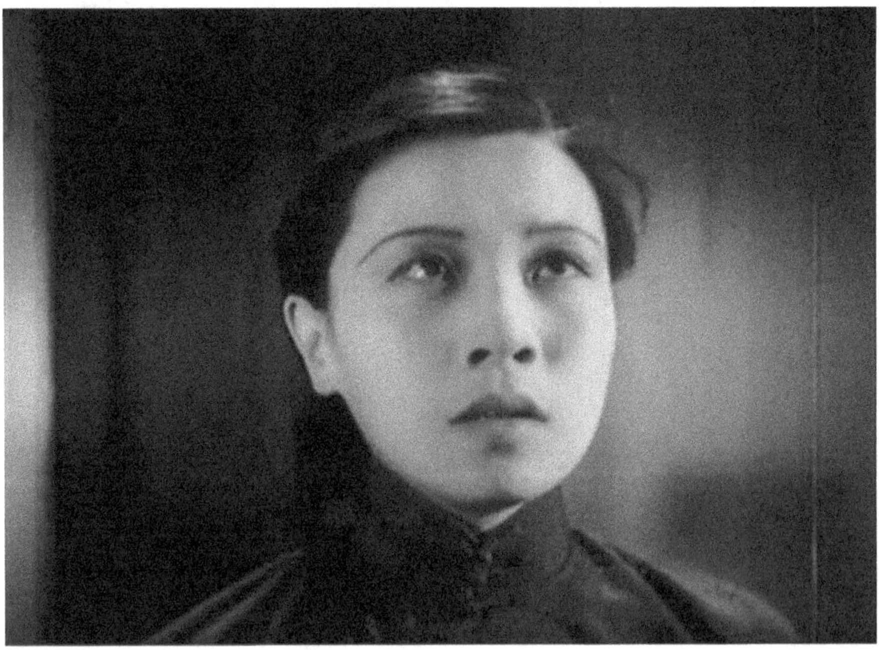

Figure 1.2 Close-up of the mother (Ruan Lingyu) looking into the distance in a trance

Whereas both the face shot and the feet shot are enchanting, their ramifications are drastically different. The interior shots aim to identify and glamorize the mother's face, thereby sanctifying the home space. The street shots, in contrast, painstakingly exclude the face by focusing on the feet, the shimmering dress, and the foreshortened body (in the perpendicular overhead shot). Undoubtedly, the enchantment of anonymous quotidian elements (the feet, the train of a dress, the pavement, and the gas light) on the pedestrian street produces unconventional and excessive visual appeal, thus triggering cinephilia. Nevertheless, whereas European cinephilia theory tends to attribute subversive potential to unexpected visual excess,[37] I understand Wu's cinephiliac streetwalking sequences as symptomatic of the difficulty of representing illegal prostitution and abject female sexuality.

To understand why these cinephiliac sequences should be interpreted symptomatically, we need first to examine the authorship of the street shots or from whose perspective(s) the shots originate. To the extent that the street shots exclude the face, rendering the nocturnal business anonymous and subjectless, prostitution becomes both decontextualized and literalized as an act of streetwalking disconnected from an identifiable agent who does the walking. The extreme low angle and extreme high angle framing that produce the truncating effect apparently exist independent of any empirical subject or character. This echoes what Slavoj Žižek describes as an "empty, a priori gaze that cannot be pinpointed as a determinate reality."[38] Drawing on Lacan's argument of the "split between the eye and the gaze,"[39] Žižek sees the a priori gaze as a function of unconscious desire, which preexists and shapes the subjectivity of what is seen. Such an a priori gaze signifies the "primordial address by the Other" and constitutes a "formal 'condition of possibility' of our seeing anything at all."[40] By defining the gaze as the "condition of possibility" for seeing, Žižek points up an underlying structure of the scopic regime.

To extend this argument for the cinephiliac streetwalking scenes in *The Goddess,* I suggest that the overarching "address by the Other" not only enables seeing, but also conditions seeing from certain angles while excluding others. That is, revelation simultaneously entails concealment. Understood in connection with Wu's reference to the hampering circumstances that made direct depiction of existential prostitution impossible, we may argue that the hampering conditions, combined with his lack of living knowledge of low-class prostitution, constituted precisely the "address of the Other" that produced the unconventional framing, the truncating and defamiliarizing effect, and the elliptical editing. Consequently, abject female sexuality and gendered subaltern existence of the urban space become deflected and disavowed.[41] In place of the prostitute on the street, Wu posited the mother at home—symbol of the normal social order—as the central figure of the film. The mother in the foreground thus fulfills two apparently contradictory functions:

(1) surrogating and repressing the prostitute in the (back)ground and (2) mediating and figuring (i.e., pointing *toward*) the unfigurable prostitute by pointing *at* itself as a surrogate (albeit inadequate) image.

Wu's suggestive sketch (*xieyi*) style (manifested in the haloed mother figure and the cinephiliac streetwalking sequences) does not simply circumvent the difficulty of representing abject female sexuality. It also encourages aestheticization and depoliticization, thus releasing the audience from the obligation of critical realism. This compromised politics was detected by some leftist critics, despite the overall praise for the film's aesthetics and the leading actress Ruan Lingyu's superb performance. Wang Chenwu (1911–1938) (aka Chen Wu), a leftist critic, for instance, argued that the focus on depoliticized maternal love "overshadowed, even annulled the film's social message," which implied Wu's "inability to confront the social structure as the root of all problems."[42]

Wang Chenwu correctly intuited the representational problem. However, his reductive diagnosis of Wu's ideological limitation foreclosed the opportunity of examining Wu's laborious negotiation with the representational crisis. This negotiation involves two aspects that can be called *Repräsentation* and *Vertretung* (both translate into "representation" in English). The crisis of *Repräsentation* resides in the difficulty of externalizing a mind picture of prostitution in the film medium owing to ideological constraints and the delimited representational scheme of the maternal melodrama or family ethics drama. The crisis of *Vertretung* has to do with the impossibility of speaking on behalf of the subaltern, given Wu's distanciation from that social sector. Wu's sketchy and evocative (*xieyi*) representational strategy is symptomatic precisely of these two aspects of representational crisis. Thus, to take the aesthetic street sequences at face value would elide the underlying geopolitical structure of colonial modernity. Through a symptomatic rereading of Wu's *xieyi* strategy of representation, I foreground *The Goddess*' allegorical connection with its geopolitical circumstances, thereby repoliticizing its sketchy, elliptical style.

The repoliticizing approach also enables a new understanding of Wu's sound remake of *The Goddess, Rouge Tears,* released in Hong Kong on December 16, 1938—one year after the outbreak of the Second Sino-Japanese War in mainland China. *Rouge Tears* has fallen into critical oblivion; both the director, Wu Yonggang, and the leading actress, Hu Die, fail to mention it in their memoirs. The few contemporary commentaries dismiss the film for its political conservatism and artistic "regression."[43] Nevertheless, back in the late 1930s, *Rouge Tears* occupied a more ambiguous position. It was pitched as a moving tragedy and "one of the most successful artworks,"[44] while also being criticized as a representative of the "poisonous," profit-oriented Hong Kong cinema that "focused on feudal, fantastical, superstitious, and sensuous subjects."[45] Such contradictory evaluations are indicative of the gap between the progressive discourses that demanded Hong Kong (cinema)'s allegiance to China's nationalist wartime ideology, on the one hand, and, on the other hand, Hong Kong's heterogeneous film practices in which leftist and nationalist cinema did not monopolize but rather coexisted and competed with genres that were less explicitly nationalist, such as folklore, fantasy, horror, and sensuous drama. Indeed, these reputedly backward and poisonous local productions mushroomed in May 1938 and climaxed in July, which provoked the mainland Nationalist government's renewed film regulation and censorship.[46]

The difficulty of positioning and evaluating *Rouge Tears* was further complicated by the fact that it was not exactly a local Hong Kong production, but more a translocal collaboration that led to Cantonese and Mandarin Chinese versions (similar to early multilanguage talkies made for different markets by Euro-American film companies). It was produced by the Shanghai-based Xinhua Yingye Gongsi 新华影业公司 (New China Film Company), headed by the King of Advertisement, S. K. Chang (Zhang Shankun) 张善琨 (1905–1957),[47] in collaboration with the Hong Kong–based Nanyue Yingpian Gongsi 南粤影片公司 (Nanyue Film Studio), founded by a Shanghai émigré, Zhu Qingxian 竺清贤. Starting out as a sound technician, in 1932 Zhu invented the Qingxian Brand sound recording system, which became Nanyue's house brand. Two directors, Xinhua's Wu Yonggang and Nanyue's Chen Pi, helmed the Mandarin and Cantonese versions respectively, with two casts that shared only the leading actress, Hu Die 胡蝶, and the actor who played her son, Li Keng 黎铿 (who also played the son in *The Goddess*).

The reason that the remake was done in Hong Kong had to do with wartime exigencies (mass migration of film workers from Shanghai to Hong Kong as well as inland) and S. K. Chang's business ambition of harnessing Hong Kong talent and its market.[48] Among the film workers who migrated to Hong Kong with the outbreak of the war were Hu Die, Shanghai's 1933 "Movie Queen," and Li Keng. To cast them as the mother and son in the sound remake necessitated shooting in Hong Kong, which also successfully harnessed Hu's bilingual capacity as a Cantonese native raised in northern China (and thus proficient in both Cantonese and Mandarin Chinese), not to mention cashing in on her residual value as the "Movie Queen."

By remaking the film in Hong Kong at a time when the rest of China was embroiled in the war and after the original leading actress, Ruan Lingyu, had committed suicide in 1935, the production crews faced two main absences, that of the figure (Ruan and her definitive rendition of the mother-prostitute), and that of the (back)ground (the Shanghai street). These absences led to the challenge of *Vorstellung*, or bringing back and imitating what was past and absent.[49] To compensate for the two absences and to take advantage of the sound technology, Wu adopted a strategy of representation that can be described as elaboration, or *gongbi*. Originating as a traditional painting style that is opposed to *xieyi*, *gongbi*, according to Wu, refers to elaborated lighting, fine delineation, and profuse colors. The strategy of *gongbi* through elaboration and excessive detailing in *Rouge Tears* leads to the reversal of the relationship between the figure (mother-home) and the (back)ground (prostitute-street), which in turn demystifies the cinephiliac moments in *The Goddess* by exposing the underlying representational crisis and geopolitical structure.

Like the *xieyi* strategy that is amply illustrated in the streetwalking scenes in *The Goddess*, the *gongbi* style is also most clearly demonstrated in the corresponding sequences.[50] In *The Goddess*, the night streetscape is conjured with the dancing neon lights of two major department stores (Sincere and Wing On). The two montage sequences of kinesthetic neon lights, one at the beginning of the film and the other toward the end, do not simply signal Shanghai's alluring urban street modernity; more important, they suggest the eruption of the (back)ground (street) into the foreground (home), posing an increasing threat to the mother figure.

To re-create the neon-lit skyline in Hong Kong, the remake mounts full-scale audio-visual elaboration. First, it adds a fast-paced, sometimes jazzy and sometimes comic nondiegetic music score, highlighting the bustling night street crowd and illicit dealings and desires. In addition, it presents an overabundance of neon signs of commodity brands popular with Chinese-speaking communities in Shanghai, Hong Kong, and Southeast Asia. These signs embody border-crossing commercial culture, which facilitates a transportable skyline. The neon signs do not directly refer to or reflect the Shanghai night skyline, but rather imply the latter through resemblance and association. Thus, they function as what the semiotician C. S. Peirce would call the icon of Nanjing Road (and commercial Shanghai by extension), contradistinguished from the neon signs in *The Goddess*, which are indexical (in the Peircian sense), that is, directly referring to Shanghai's urban night life.[51]

The third aspect of re-presenting (in the sense of *Vorstellung*) the absent Shanghai urban streetscape is the addition of a new character—a salacious rural man whose perspective focalizes the commercial attractions. Unlike *The Goddess*, in which the street and streetwalking scenes are mostly shot from a distanced and/or contrived perspective, manifesting what Žižek calls the "primordial address of the Other," *Rouge Tears* presents the street scenes at a much closer range, from the country rube's perspective. His gaze not only interweaves various street attractions, but also occupies an ambiguous position, being simultaneously privileged as a male gazer with moderate purchasing power and discriminated against and exploited as a low-class, vulnerable rube. Thus, even as he is ogling the scantily dressed female mannequin (whose bare legs are planted in the foreground), he is spotted by the urban thug, who subsequently steals the rube's wallet. His desire for "commodity-experience" (to borrow Anne Friedberg's term)[52] ironically coincides with his being turned into a commodity by the urban gaze that originates from street modernity and the streetwise commercial drive.

These graphic audio-visual insertions and additional peripheral plot conjure Shanghai's night streetscape in excessive detail. By deploying an embodied perspective (from the country rube), the remake reconnects the gaze and the eye, rendering scopophilia (i.e., the desire to see, often associated with voyeurism) explicitly male, possessive, and objectivizing. This is demonstrated in the remake's detailed visualization of the commercial and exploitative trade that animates the night street. In *The Goddess,* the exploitative streetside flesh trade is implied through cinephiliac streetwalking scenes, as discussed earlier. It is also prefigured by the semantic interchangeability that emerges from the juxtaposition of the prostitute, the pawnshop, and the swimsuited female mannequin displayed in a store window. The analogy between these images rests on the audience's interpretation. *Rouge Tears,* on the contrary, parades images that are rendered emphatically exchangeable commodities by the rube's salacious gaze. These fetishized images include the neon lights, the scantily dressed female mannequin, meat being chopped by a butcher, and, finally, the prostitute. The buxom physique of Hu Die, the leading actress in *Rouge Tears,* in contrast to the light build of Ruan Lingyu, makes the pun on the meat/flesh trade all the more pungent, even inappropriately comic.

Along with the night streetscape, the streetwalking scenes are also more elaborated. Contrary to the de-faced, elliptical, and aestheticized streetwalking sequences in *The Goddess,* Hu Die's prostitute puts on her signature single-dimpled smile to all male passers-by who visibly despise and ridicule her. She is also shown accepting money from the thug, then sleeping soundly with him, only to lose the money again when the thug gets up early and takes it back. These details materialize the flesh-for-money business and the prostitute's pathetic failure. They do not suggest the director's better understanding of existential conditions of prostitution but are rather intended to emphasize the prostitute's vulnerability and exploitation. Nevertheless, by making the mother's prostitution disconcertingly unaesthetic and undeniable, these details also inadvertently suggest her incompetence and irredeemability. The excessive elaboration produces what Roland Barthes calls the "reality effect," or "contamination by the real."[53] The "real" here refers to the unmotherly, illegal, and undeniable streetside low-class life, and the economic, geopolitical circumstances that spawn the sex industry.

The "real" also literally taints the son's memory of his mother in *Rouge Tears.* When the thug robs her of her last earnings, she confronts him and accidentally kills him in the presence of her son (the son is absent in the corresponding sequence in *The Goddess*). In the spirit of elaboration, the violence is graphically visualized for the son and the audience as the camera captures the thug's bloody head in extreme frontal close-up. Twelve years later, the grown-up son is to remember the mother's tearful face in combination with the gory scene of murder. The layering of the abject over the virtuous encapsulates the entire film's "contamination by the real," which undermines the theme of sublime motherhood.

Thus, contrary to Wu's suggestive aesthetics in *The Goddess,* which shifted the spectatorial interest from prostitution to motherhood, *Rouge Tears* breaches the representational convention of the maternal melodrama (and the family ethics drama initiated in Shanghai) by inadvertently drawing the audience attention to the unmotherly figure. The resulting frustration of the audience's expectations may have contributed to the obscuration of *Rouge Tears,* contrary to *The Goddess'* canonization as a landmark leftist film from the silent era. This contrast has also dominated the audience's perception of Hu's acting in *Rouge Tears* vis-à-vis Ruan's acting in *The Goddess.* A 1939 Shanghai review made this clear in comparing the Mandarin version of *Rouge Tears* with *The Goddess,* when both were simultaneously rerun in different theaters. According to the reviewer, *Rouge Tears* demonstrated more sophisticated techniques (possibly resulting from the sound technology), yet Hu's acting paled next to Ruan's.[54]

This comparison reinforces the essentialist discourse of fit between the actor and the role. It privileges Ruan's supposedly natural and innate match with the tragic mother role over Hu's natural mismatch. Yet, as I demonstrate below, just as the unmotherly streetwalker can easily contaminate virtuous motherhood, Hu's "misfit" also works to denaturalize Ruan's "fit." This reversal enables us to reevaluate *The Goddess* vis-à-vis *Rouge Tears* and *Stella Dallas,* thereby politicizing the subaltern remaking of the genre of maternal melodrama in 1930s Shanghai and Hong Kong.

To demystify Ruan's "fit" with her character, I start with Roy Armes' contention that whereas "the star and all the things he or she represents are *not* an *inevitable* part of the cinema," the establishment of a star means that his or her communication with the audience is "direct and total—to be a fan is in a way to be *in love* with the star."[55] In the case of Ruan, the "love" makes the audience forget the initial arbitrary relationship between the star and the role, resulting in reification of the fit. Ruan's presumed genetic link with her muted "goddess"[56] is premised precisely on the audience's participation in constructing the "fit" and then taking the construct for a fact. Overshadowed by Ruan's naturalized rendition of the mother-prostitute character, Hu Die's reenactment becomes what Marvin Carlson would call "ghosting," a form of acting that trails external associations linked with another context.[57] Hu's ghosting is two-layered—as a well-known actress in a new role and as a different actress rehearsing an old role. In both cases, her ghosting involves incongruence between what is presented and what is expected. This leads the audience to conveniently dismiss Hu's rerendition of the mother-prostitute figure as a misfit.

In addition to Ruan's reified acting style, the negative reception of Hu's reenactment can also be attributed to the audience's anxiety with the sound technology and its potential destruction of the quiescent aesthetics of silent cinema. Armes' description of the impact of sound on the star image is again instructive. He argues that sound brings dreamlike silent-era stars "down to earth," making them "more ordinary and more human."[58] As if to illustrate Armes' description, Barthes contrasts Greta Garbo and Audrey Hepburn in terms of "concept" versus "substance," "Idea" versus "event," the former being distant and transcendental whereas the latter is rooted in materialist, mundane reality.[59] This sound-induced earthy turn parallels the shift from Ruan's "'metaphysical' figure, inspired by a noble self-sacrificial spirit, untainted by any base desire," to Hu Die's unapologetically corporeal and contaminated rendition.[60]

As a result of audio-visual elaboration (achieved through the use of sound and detailed overcompensation for the absences of the Shanghai street and the original leading actress), Hu's excessive mimesis of Ruan's mother-prostitute figure ends up both bearing and baring the "contamination by the real." This is manifested in the interpenetration between the figure and the ground, or between the noble mother at home and the base prostitute on the street. Jean Baudrillard describes such dedifferentiation in terms of "the obscenity of the visible," which amounts to a "pornography of information."[61] In *Rouge Tears,* the "pornography of information" redoubles the pornography of prostitution, not in the sense of excessive sexualization but rather in the sense of excessive audio-visualization of abject desires and transactions that animate the street and streetwalking sequences.

On the surface, *Rouge Tears* may be a "failure" (compared to *The Goddess*) in terms of aesthetics and audience's reception. Nevertheless, the failure is productive because it demystifies the quiescent aesthetics of *The Goddess* and contributes to exposing the underlying geopolitics of Wu's remaking. The subversive power of *Rouge Tears* stems from its strategy of elaboration or excessive mimesis (*gongbi*), which is used to remediate the predecessor film and to represent abject female sexuality. As discussed in my introduction, translation produces *Nachleben,* or afterlife, that unfolds and fulfills what is encrypted in *Urgeschichte,* or prehistory, according to Walter Benjamin.[62] In my context, a remake, as a form of translation, develops and brings out what is implicit in its filmic predecessor(s). Such fulfillment does not end in a unified vessel made up of matching pieces of texts and translations, as Benjamin envisions.[63] Rather, it produces what Derrida calls the "dangerous supplement,"[64] which supplements while also replacing the "original." The afterlife's fructification and reorientation of its prehistory challenge us to analyze the ways in which *Rouge Tears* repositions and resignifies *The Goddess.*

We may start by examining how Hu Die's ghosting deconstructs Ruan's quiescent aesthetics and "natural fit" with the muted mother-prostitute character.

To understand Hu's ghosting as Ruan's "dangerous supplement," I refer to John O. Thompson's concept of the "commutation test," which is a method of testing the effects of a particular type of acting by substituting one actor with another.[65] This test allows us to denaturalize the first actor's "fit" and to "grasp units which were previously invisible, submerged in the smooth operation of the sign system in question."[66] In this context, what is made invisible and naturalized through Ruan's transcendental acting is abject female sexuality, which resurfaced through Hu's excessively corporeal reenactment. Hu's "dangerous supplement" derived from her "body too much," which, according to Jean-Louis Comolli, is the "surplus" that thwarts "the apparent naturalness, the familiarity of the body" by becoming "problematic, paradoxical . . . strange to itself."[67] Hu's surplus body (vis-à-vis Ruan and her noble mother figure) thus produces a discomforting position for the audience, forcing the latter to recognize the intractably base and materialist body of the prostitute even when the audience chooses to disavow it.

The Hu-Ruan "commutation test" brings Ruan's reified "fit" into question. That is, Hu's reenactment supplements yet also threatens to replace Ruan's acting. This Derridian "dangerous supplement" can be extended to understand *Rouge Tears*' supplementary power as a remake vis-à-vis *The Goddess*. By replacing the sketchy representation in *The Goddess* with excessive mimesis and elaboration, the street scenography (including the streetwalking scenes) in the remake seems to leap into the foreground as if through rack focus, which renders the background in sharp focus, blurring the foreground. On top of the proliferating commodities, the reconstructed Shanghai street also includes movie posters,[68] signs for the "national goods store" (*guohuo dian*),[69] and the pawnshop boss' passing observation on the cheap artificial silk that Japan is dumping into the Chinese market. By showing the street (background) erupting into the home (foreground) and allowing the prostitute to overshadow (or contaminate) the mother figure, *Rouge Tears* defamiliarizes the cinephiliac aesthetics of *The Goddess,* bringing back the unrepresentable and obscured geopolitics that underpin the predecessor film.

For Fredric Jameson, the reversal of the (back)ground and the figure brings out "something more fundamental in what might otherwise simply seem the background itself."[70] In my case, the "more fundamental thing" is the tension between semicolonialism and escalating nationalism. On the one hand, the street scenography displays prevalent commercialization, which reifies a human relationship into a human-object relationship (as illustrated in the country rube's gaze at urban attractions/commodities and his being turned into yet another commodity by the urban gaze). On the other hand, the "national goods" store, the movie posters, and the pawnshop owner's observation imply a deteriorating economy, the war, and the nationalist interpellation. Such tension and symbiosis between urban commercial culture and the urban poor, between distracting entertainment and sociopolitical discourses in the semicolonial "contact zone" (Shanghai or the Shanghai look-alike re-created in Hong Kong) produces variegated experiences of urban modernity, which encompass deprivations, desires, and agitation. On the plebian level, this tension characterizes what I am calling urban China's "street modernity," which summarizes experiences that are oftentimes gendered female and related to the lower class in film representations.

Even when this tension, or what Jameson calls the "more fundamental thing," is brought out in the remake through the reversal of the figure and the (back)ground, its effect and topicality still depend on the audience's discernment and sociopolitical sensitivity. For after all, the layered street signs within the scenography are commonplace, scattered, and embedded within the thick texture of the mise-en-scène. That is, the elaborated (back)ground does not offer an in-depth revelation of or commentary on existential prostitution or "street modernity" per se. Rather, it registers the director's continued negotiation with the problematic of representing abject female sexuality, this time in the pre–Pearl Harbor Hong Kong. Such negotiation is further manifested in the two films' utopic vision—in the form of the mother-prostitute's hope for the future.

Utopia: What Does an "Unknown Woman" Want?

Stella Dallas ends with the mother's enraptured look after witnessing her daughter's marriage into a higher class. Her satisfaction can be read in two ways (as laid out in the first section of this chapter): as her vicarious wish fulfillment through her daughter, which would reinscribe the gender hierarchy and patriarchy, or as her freedom to pursue her "difference of existence" independent of the bourgeois, patriarchal system of marriage and family. Whereas Stella walks away with an ecstatic smile, the mother-prostitute in *The Goddess* ends up with twelve years' imprisonment for accidentally killing the exploitative urban thug. In the concluding sequence, the jailed mother entrusts her son to the righteous school headmaster (the ideal father figure, equivalent to Stella's former husband) and requests that her son be informed of her "death" and provided with a decent education. After the headmaster's departure, she is left alone in the cell, framed behind the bars, looking toward frame right, where an image of her son appears, smiling back at her, with his arms contently folded (Figure 1.3).

The last shot shows her turning around to the audience, slowly looking down, closing her eyes, seemingly reconciled with her situation. As she closes her eyes to the camera, to the audience, and to the world, the son's image in right frame

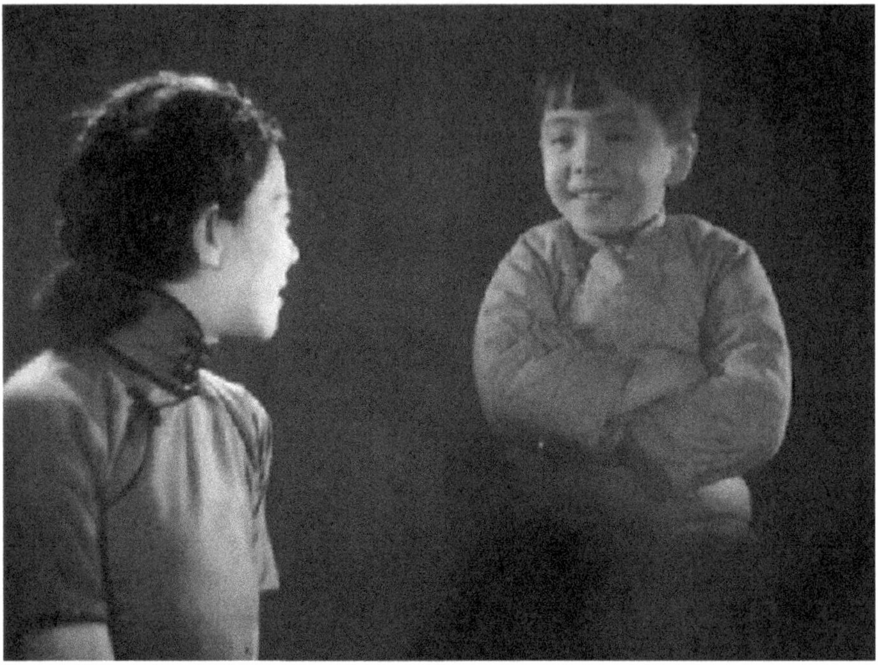

Figure 1.3 The mother in prison has an illusion of her cheerful son

vanishes, leaving a dark void that is also pregnant with an undefined hope. Her morphing into a blind-mute statue mirrors Norwegian sculptor Stephan Abel Sinding's *The Captive Mother*—the background image of the title cards.

This image of the happy son is usually seen as a straightforward representation of the mother's vision, which redeems her self-abnegation. Following Cavell's optimist take, William Rothman argues that in *The Goddess,* the mother's self-denial "*gives* her a self on film," and that the film ultimately demonstrates "acknowledgement and affirmation of the woman herself."[71] Like Cavell, Rothman emphasizes individual choice while ignoring how an individual's agency is imbricated in and circumscribed by sociopolitical conditions. Consequently, the statement that the film ends with "acknowledgement and affirmation of the woman herself" homogenizes "the woman's" experiences and fails to address a lower-class mother-prostitute's experience with the "street modernity" in semicolonial China.

To emphasize the lower-class unknown woman's experience, we must emphasize her self-exclusion from the utopic image that is apparently attributed to her. Unlike Stella's walking away, the mother-prostitute's incarceration indicates the impossibility of what Cavell calls the "feminine difference." Furthermore, it suggests that she cannot partake in modernity without also falling prey to the semicolonial urban street. To displace her from the street into the prison not only deprives her of her family, but also blocks her access to commercial and political modernity (barring her from participating in the commercial culture or in nation-state building).

The mother-prostitute's exclusion from the future calls into question her apparent authorship of the vision. Indeed, to the extent that the film originated from director Wu Yonggang's chance sighting and subsequent interest in street-side "painted" women and that the film script was encouraged and revised by leftist critics (according to Wu's 1980 account), we may see the vision and the power of anticipation as ultimately resting with the director and the supportive leftist critics. Whereas Wu and the leftists might have different attitudes toward class conflict, the former being a humanist artist, the latter more or less leaning toward Marxism, they shared a discontent with China's subjugated status. In aspiring for a strong, independent nation-state, they similarly mobilized the victimized "unknown woman" as the vehicle of their social exposé. Unsurprisingly, therefore, the utopic vision of the happy son (embodying the male-centered future of the Chinese nation-state) is ultimately lodged in the male director and his supporters, even though it was framed as the mother's vision.

Yet, to understand the male-authored utopic vision as being exclusively geared to male intellectuals' interests would negate the enduring power of the vision. This power, I would argue, derives from Wu's painstaking negotiation with his subject instead of a mere ventriloquism of her. And it endures owing to its subjunctive and provisionary nature. As Ernst Bloch suggests, utopia or the principle of hope is defined precisely by the "power of anticipation" that operates subjunctively without prescribing the future.[72] This principle is manifested in the mother's look of longing that evokes the son's image, apparition-like, with a responding smile. The mother's content face after seeing the vision suggests a subtle exchange with the son. To that extent, she does indeed have the power of anticipating a happy future within the diegesis.

The very vagueness and ephemerality of the vision do not annul but rather define the utopic thrust. By confronting the audience with an image that does not yield an explicit message, the vision foregrounds its own illegibility, which produces an affective impact. As Peter Brooks argues in his seminal study of novelistic melodrama, the "text of muteness," embodied in a mute character or a tableau at the climax of a melodrama, does not function as a semantic sign to be decoded but rather as a mute gesture pointing toward something beyond. It is an as-if proposition linking up the literal with the envisioned, hinting at "another reality."[73] In this sense, the mother-prostitute's muteness and self-blinding (closing her eyes to the world) literalize Brooks' "text of muteness," and the vision of her happy son can be seen as her as-if proposition that points toward a future beyond her current incarceration. Such a nonsemantic address to the audience challenges the conventional hermeneutic approach and demands a new understanding of the utopic drive that is not so much based on the vision's meaning and materialization as on its affective virtuality, even near impossibility of materialization. In short, the undefined vision, like Brooks' notion of the as-if proposition, points to "another reality."

In *The Goddess,* the vision necessarily remains subjunctive and virtual owing to its conditions of production, especially the director's sociopolitical positioning vis-à-vis that of his subject. If the mother-prostitute's subaltern position (being deprived of all social resources and of direct representation) and her inability to define her hope clearly serve to overdetermine the vagueness of her vision, then preserving such vagueness could indicate Wu Yonggang's admission of his own lack of understanding of his character and his decision to respect the distance and to present the vision as it appears to her rather than spelling it out by putting thoughts in her mind. We might also go further and argue that the insistence on vagueness was actually necessitated by Wu's own inability to define a clear future caused by two factors: (1) his own marginal position as a novice director with limited experience with lower-class life despite his social conscience and (2) the association of his social conscience with the emerging leftism in the early 1930s, when it operated as what Raymond Williams would call a "structure of feeling" rather than a reified, homogenized ideology. To the extent that a structure of feeling often emerges with the rise of a class, or a contradiction, fracture, or mutation within a class, as Williams suggests, it tends to be inchoate, affective, unformulated, and preideological.[74]

Since Wu made *The Goddess* at a time of political instability and rapid shifts, it is not surprising that the vision remained an embryonic "structure of feeling." In this sense, the male, humanist, intellectual director and his subaltern character share the similar difficulty of imagining a concrete better future, despite their different gender, class, and ideological positions. Their gap transforms into intersection, even affinity. Antonio Gramsci describes this as the "*unwitting reflection* of the most elementary and profound aspirations of even the *lowest subaltern social groups*" by intellectuals who have other preoccupations.[75] What grounds this "unwitting reflection" in *The Goddess* is precisely the director and his subaltern character's shared geopolitical circumstances, that is, colonial modernity experienced as "street modernity."

Moving from *The Goddess* to *Rouge Tears,* the previous vague utopic vision is now materialized with elaborated details, enabled by the strategy of elaboration. In the closing sequence, which closely duplicates the internal-versus-external setup at the end of *Stella Dallas,* the aged mother, released after twelve years of imprisonment, stands outside the school headmaster's house, gazing through the window at her adult son's engagement party (Figures 1.4, 1.5). This window frame

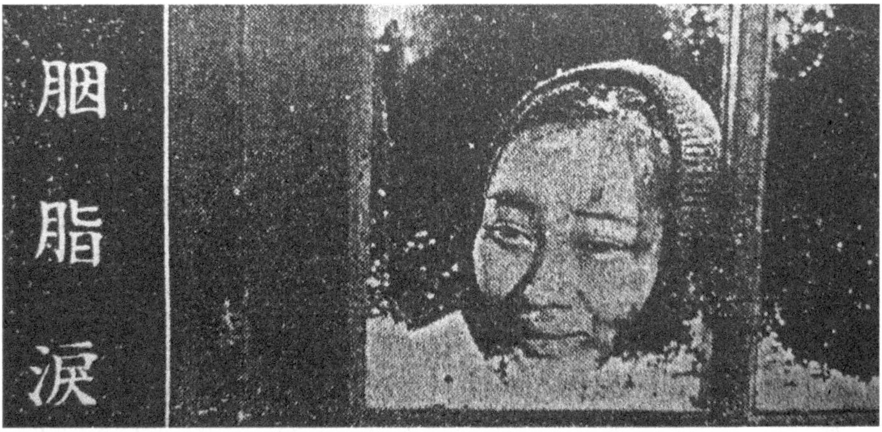

Figure 1.4 The mother looking in from outside the window bars in *Rouge Tears* (*Nanyue* special issue, n.p., courtesy of Hong Kong Film Archive)

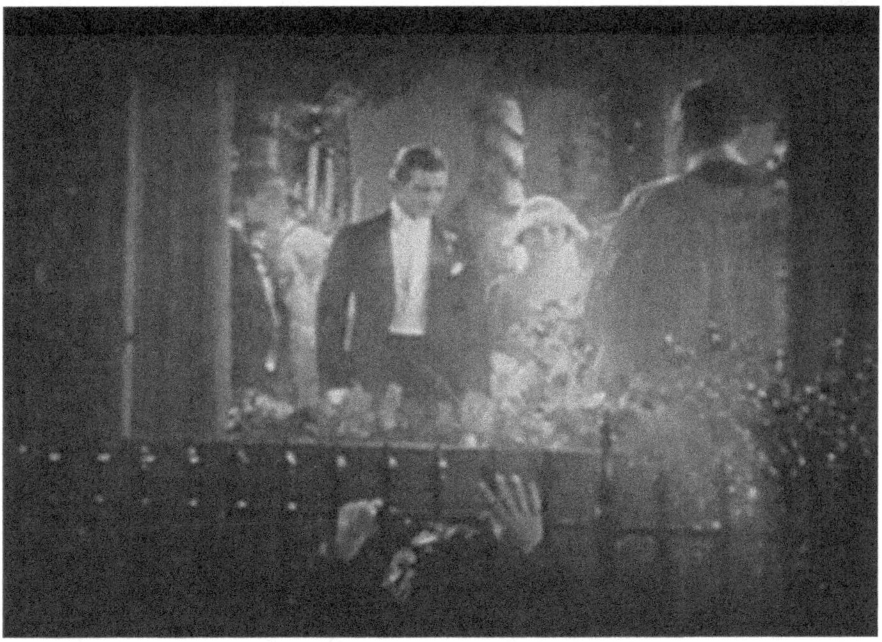

Figures 1.5 The mother, at bottom, witnessing her daughter's wedding from outside, her hands gripping the bars, in *Stella Dallas*

resembles the prison cell bars in that they both separate her from social normality, rendering her the abject "Other" on the wrong side. It also evokes the film screen that is projecting a success drama in which she has no part, and her perspectival shots meet no reverse/response shots from the other side of the window. Having witnessed her son's "success" silently, she chooses to vanish. With a close-up shot of her face superimposed on the snow-laden tree branches, she raises a finger to her lips, hushing with a smile, while snowflakes dance around her face, which gradually evaporates. The film ends with a theme line: "The greatest of human nature is maternal love."

At the son's engagement party, the erstwhile undefined hope for the future now pans out in two ways: his engagement with a well-educated classmate (which promises a respectable domestic life that the mother-prostitute is denied) and the prospects of continued music education overseas on graduating from the music conservatory. In anticipation of the promising yet prescribed future, the former school headmaster, or the surrogate father, urges the son to forget past memories and suffering (associated with his "dead" mother) in order to enjoy his youth and to dedicate himself to improving China's musical culture. With such a national-international outlook, the success story inscribes a present and a future that both center on male achievement while disavowing the past associated with the pathos of the mother-prostitute-turned-murderer. Consequently, the mother can only enjoy the "show" from the external side of the window/screen/divider, a "show" that promotes intellectual humanism laced with middle-class fantasy of individual and national improvement, completely exceeding her imagination.

Paradoxically, the solidification of undefined, virtual futurity into fait accompli (the future realized here and now with all details) deconstructs the utopic thrust. The future is now revealed as a middle-class, male-centered, male-driven society in which the poorly educated working-class woman has no role to play. In other words, this homogenous ideal society does not come from the elimination of class or gender inequality but rather from disavowal of what is perceived as the abject Other. Contrary to the vague vision in *The Goddess* that keeps alive the utopic thrust and the power of anticipation, the elaborated accomplishment in *Rouge Tears* demystifies the utopic thrust as essentially elitist patriarchal ideology that promotes male subjectivity, upward mobility, and male responsibility for nation building.

In his study of the *Godfather* series, F. Jameson similarly argues that the Utopian impulse that coexists with the ideological impulse in *Godfather I* becomes deconstructed in the sequel where the ideological content becomes undisguised and unmasked through "aesthetic representation and figuration."[76] That is, the Utopian impulse is invalidated when its ideological content is bared through representation. In *Rouge Tears,* the "aesthetic representation and figuration" that reveals the ideological premise of the utopic vision in *The Goddess* is precisely the strategy of *gongbi,* or excessive elaboration.

Such excessive elaboration does not make *Rouge Tears* an inferior film but rather a critical and dangerous supplement to *The Goddess.* Like an anamorphic lens that reorients our perception, the remake racks the focus, so to speak, by reversing the figure and the ground, utopia and ideology, thereby exposing the predecessor film's more fundamental ideological premise that has long been glossed over by the much celebrated manifest text (i.e., the theme of noble motherhood and the quiescent, subtle aesthetics). Through a comparative study with *Rouge Tears,* Wu's aesthetic tour-de-force, *The Goddess,* comes to be repositioned and repoliticized as a cultural product that is allegorical of the crisis of representing abject female sexuality and the gendered, lower-class experience of China's colonial modernity. In this sense, the entire remaking process can be viewed as a "commutation test" that alters certain audio-visual and representational aspects, with the result of bearing and baring the political subtext of the predecessor film.

Conclusion: An "Unknown Woman" from Shanghai Finds an Unexpected Dream in Hong Kong

In this comparative study of *The Goddess* vis-à-vis its Hollywood "before"—*Stella Dallas*—and its Hong Kong "after"—*Rouge Tears*—I have stressed the "critical act"[77] of positioning and politicizing the films. By defamiliarizing and excavating the politics of variant representational strategies, I attempt not simply to rescue the Hong Kong–made *Rouge Tears* from oblivion but rather to deploy it as a critical, anamorphic lens for repositioning and repoliticizing its silent predecessors made in Shanghai as well as Hollywood.

As my study demonstrates, the strategies of figuration and representation in *The Goddess* and *Rouge Tears* (sketch and elaboration respectively) register the director's negotiation with the crisis of representing abject female sexuality, a crisis revolving around the vexed relationship between the humanist, male authorship, the lower-class "unknown woman's" experience with China's colonial modernity, and the genre of melodrama or family ethics drama. By grounding the strategies of figuration in the politics of representation and representability, and in the ideological parameters of the melodrama genre, I stress that the transcendentalist "feminine difference" that Cavell sees in *Stella Dallas* hardly exists in Wu's films. On the contrary, both films underscore the low-class prostitute's experience of deprivation on the urban street, which in turn serves as a trope for addressing China's semicolonization.

Yet a question remains: how do we understand the role of Hong Kong in the making of *Rouge Tears*? To what extent does Hong Kong's colonial situation (in comparison with Shanghai's semicolonization) shape the remake? Can we see the remake as not only Hong Kong–made, but also Hong Kong–related? Finally, how might these questions help us understand filmmaking in pre–Pearl Harbor Hong Kong in relation to Hong Kong's regional collective subject positioning?

I have suggested that the decision to make *Rouge Tears* in Hong Kong in collaboration with the local Nanyue Film Studio had to do with war exigencies. Yet, in terms of narrative and thematic concerns, the remake replicated *The Goddess,* continuing Shanghai's prewar social exposé tradition driven by intellectual humanism.[78] As such, the remake inherits the mainland China orientation and does not exhibit specific interest in Hong Kong's geopolitics. Nevertheless, a different spin becomes noteworthy when we consider the film's publicity materials.

The film's publicity materials in Hong Kong emphasize its southern Chinese quality, which was related to yet not equivalent with Hong Kong's locality. That quality involves the leading actress Hu Die's switch from Mandarin Chinese to Cantonese (her native dialect) in the Cantonese version.[79] Hu Die is reclaimed as a Cantonese native, as a publicity poster affirms: "When a Cantonese hears Cantonese, things become crystal clear" (*Guangdong ren ting Guangdong hua, gewai liaoran*) (Figure 1.6).

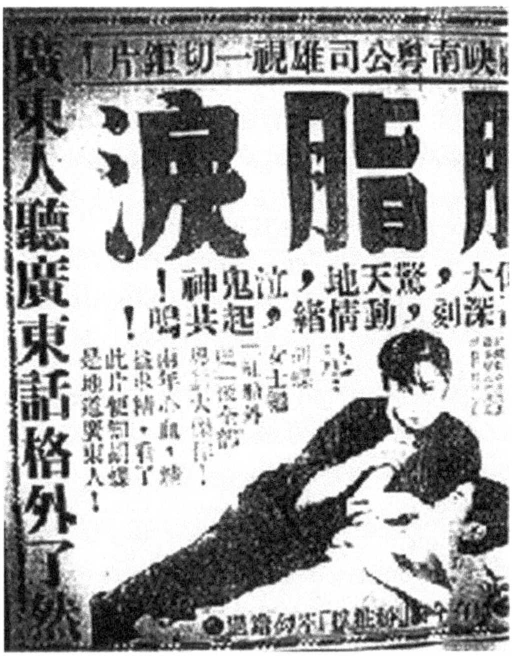

Figure 1.6 A poster of *Rouge Tears* showing Hu Die's mother character cradling her son. The blurb on the left declares, "When a Cantonese speaks Cantonese, things become crystal clear." The description above the image claims *Rouge Tears* as a Cantonese masterpiece, which proves Hu Die to be a full-blooded Cantonese native. (Courtesy of Hong Kong Film Archive)

The publicity also highlights the Qingxian brand sound recording system developed in 1932 in Shanghai by Zhu Qingxian—founder of Nanyue Film Studio in Hong Kong. The Qingxian brand was acclaimed as a locally made sound recording technology that allowed the Hong Kong film industry to offer significant help to the dislocated Shanghai film workers during the war. Such publicity tapped into and boosted the regional pride in southern Chinese culture, which prevailed in Hong Kong.

Contrary to the emphasis on southern Chinese pride and Hong Kong's film resources as industrial support, Hong Kong's colonial geopolitics was hinted at, yet ultimately remained a nonissue. This lack of concern with Hong Kong's specific locality means that Hong Kong was not yet seen as a positive reference point in the filmic interactions. This is reflected in the fact that Cantonese films made in Hong Kong at the time were categorized either on a linguistic basis as "Cantonese cinema" (*Yueyu pian*) or according to their larger regional cultural allegiance as "southern Chinese cinema" (*Hua'nan dianying*).[80]

The historical and geopolitical imbrication between Hong Kong–made Cantonese cinema and southern Chinese lingua-culture requires that we dereify Hong Kong cinema and reassess its intricate interactions with mainland China, Southeast Asia (a major destination for early southern Chinese emigrants), as well as Hollywood. The connection between *The Goddess* and *Rouge Tears,* being one example of such interactions during the silent-to-talkie transitional period, demonstrates the submergence of Hong Kong's locality in the regional matrix of "southern China" (*Hua'nan*). In other words, the Hong Kong–specific collective consciousness was not an a priori, tangible existence or telos to begin with. Rather, when it does gradually emerge into filmic representation and critical discourses, its content, import, and agenda continue to shift with time. Thus, Hong Kong's localized geopolitics and collective consciousness should be examined as an inchoate and fluid "structure of feeling" (à la Raymond Williams). This "structure of feeling" portends a mode of experience and affect that, on the one hand, stems from the lingua-cultural matrix of the larger southern Chinese culture and, on the other hand, registers a new geopolitics and subjectivity.

In the following three chapters, I study the ways in which the Shanghai and Hong Kong remakes increasingly participate in producing and reformulating location-specific collective subject positions. Since the Hong Kong remakes in these chapters are helmed by locally grown Cantonese filmmakers, I specifically focus on delineating Hong Kong's subject positioning through the continuous filmic interactions in the Shanghai–Hong Kong corridor and the Shanghai–Hong Kong–Hollywood triangulation.

CHAPTER 2

Family Resemblance, Class Conflicts

Re-version of the Sisterhood Singsong Drama

It is us poor people and us women who suffer the most after all.
—*Sister Flowers,* 1933

A year before Ruan Lingyu's "goddess" transforms herself into a blind-mute "captive mother" behind prison bars in 1934, Hu Die, the 1933 "Chinese Movie Queen," who was to reprise Ruan's role in both Cantonese and Mandarin Chinese in 1938, had already played a talking *and* singing mother, or, more precisely, two mothers (one rich, one poor) who are also twin sisters, in *Sister Flowers* (*Zimei hua*) (1933).[1] Directed by Zheng Zhengqiu (1888–1935), a dramatist-turned-filmmaker and a founding member of Shanghai's Mingxing (Star) Motion Pictures Co., *Sister Flowers* broke the box office record, showing to a full-house audience in Shanghai for over sixty days consecutively. It not only led Zheng to produce a sequel the next year, *A Flower Reborn* (*Zaisheng hua*) (1934), starring Hu Die again,[2] but also spawned a string of explicit and implicit remakes.[3] In this chapter, I compare the 1933 *Sister Flowers* with two Hong Kong remakes, *The Sister Flowers from the South* (*Nanguo zimei hua*) (dir. Li Bin, Liang Chen, 1939) and *The Happy Reunion* (literally, *New Sister Flowers, Xin zimei hua*) (dir. Hu Peng, 1962), and a postrevolutionary Shanghai film, *Stage Sisters* (*Wutai jiemei*) (dir. Xie Jin, 1964), all of which develop the sisterhood scenario with reference to different political agendas.

The decades of the 1930s and 1960s, in which the four sisterhood films were made, mark the (semi)colonial and Cold War eras, which unfolded in different directions in mainland China and Hong Kong. Compared with Wu Yonggang's *Rouge Tears,* made in Hong Kong in 1938, the two Hong Kong sisterhood films from 1939 and 1962 demonstrate an increasing interest in the locality of "Hong Kong" (distinguished from China) as both a setting and a thematic concern. The 1964 Shanghai film continues the theme of sisterhood solidarity, yet drastically reconfigures the sisters' social status and realigns the narrative with the socialist ideology of revolutionary China. The narrative premise of twin sisters being born identical yet becoming very different owing to their divergent social environments serves as a metaphor for the relationship between the Shanghai and Hong Kong cinemas. Originated under similar geopolitical circumstances—both Shanghai and Hong Kong being contact zones between China and the West—these two film cultures interacted throughout the first half of the twentieth century, yet eventually developed divergent (albeit still co-implicating) trajectories because of Shanghai's and Hong Kong's radically different politics during the Cold War era.

Given that the two Hong Kong remakes were made by Cantonese casts and crews that were not interested in replicating the 1933 *Sister Flowers* and that the postrevolutionary *Stage Sisters* was made in a drastically different political context from that of all the other versions, the remakes demonstrate greater latitude and closer engagement with their individual and immediate conditions in reworking the sisterhood scenario. Thomas Leitch describes this type of remaking as "updating," which often positions itself as a "revisionary" competitor vis-à-vis its predecessor by addressing "the audience's changed desires," and "transposing [the preceding film] to a new setting, inverting its system of values, or adopting standards of realism that implicitly criticize the original as dated, outmoded, or irrelevant."[4] Leitch's term usefully underscores the contention between the films; however, it implies a teleological trajectory that prioritizes the more recent film while relegating the predecessor films to the past or marking them as passé.

To emphasize the intersectional translation and revisionary transposition without assuming a teleological progression, I use the term "re-version" to describe the method of remaking in this chapter. Etymologically, "version" means rotation, turn, transformation, and "translated rendering" or, more specifically, "put[ting] something foreign into the mother tongue."[5] Thus, I use "re-version" to emphasize continuous transformation and localization, each version presupposing and negotiating an archive of one or more similar films and yet constituting a different repetition. It is through re-version that the "Hong Kong" locality comes to be imaged, articulated, and recognized as such by local *and* overseas Cantonese audiences. Likewise, re-version facilitates the "new" socialist China's self-differentiation from the "old," semicolonial China, on the one hand, and the capitalist West, on the other.

Since all four films fall roughly under the rubric of *gechang pian*, or singsong drama, that spices a melodramatic scenario with musical interludes, my study of the border-crossing and transhistorical re-versions will focus on two nodal points, each signifying one genre component. They are (1) the staging of the recognition scene, which instigates the melodramatic reversal of fate and reconfiguration of the social as well as domestic space, and (2) the acoustic spectacle of singing sequences and its affective mode of constructing and addressing the audience.

In analyzing these key scenes, I am centrally concerned with the ways in which social tensions regarding gender and class are disavowed, inscribed, negotiated, and imaginarily resolved through a utopic projection for a more desirable social as well as domestic space. On this basis, I further dissect the ideological limitations of each utopic vision and explore how the ideology-utopia complex in each re-version gestures toward specific, localized collective subject positioning in the intersections of modernity and (semi)colonialism, regionalism and nationalism, and the Cold War binary politics of capitalism and socialism.

In view of the films' dual genre registers—musical (or singsong film) spliced with melodrama, I choose to focus on gender and class inequalities as the underlying contradictions.[6] The issue of class, according to Richard Dyer, is disavowed and rendered unfigurable in Hollywood (capitalist) musical.[7] In my study of the four singsong dramas made in Shanghai and Hong Kong, I demonstrate that class (along with gender) is not uniformly disavowed, but is rather foregrounded or marginalized according each film's agenda.

Furthermore, class and gender issues fuel these films' melodramatic appeal. As Zheng Zhengqiu, scriptwriter and director of *Sister Flowers* (1933), contends in response to critique of his film's reliance on coincidence: coincidence—a structural principle of the genre of melodrama (or its Chinese counterpart, the family ethics drama)—should not be shunned as contrivance; rather, it can be mobilized to elicit a convincing performance, thereby generating audience identification and sympathy.[8] Zheng argues that the power of melodramatic coincidence comes precisely from its affective resonance with the audience, which transports the diegetic space into the social realm and thereby transforms the twin-sisters scenario into an apt vehicle for the social-problem melodrama. Implicit in the social melodrama is his exposé of the gender and class tensions in 1930s Shanghai and his aspiration for social justice. This social concern is reinflected in different directions in the three re-versions subsequently made in Shanghai and Hong Kong.

Melodramatic Doubling and Recognition: Sisterhood Lost and Regained

The first three films, *Sister Flowers, The Sister Flowers from the South,* and *The Happy Reunion,* all center on twin sisters separated at a very young age, growing up in different environments, and coming to represent divergent, even conflicting, outlooks. Their ultimate mutual recognition and reunion lead to the reconfiguration of familial, social relationships and the realignment of class and gender interests. Before attaining a new equilibrium, the sisters have to traverse broad sociopolitical domains and negotiate class-gender stratifications. This process offers the audience an opportunity to witness, fantasize, and assess the ramifications of young women's increasing visibility as laborers, victims, participants, and potential social agents in the striated public space that is emerging and taking on different forms in rural and urban interactions from the early to mid-twentieth century.

Sister Flowers (1933), produced by Star Motion Pictures Co., was adapted from a "civilized play" (*wenmingxi* 文明戏), *The Noble and the Criminal* (*Guiren yu fanren* 贵人与犯人), written and staged by Zheng Zhengqiu.[9] Following the theme line "The noble and the criminal originate from the same family" (*guiren yu fanren tongshi yijia ren* 贵人与犯人同是一家人), the film stages social conflicts in the domestic setting, as demonstrated in the climax recognition scene that shows reunion and realignment of the four family members who now belong to different classes. The family consists of the twin sisters (Da Bao, Er Bao) and their parents: the impoverished mother from the countryside and the opportunistic father who has become wealthy and powerful through trafficking weapons and marrying Er Bao off to a general.[10] While Er Bao becomes a manipulative mistress, Da Bao grows up with the poor mother and marries a carpenter in the countryside. They then move to the city as war refugees. In order to raise her twin infants, Da Bao finds work as a wet nurse for a rich woman, who turns out to be none other than her long-lost twin sister, Er Bao. When her husband suffers an injury and needs urgent medication, Da Bao turns to her mistress for a wage advance, only to be rejected. In despair, she tries to steal a gold neckband from Er Bao's son but is spotted by the general's sister. In an attempt to hush her, Da Bao accidentally knocks over a large porcelain vase that drops and instantly kills the general's sister. Da Bao is subsequently arrested and investigated by the police chief, who is none other than her long-lost father.

In the family recognition and reunion sequence, the family members are brought together in the father's living room as antagonists: the poor "criminal" elder sister versus the rich "noble" younger sister, the powerless rural mother versus the powerful urban father, the "criminal" daughter versus the "police chief" father, and the wealthy daughter versus the poor mother. This sequence (and the film as a whole) has oftentimes been criticized for being overly stagy owing to the largely fixed and interior camerawork, which can be attributed to the clunky recording system used in the early talkie era, yet is also seen as symptomatic of the director Zheng's theatrical background. My contention, however, is that the "stagy" setup actually serves effectively to visualize the tension between the characters, who represent conflicting class and gender interests. By regrouping the characters along different spatial axes within and beyond the screen, the family recognition/reunion sequence visually simulates various scenarios of gender and class realignment.

The sequence begins by centering the father and Er Bao, implying their alliance based on class and power. Then the mother enters the frame from the left, seeking to prove her relationship with the long-lost daughter, while the father is positioned between them, yet receding to the background as an obstacle with a decreasing presence. The turning point comes when the mother successfully matches a scar on her left arm with Er Bao's scar on her right arm (framed in extreme close-up) (Figure 2.1). The mother explains that the scar was inflicted by the father, who tried to punish Er Bao as a child, and that when the mother intervened, she and Er Bao were both scorched in one stroke. At this, Er Bao comes to realize that she is not only bound to this poor woman by blood; more important, they are both victims of patriarchal power. At this realization, the repentant Er Bao sobs on her mother's shoulder while blotting out the father's figure in the background.

Having visually reunited the mother and Er Bao, the camera pans left to frame the mother mediating between the indignant Da Bao and her wealthy sister (who is now outside of the frame). The next frame shows the mother and Da Bao on frame left, opposite the father on frame right, who suggests bringing the sisters together for a drink at the table. Still antagonists even when seated around the

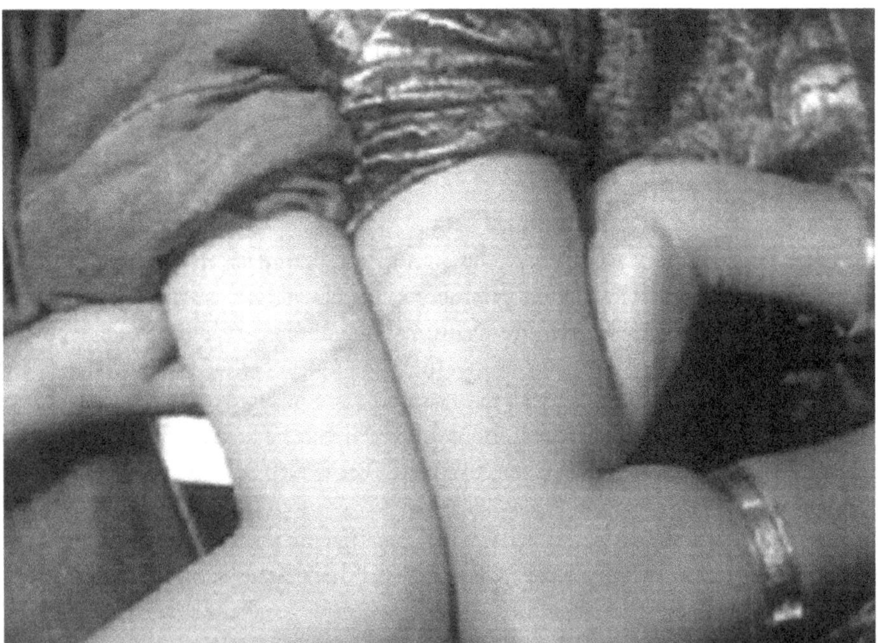

Figure 2.1 Mother's and daughter's scars match in extreme close-up in *Sister Flowers*

same table, the two sisters literally occupy different frames. In the first frame, when Er Bao, grouped with the father (in the background), offers a drink to her criminal sister (off screen), it has to be relayed by the mother, whose hand enters frame left to take the glass. In the next frame, the mother's hand enters Da Bao's frame right to pass the drink to her (Figures 2.2, 2.3).

The mother's mediation leads to the most publicized shot of this film. In this full shot, the three women sit around a table, with the father significantly missing (Figure 2.4). Da Bao and the mother, dressed in rags, are grouped on the left, while Er Bao, with permed hair and a flashy *qipao,* is isolated on the right, looking down, as if she feels guilty for what she has done to her rural twin sister. Again, the mother mediates by looking pleadingly toward both daughters in turn. Finally, the three women are reconciled and united with the consensus that "It is us poor people and us women who suffer the most after all" (*Shouku de haishi women qiongren; shouku de haishi women nüren*). By letting Da Bao deliver this punch line in an ostensible domestic setting, the film implies a women's alliance that is based on shared dual subjugation (in class and gender) and that goes from home to the larger society, leaving behind the wealthy patriarch.[11]

Regarding the dual hierarchies of gender and class, Vivian Shen argues: "Class is above kinship when it comes to dealing with the opposite sex. But women are consolidated regardless of their class differences."[12] However, in view of the ascendance of leftist cinema in early-1930s Shanghai (with its emphasis on class consciousness), I believe that the characters' ideological realignment stems from the interweaving of class and gender interests. It is through the gender-class analogy that being a woman is perceived as equivalent to being poor and oppressed, even if an individual woman (like Er Bao) may temporarily enjoy the illusion of power. The gender-class analogy suggests Zheng Zhengqiu's tentative adoption of a leftist perspective, which led to his efforts to inject class consciousness into his abiding humanist concern with women's subjugation in China's patriarchal society. In a key essay titled "Ruhe zoushang qianjin zhi lu" (How I Found the Progressive Road), Zheng proposes "Three Anti-isms" (*san fan zhuyi*), namely, anti-imperialism, anticapitalism, and antifeudalism. Based on his newfound radicalism, he asks that filmmakers stop pandering to the tastes of petty urbanites (*xiao shimin*) and instead try to transform their tastes.[13] Zheng's transition signals a new understanding of realism as a representational strategy that prefigures a not yet "real" world, rather than simply reflecting or succumbing to existing circumstances.

Zheng's radical turn apparently facilitates a form of subaltern speech, articulated by the doubly subjugated poor sister through her diagnosis of the social problem—"It is us poor people and us women who suffer the most after all." Yet, the resolution to the problem still resides in a powerful man. At the end of the film, the triumphant female trio walk out on the old patriarch, accompanied by upbeat,

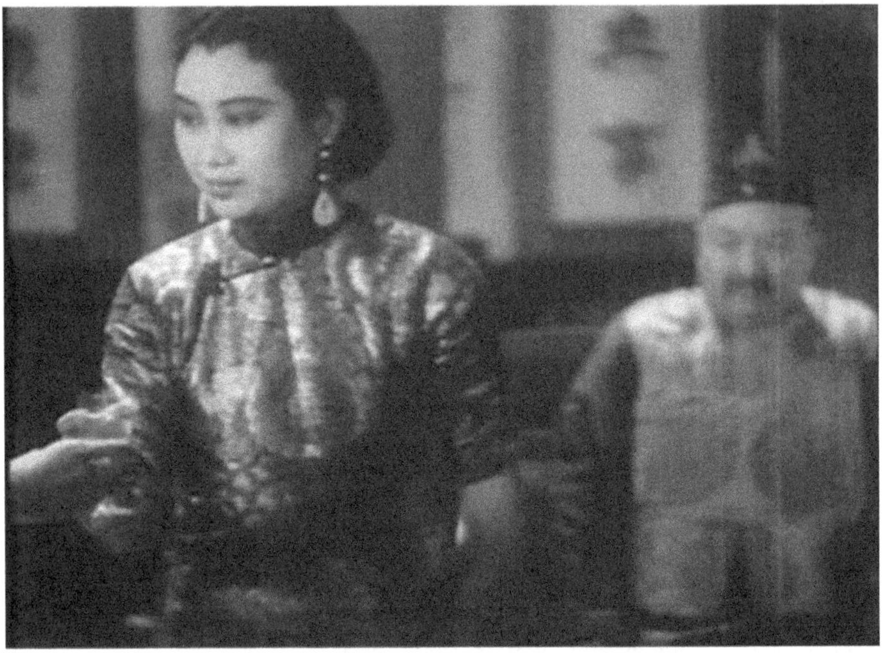

Figures 2.2 The mother's hand receiving the glass from Er Bao, frame left

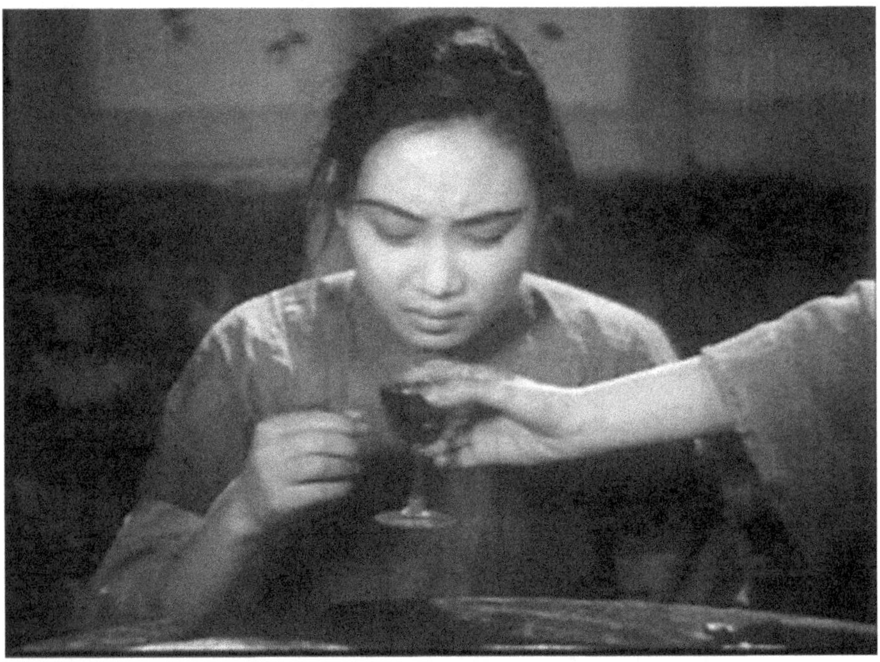

Figure 2.3 The mother's hand passing the glass to Da Bao, frame right, seeking to mediate between the two antagonist sisters, who occupy different frame spaces

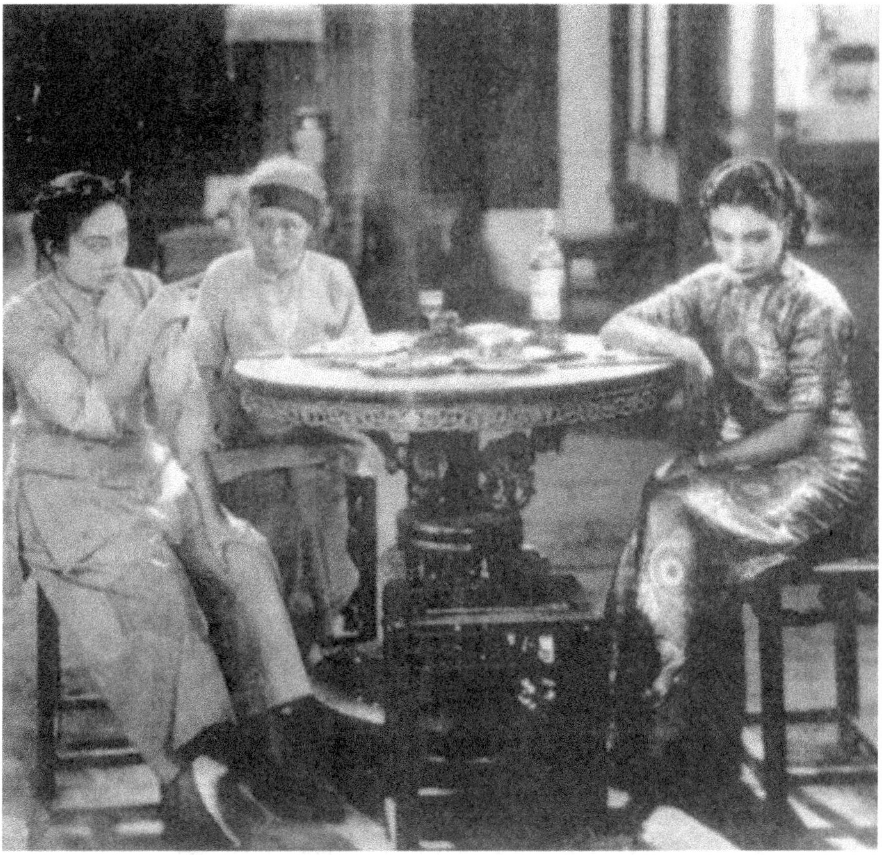

Figure 2.4 Full shot of mother and two daughters seated around the table, with Hu Die playing the twin daughters. The father is absent.

nondiegetic music, only to turn to Er Bao's husband, the warlord general, for help. The women's alliance is thus ultimately predicated on the delusive trust in a more powerful man. By posing the patriarchal system first as the problem, then as the solution, the film raises the question and imaginarily absolves it by purging the bad father; yet it falls short of questioning the patriarchal system per se. The utopic ending of female solidarity thus reinscribes the ideology that it sets out to critique.

Thus, despite its box office success and its election as the best Mandarin Chinese sound film in May 1934,[14] some critics faulted the film for "unhealthy sensibility" (*bu jianquan de yishi* 不健康的意识) and "conciliationism" (*tiaohe zhuyi* 调和主义).[15] Tang Na (1914–1988), a newspaper journalist, scriptwriter, actor, and film reviewer, attacked its "poisonous didacticism derived from escapist conciliationism."[16] Lu Xun (1881–1936), a leading writer and critic in modern China, highlighted the film's fatalism (when the mother tells the poor daughter: "The poor shall always be poor. You have to tolerate it patiently."), and satirized such fatalism as a quintessential weakness of the Chinese national character.[17]

Some other reviewers maintained that precisely because the film generated great profit and delivered Star Motion Pictures Co. from its financial crisis, its excessive sentimentalism and crude technology could become a dangerously misleading model for the Chinese film industry. Luo Yunwen, for instance, was disturbed by the film's display of tear-jerking scenes combined with its technical retrogression (manifested in the static camerawork that evoked the outdated "civilized play"). He considered these to be indicative of the director's pandering to a petty bourgeois audience's conservative appetite, even though the director explicitly emphasized the importance of transforming the audience's tastes (as quoted earlier). Luo concluded that the film excluded the proletarian audience, whose everyday pressures prevented them from enjoying such petty bourgeois entertainment.[18] In summary, the utopic union of the oppressed women was seen as facile and inane, gratifying only to a sentimental audience.

The ideological conciliationsim that the 1930s critics pinpointed in *Sister Flowers* seems to be corrected in a distant echo over three decades later in *Stage Sisters* (1964), a film produced by Shanghai Tianma Film Studio under the new socialist regime. The director, Xie Jin (1923–2008), a key figure in the first generation of directors in postrevolutionary China, was well versed in the 1930s family ethics drama (established by Zheng Zhengqiu's Star Motion Pictures Co.). He also received a dramatic education in the tumultuous 1940s from socially committed playwrights and critics. Therefore, it is not surprising that Xie's oeuvre, spanning half a century, is largely composed of social melodramas that address social events and problems through the lens of domestic drama.

Stage Sisters, one of Xie's best-known social melodramas made before the Cultural Revolution, reprises the sisterhood scenario with a similar focus on women's social role. By tracing the friendship and alienation of two lower-class Shaoxing opera actresses in pre-1949 "old" China and their ultimate reunion and common hope for a new future in the post-1949 "new" China, the film contrasts the women's fates under different social systems, emphasizing women's acquiring political consciousness and agency through new proletarian art. If the contrast between the twin sisters in *Sister Flowers* mainly consists in their opposite class affiliations, *Stage Sisters* revolves around a series of binaries between the "old" and the "new," the rural and the urban, the poor and the rich. These binaries drive the two stage sisters' meeting, alienation, and reunion. The stage sister who progresses with the times becomes a revolutionary actress serving the masses in the "new" rural China, whereas the other stage sister, who stagnates in the "old" parasitic and degenerate urban lifestyle, eventually loses her political as well as artistic "stage."

To recuperate the degenerate sister means to reeducate and radicalize her for the revolutionary rural audience in the "new" China.

A related key difference Xie introduces into the sisterhood scenario is that the "sisters" are not related by blood; rather, they become bonded through shared sufferings in the "old society," which enable them to acquire agency when they complete their reeducation in the "new society." The replacement of the blood lineage with shared sociopolitical experience and vision allows the film to expand the women's alliance to include not two but four sisters: Chunhua and Yuehong as the two stage sisters, Little Chunhua—a minor actress in the traveling Shaoxing opera troupe—and Jiang Bo—a progressive woman journalist.

Chunhua starts as an indomitable child bride who escapes from the feudal family, joins a traveling Shaoxing opera troupe, and becomes an accomplished actress specializing in young female roles. Her reputation eventually brings her from the rural stage to Shanghai's major theater. Resistant to metropolitan temptations, she eventually becomes radicalized by the progressive woman journalist Jiang Bo. In the socialist "new society," she becomes an active cultural worker committed to "self-reforming and performing revolutionary plays." Chunhua's stage sister, Yuehong, specializes in impersonating young male roles and plays Chunhua's companion on stage. Yet she falls prey to Shanghai's urban lure and slips into a parasitic life as the mistress of the exploitative theater manager. In 1949, when the manager escapes to Taiwan with the Guomingtang after its defeat by the Communist Party, Yuehong is abandoned, and eventually repents and is refolded into the revolutionary camp following her reunion with Chunhua during the latter's trip to the countryside.

The third sister, Little Chunhua, is the symbolic double of Chunhua. She also begins as an abused child bride. On seeing Chunhua being punished and pilloried in public, Little Chunhua offers her a bowl of water as well as commiseration. She reappears toward the end of the film, witnessing and expanding the revolutionary sisterhood. Finally, the "sister" responsible for inculcating revolutionary consciousness is Jiang Bo, a progressive journalist who helps Chunhua to understand her personal suffering in terms of class-gender suppression aggravated by Western (especially American) imperialism. Thus, she channels Chunhua's personal frustration toward a collective political goal.

Given the malleability, expandability, and political basis of the sisters' class-gender alliance, *Stage Sisters* sets the scenes of the sisters' mutual recognition and commitment in nondomestic settings. These scenes of recognition are captured in a set of two-person shots that evoke the reframing and regrouping of the family members in the climax recognition sequence in Zheng Zhengqiu's *Sister Flowers,* yet transcend the latter's familial, indoor confines. These two-person shots include a photograph of Chunhua and Yuehong in medium close-up, a close-up shot of

Little Chunhua offering water to the pilloried Chunhua, and a long tableau shot of Chunhua and Jiang Bo framed by a door on a rainy night, facing toward the audience while immersed in discussion about women's self-empowerment, which is conveyed not through their dialog, but rather through the extradiegetic chorus singing in Shaoxing opera (I shall discuss the acoustic address to the audience in the section below).

If *Sister Flowers* uses the mother's and daughter's conjoining scars to clinch their mutual recognition, *Stage Sisters* deploys the two-person framings as visual emblems of the sisters' self-rerecognition as well as mutual recognition, which also invites the audience to recognize the sisters' shared suffering, desire, and vision. Just as the indelible scars in *Sister Flowers* symbolize the mother's and daughter's common suppression by the patriarch, the shot of Little Chunhua offering water to the pilloried Chunhua underscores their shared sufferings under feudal patriarchal oppression. Furthermore, the long tableau shot of Chunhua and Jiang Bo framed by the door marks a threshold moment when the audience is invited to join the collective reflection on the vision of politicized sisterhood, a vision articulated by the Shaoxing opera chorus singing (Figure 2.5).

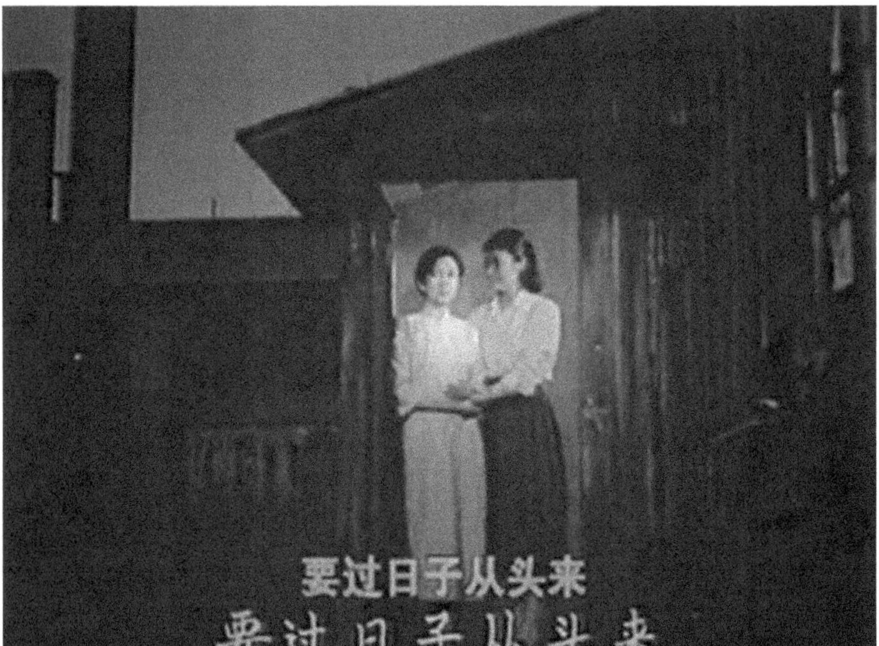

Figure 2.5 Long shot of politicized sisterhood, accompanied by a chorus singing "And to start a new life," in *Stage Sisters*

Gina Marchetti associates the self-reflective power of this shot with the Brechtian "alienation effect"[19] and Roland Barthes's *découpage* (i.e., cutting-out) effect. It throws the naturalized status quo into perspective and invites the audience to contemplate the "pregnant moment" characterized by the "presence of all the absences (memories, lessons, promises) to whose rhythm History becomes intelligible and desirable."[20] The same goes for other two-person shots. By arresting and denaturalizing the flow of realism that focuses on the present time-space, these pregnant moments suggest an "other" time-space that opens up ways of imagining and generating social and historical transformation. Thus, the two-person shots of sisterhood beyond the sheltered domestic sphere not only encourage recognition of the here and now, but also instigate and provisionally enact desirable future sociopolitical formations.

Yet, like the vision of female solidarity in *Sister Flowers* that ends up reinscribing the patriarchal structure, the vision of politicized sisterhood in the "new" society also has its ideological limitations. It is ultimately predicated upon excluding both domestic life and women with too much of a past in the "old" society. Shang Shuihua, an aged, fallen Shaoxing opera star, for instance, is pitied as a victim of the "old society" but is excluded from the young women's "sorority." Her suicide conveniently puts an end to her era and clears the space for the "new" youth. Along with the aged woman from the past, marriage also becomes invalidated or simply obviated. Young women in New China are liberated from the status of being men's sex objects or property and have become workers for the leftist political cause. The stage sisters' mutual recognition and reunion in the concluding sequence posit a reversal of class and gender hierarchies in "old" China. Yet, it is only through disavowing the "old" (including the older actress) that the "new" is established as a compulsive desire. In other words, the empowerment of the selected subaltern by making them "new" simultaneously produces another subaltern sector that is relegated to further obscurity.

Contrary to *Stage Sisters,* which reverses the class and gender conflicts in "old," pre-1949 China and stresses the empowerment of selected subaltern groups in "new" China, the two Hong Kong re-versions not only tone down class and gender conflicts, but also depart from the leftist ideology by divesting the downtrodden of sociopolitical agency. Instead, they demonstrate increasing investment in urbanity and Western-style modernity as desirable markers of Hong Kong's future subject positioning. Made six years after Zheng Zhengqiu's *Sister Flowers, The Sister Flowers from the South* (1939) relocates the twin sisters scenario to the "south" (i.e., Hong Kong), and the drama revolves around their inadvertent identity switch. The sisters' subsequent traversing into strange public spaces allows the film to underscore Hong Kong's locality by displaying its rural-urban contrast.

The elder sister, Da Die, adopted by a rich Mr. Zhou and renamed Zhou Yunying, is urban, well educated, and self-confident. The younger sister, Xiao Die, however, is wimpy and dependent, living with her poor father in the countryside and bullied by a stereotypically difficult stepmother. The identity switch begins when they simultaneously run away from their respective homes, Da Die escaping from a marriage that her foster father has arranged for the sake of his own upward mobility and Xiao Die fleeing after accidentally injuring her envious stepsister. Drifting into each other's space, Xiao Die is mistaken as Da Die and taken to Zhou's home, whereas Da Die is mistaken for Xiao Die by the latter's lover, Zhongqing, who takes her to her biological father in the countryside. The place and identity switching produce very different effects. The sophisticated Da Die takes the initiative in proving herself the long-lost twin daughter by showing a jade piece that forms a pair with Xiao Die's jade. As a talented singer, she also proves herself a better match for Zhongqing, a Westernized musician dressed in a suit and tie. Thus, Da Die not only initiates the family members' recognition and reunion in Xiao Die's absence, but also virtually threatens to replace Xiao Die as both a daughter and Zhongqing's girlfriend.

In contrast, Xiao Die's transformation into a high-class urban lady entails painful displacement and exploitation. Her discomfort with high heels and the dandy fiancé's advances illustrates the rural-urban gap. Exploited as a piece of commodity exchanged between men (Mr. Zhou and the fiancé), she helplessly allows herself to be framed in a newspaper photo that announces the "wedding of the patriotic Miss Zhou." She is delivered from this externally imposed role only when Da Die and Zhongqing come to her rescue upon seeing the photo. Xiao Die's return to the countryside and reunion with her twin sister, however, involve another displacement: Zhongqing's affection has now switched to Da Die. The triangular tension is resolved when Da Die once again demonstrates full agency by absenting herself and traveling to mainland China to join the national defense against the Japanese invasion. Her departure from Hong Kong not only solves the knotted romantic relationship, but also allows her to live out the title of "patriotic Miss Zhou," which fits well with the wartime nationalism. The film ends by cross-cutting between the lovelorn Xiao Die climbing up a stony mountain in an attempt to leave the home that no longer seems to need her and Zhongqing trying to retrieve her, after seeing Da Die off at the port. Meanwhile, the helpless rural father watches as Zhongqing catches up with Xiao Die, who instantly flies into his arms in a happy ending.

In this Hong Kong re-version of the family drama, class hierarchy is played down, resignified, and refigured as a rural-urban divide. Agency, now defined in individual terms (as opposed to collective conscientization), belongs to the well-educated, urban upper-middle-class, young characters rather than to the subaltern rural family. Furthermore, family reunion is predicated not on the purging of the wealthy urban patriarch (as in *Sister Flowers*) but rather on the elimination of the rural, non-blood-related stepmother in a stroke of poetic justice (she gets herself killed in an attempt to kill Da Die and Zhongqing). Poshek Fu sees this change as the film's refusal to romanticize the countryside as the site of subaltern power/speech.[21] It counters *The Sister Flowers* and other early- to mid-1930s left-leaning films, which tend to portray the countryside as the desirable, pristine China, while associating the city with Western corruption. In *The Sister Flowers from the South,* class tension is refigured from a prourban, nonleftist perspective.

Given the historical circumstances—the year was 1939, and, while the Second Sino-Japanese War was surging in mainland China, Hong Kong was relatively peaceful despite being subjected to China's nationalist call—*The Sister Flowers from the South* painstakingly negotiates between Hong Kong's locality and China's wartime nationalism. The twin sisters' divergent fates (one staying in Hong Kong, the other joining the nationalist cause in China), according to Poshek Fu, allegorize precisely Hong Kong's "ambiguous, almost schizophrenic" position "between centralizing nationalism and local consciousness."[22] Based on this reasoning, Fu argues that the "incipient sense of Hong Kong identity shaped by its hybridized culture and colonization" started not with the 1997 crisis but rather as early as the 1930s.[23]

Fu's equation between Hong Kong identity and concerns for Hong Kong's locality in the late 1930s could be premature and anachronistic. As I have argued in the previous chapter, Hong Kong–related collective consciousness in the late 1930s was largely embedded in the southern Chinese socio-lingua-cultural matrix rather than being specific to Hong Kong. The fact that the film ends with Xiao Die's settlement in Hong Kong while leaving Da Die's nationalist cause off the screen does seem to privilege Hong Kong's local experience. Yet, this local emphasis does not presume a defined Hong Kong identity; rather, it consists in flexibly engaging with the local and translocal resources and circumstances, which necessarily develop in relation with yet remain irreducible to nationalism (or allegiance to a remote Chinese government).

Similarly, the film's production and distribution were firmly grounded in local and translocal Cantonese resources. It was the debut production of Hu Dieying Film Company (Hu Dieying Yingye Gongsi 胡蝶影影业公司), founded by Hu Dieying, who played the twin sisters in the film. The company was located within Nanyang Film Company (Nanyang Zhipianchang 南洋制片厂)—the Hong Kong reincarnation of Shanghai's Tianyi (Unique) Film Production during the war.[24] The crew and cast behind the film were completely Cantonese. Given Hu Dieying Film Company's reliance on Nanyang Film Company, it is not surprising that the film was distributed in Singapore by Shaw Brothers—Tianyi's Southeast Asian distribution arm set up in 1930 by Run Run Shaw.[25] Thus, the film was specifically targeted at the Cantonese audience in Hong Kong and overseas.

The film's engagement with localness is also manifested in the mise-en-scène that showcases Hong Kong's landscape and in Hong Kong's striated social space that Xiao Die painfully negotiates. The film is among the earliest Hong Kong examples that feature exterior shooting, offering panoramic views of Hong Kong's bay, port, and rocky hills. This scenery hardly prefigures the easily recognizable Hong Kong trademark spots paraded in later films. On the contrary, it registers a quasi-documentary drive to depict the here and now and a distinct local look that would invite the Cantonese audience both within and without Hong Kong to recognize and relate to it.

Furthermore, the "local" Hong Kong social landscape is depicted as striated, and the local consciousness, as embodied by Xiao Die, is inchoate and evolving. Contrary to the cosmopolitan Da Die's unproblematic shuttling from the city to the countryside and from Hong Kong to the off-screen Chinese mainland, Xiao Die's spatial traversing involves a more painful (mal)adjustment. The perils she experiences during her urban adventure not only illustrate the rural-urban gap, but, more importantly, underscore Hong Kong's rapidly changing society, which entails the larger issue of female labor migration and displacement resulting from urban economic development. The film's conclusion in the countryside seems to indicate the impossibility for the rural poor to adapt to a new social position in a totally different urban environment. Yet, by reserving the urbane Zhongqing for Xiao Die, the film suggests a gradualist approach to urbanization, conjuring a local position that derives from the rural yet is expected slowly to approximate modern urbanity and individualism.

Shot over twenty years later, *The Happy Reunion* (1962) is another Cantonese twin-sisters film that combines domestic melodrama and musical spectacles. It continues and furthers the dramatic twists of identity confusion and place switching, expands the singing interludes, and introduces components from the detective genre. The film opens with the attempted murder of the urban sister, Yu Lanfen, and ends with the detective's timely arrival at the final showdown and successful elimination of the murderer. At this point, the film switches to melodramatic mutual recognition and the happy reunion of the wealthy mother, Mrs. Yu; the lost rural sister, Lanfang; the urban sister, Lanfen; and Lanfen's fiancé.

Once again, the sisters' differences symbolize the rural-urban contrast in early-1960s, preindustrial Hong Kong—this time with a humorous twist. Following the 1939 Hong Kong re-version, this film largely eliminates the issue of class conflicts and demonstrates no apparent political interest. Yet it also converges with the socialist *Stage Sisters* in that they both foreground the sisters' singleness,[26] which frees them from the wife-mother position and enables their social mobility and flexible, protean identity. If *Stage Sisters* multiplies radicalized young single women in order to underscore the emergence of a new revolutionary social sector in postrevolutionary China, the Hong Kong re-version uses this flexible singleness to facilitate the sisters' shifting personae and multiple layers of performance. The playful identity masquerade makes the melodramatic recognition more difficult, yet also more entertaining. Two elements are crucial in the identity game: latex mask technology and the leading actress He Lan's versatile acting, which lead to pleasurable and wondrous visual spectacles.

The latex mask was a new technical development that facilitated facial transformation and identity confusion. The murderous cousin, Guoji, seeks to plant the crime on Lanfen's fiancé, Jiaxiang, precisely by wearing a latex mask that resembles Jiaxiang's face.[27] Additionally, the visual spectacles of identity sliding hinge on He Lan's versatile portrayal of characters of both sexes from different class backgrounds. He Lan was contracted by the film's production company, Taoyuan Film Company (Taoyuan Dianying Qiye Gongsi 桃源电影企业公司), and nominated one of the ten hottest Cantonese movie stars in 1963.[28] In *The Happy Reunion,* she plays the twin sisters, following Hu Die in *Sister Flowers* and Hu Dieying in *The Sister Flowers from the South* (Figure 2.6). As the urban sister, Lanfen, disappears after her cousin, Guoji, tried to kill her, the rustic Lanfang travels to the city to

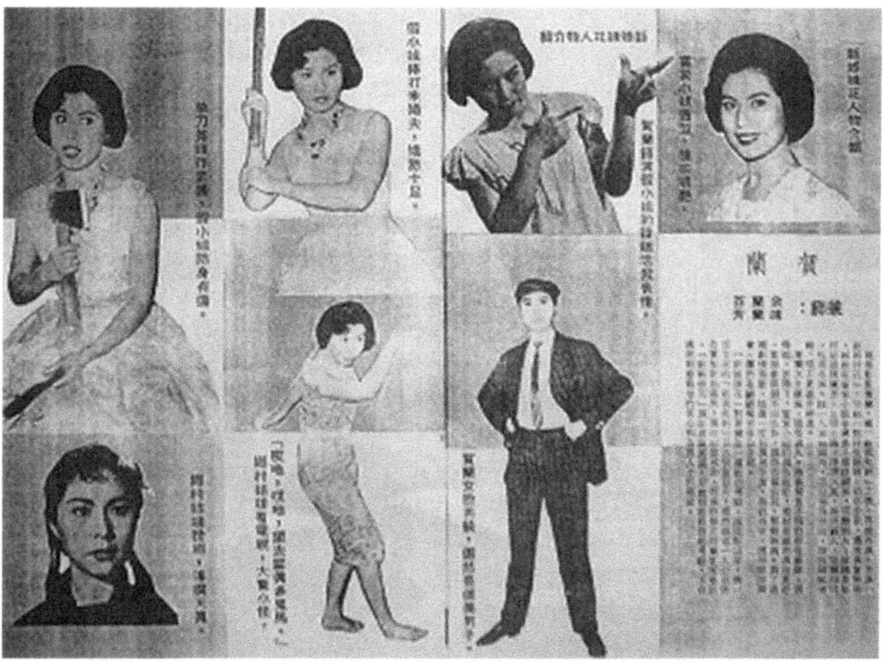

Figure 2.6 He Lan's multiple appearances as the twin sisters in *The Happy Reunion* (*"Xin zimei hua" dianying liantu xiaoshuo* [The Happy Reunion: An Illustrated Fiction], n.p., courtesy of Hong Kong Film Archive)

look for her biological parents. Despite her rustic garb and worn shoes, Lanfang is immediately mistaken for Lanfen, pictured in the "missing person" notice that Mrs. Yu posts in the newspaper, and she is summarily tied up and carried to the Yu family in a sack. Meanwhile, the injured Lanfen recovers at a fisherman's rural home while trying to uncover why her fiancé Jiaxiang would try to murder her. (In fact, it is her cousin, Guoji, wearing a latex mask that resembles Jiaxiang's face in the murder attempt.)

To find out the murderer's motive, Lanfen engineers an identity performance by cross-dressing as a gentleman attending the Yu family party, which is held in an attempt to revive the memory of Lanfang, who is mistaken to be the amnesiac Lanfen. In the film's publicity materials, Lanfen/He Lan's cross-dressing is touted as an attraction especially titillating to the female audience.[29] To accompany Lanfen's gentleman, the fisherman's daughter, who has befriended Lanfen, dresses up as a city girl at the party. The girl's newly bobbed hair and fashionable dress resonate with Lanfang's initial attempt to urbanize herself upon landing in Kowloon Peninsula.

A further layer of visual masquerade and role playing involves He Lan playing the rural Lanfang playing the urban Lanfen. After the family party, Lanfen secretly meets with Lanfang (seeing her as a look-alike, yet not recognizing their twinship) and asks the latter to continue playing the imposed identity so as to expose the murderer. To facilitate Lanfang's masquerade, Lanfen coaches her on urban upper-middle-class habits such as showering in the morning, drinking chocolate milk, kissing *ma-mi* (or mommy), and relishing expensive delicacies. All these habits contrast comically with Lanfang's aversion to kissing and high heels, and her rustic preference for lower-class snacks. Lanfang's awkward rehearsal of kissing (forcefully charging with a Mickey Mouse sound effect toward Lanfen, who pretends to be the *ma-mi* to be kissed) not only caricatures the gap between the city and the countryside, the local and the Western, but also offers a light-hearted portrayal of identity "upgrade" driven by Westernization. Meanwhile, the fact that Lanfang's mimicry must remain inferior and ludicrous (compared to Lanfen's naturalized everyday habits) indicates the importance of class and rural-urban differentiation, despite the film's ostensible drive toward uniform modernization and urbanization. (Later in this section, I will return to this subject to analyze the film's simultaneous disavowal and assumption of class conflicts and the rural-urban discrepancy, which is overdetermined by Hong Kong's Cold War geopolitics.)

He Lan's playful performance of characters of different sexes and class backgrounds displays her versatility as an actress with various skills including yachting, singing, dancing, playing basketball, fighting, as well as acting. All of these activities conjure a new image of youth and urban modernity that was becoming increasingly popular with the expanding young audience group in the 1960s.

Furthermore, He Lan's visual metamorphosis and Guoji's latex mask are emblematic of the cinematic medium's capability of developing ever-shifting images and spectacles of attraction, which postwar Hong Kong filmmakers were actively exploring.

If the bulk of the film is dedicated to entertaining identity masquerade that elides the issue of class and gender conflicts through cross-class and gender-bending performance, then the concluding recognition and family reunion sequence briefly introduces "real-life" issues of class and history, then once again displaces them. This brief interjection of the "real" combined with Lanfen/Lanfang/He Lan's carnivalesque visual masquerade lead to light-hearted treatment of the rural sister's double bind with regard to her class identity. This treatment in turn refracts the ideological premise of the modernization drive in 1960s Hong Kong.

The recognition and family reunion of the wealthy mother and the twin sisters ensue when the mother produces an old photo showing three men, Mr. Yu (the father), Mr. Chen, and the father of Jiangxiang—Lanfen's fiancé. This all-male photo reveals a hidden family history. The three men used to work as coal miners in Singapore; in a mine explosion, Jiangxiang's father sacrifices himself to save Mr. Yu; consequently, the Yu family adopts the orphaned Jiangxiang, while giving the younger daughter, Lanfang, to Mr. Chen. The sisters' separation, or, more precisely, redistribution, therefore results from the three men's friendship in hard times, when Hong Kong (and southern China) was exporting cheap labor to Southeast Asia (as well as North America).

The reference to exported cheap labor, brief as it is, may very well have resonated with the overseas Chinese audience in Southeast Asia.[30] Yet, by confining the experience of suffering (as diasporic coal miners) to the "past" and elsewhere (Singapore), and stressing the men's hard work and selfless brotherhood, Mrs. Yu's story brings up the obscured chapter of history only to justify the family's current affluence (and contemporary Hong Kong's rush toward Westernization). After all, Yu's wealth comes from honesty, loyalty, and hard work, as opposed to the patriarch's weapon-mongering and sponging off of the daughter's marriage (as in *Sister Flowers*). The justification of wealth and Western-style modernity, however, does not completely do away with the issue of class. With the reunion of the wealthy Yu family comes the imperative for the rural Lanfang to assume a new upper-class position as Miss Yu Number 2. Meanwhile, however, Lanfang's upward class mobility is shown to be not entirely desirable when Lanfen's fiancé jokes that Lanfang must not dress or behave like Lanfen in order to avoid confusion. In other words, class and rural-urban distinctions must be preserved for maintaining the proper social order. Thus, social hierarchy is reinscribed (through Lanfang's necessarily inferior mimicry of her wealthy twin sister) even as it is disavowed by the illusive drive toward a homogenous upper-middle-class lifestyle.

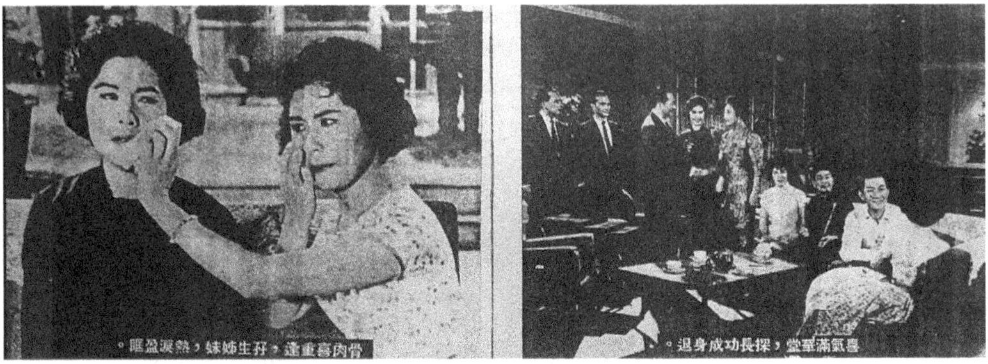

Figure 2.7 The happy reunion here and now (contrary to the tension-ridden roundtable scene in *Sister Flowers*). Rich sister wipes tears for poor sister in sympathy (left); all inclusive reunion (right) ("*Xin zimei hua" dianying liantu xiaoshuo*, n.p., courtesy of Hong Kong Film Archive)

Since the film shies away from a fundamental social tension that demands instant resolution, the sibling recognition and family reunion do not gesture toward a systemic transformation but rather occur as happenstance, tacked onto the detective's foiling of Guoji's second murder attempt. Consequently, the utopic thrust, or the gesture of anticipation, is short-circuited in *The Happy Reunion,* and the here and now (of a Westernized, urban Hong Kong) is presented as the ideal state (Figure 2.7).

Interestingly, the here and now of upper-middle-class Hong Kong is justified and idealized through its contrast not only with hard labor in Southeast Asia, but also with Shanghai and its film culture. Here the casting of Hu Die as Mrs. Yu, the wealthy mother, takes on historical and symbolic significance. Having played the lower-class mother-prostitute in *Rouge Tears* (1938) and the twin sisters in *Sister Flowers* (1933), the 1933 "Chinese Movie Queen" emblematizes early-twentieth-century Chinese cinema. Thus, her casting in *The Happy Reunion* not only cashes in on her residual star value and her native command of the Cantonese dialect (a strategy already employed in *Rouge Tears*), but also constitutes a remote echo of early Chinese film history. Meanwhile, Hu's almost exclusive portrayal of elderly mothers in supporting roles in 1960s Hong Kong not only corresponds with her aging,[31] but also signals the temporal, generational, and spatial shift from 1930s Shanghai to 1960s Hong Kong. As Hu's revival simultaneously spells her marginalization in films that feature Hong Kong–raised young actors and recenter on Hong Kong–specific concerns, the Shanghai–Hong Kong filmic "kinship" is both acknowledged and reoriented to focus on Hong Kong's increasing claim for independent local consciousness and postwar capitalist modernity.

The Acoustic Allure: Fashioning and Addressing the Audience

The melodramatic moments of identity confusion, multiplication, and recognition deployed in these four films are complemented by musical interludes that lure and address the audience on the affective level as technical novelty, popular entertainment, trigger of regional resonances, and/or vehicle of ideological indoctrination. The musical interludes initially became a popular additional technical novelty in film with the inception of sound in early-1930s Chinese cinema. It led to a fad of singsong cinema (*gechang pian*) both inside and outside of China.[32] The first Shanghai-made Vitaphone film was *The Singsong Girl Red Peony* (*Genü hong mudan*) (dir. Zhang Shichuan, 1931), starring none other than Hu Die, who performed set pieces drawn from the Peking Opera repertoire, which garnered an enthusiastic response from the domestic and diasporic Chinese audience.[33] Almost simultaneously, Cantonese songs were incorporated into films adapted from Hollywood's early fantasy musicals (a mode of remaking studied in my next chapter).

Given the commercial success of these early singsong films throughout China, Hong Kong, and the Southeastern Asian region, it is not surprising that *Sister Flowers* was advertised as "an all talking and singing masterpiece," featuring a long singing sequence as a major spectacle. In this prolonged two-minute song sequence, Hu Die, one of the earliest actresses heard on the screen, plays Da Bao, the impoverished yet loving mother who sings a lullaby while rocking her twin babies. The sequence is largely done in one long take, framing Da Bao in a medium shot, singing about poor parents' unbounded love for their children (Figure 2.8).

The a cappella song was meant to demonstrate the perfect marriage of Hu's vocal skills and the Movietone sound-recording technology. To underscore the film's acoustic attraction, the Central Theater (Zhongyang Da Xiyuan 中央大戏院) broadcast the song to the public through loudspeakers as a form of preview. Bonus printed lyrics and newspaper advertisements further emphasized the acoustic allure as well as the "unprecedented" visual spectacle of Hu Die playing two roles in the same frame.[34] The film ran consecutively for over sixty days in Shanghai's first-run Strand (Xinguang 新光) Theatre, then continued to attract full-house audiences for more than twenty days in the second-run Central (Zhongyang) Theater, setting a box office record.[35] Hu also toured the film in Hong Kong in 1935, making it available to the Hong Kong audience.[36] This tour could have contributed to the spate of 1940s Hong Kong remakes of the twin-sister scenario.

As an audio-visual spectacle and a social-exposé film, *Sister Flowers*, along with seven other Chinese films, was selected for the Moscow International Film Festival in 1935, followed by a tour in major European countries, accompanied

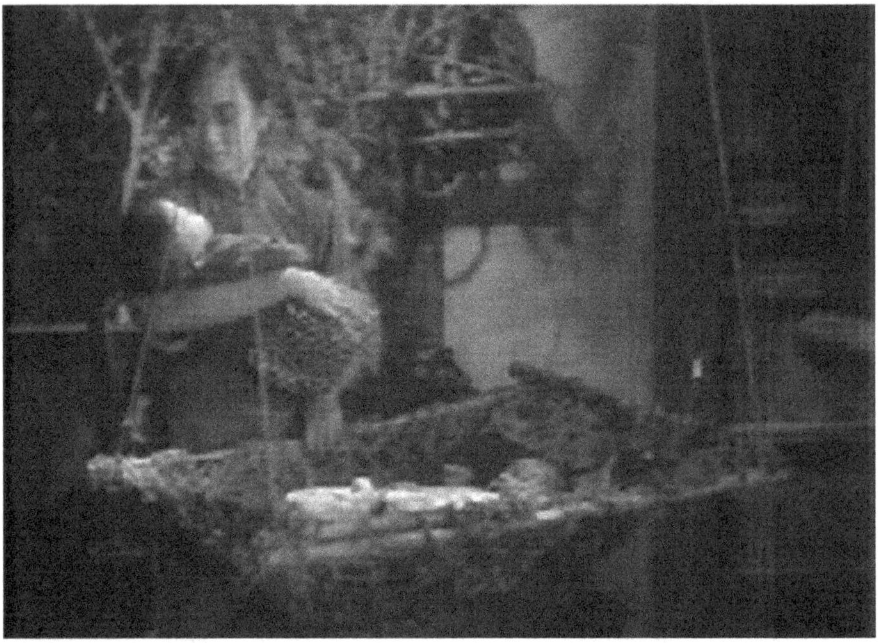

Figure 2.8 Hu Die's Da Bao singing a lullaby while rocking her twin babies in a long take in *Sister Flowers*

by Hu Die and Star Motion Pictures Co.'s producer Zhou Jianyun 周剑云. It was rumored that *Sister Flowers* and another Star Motion Pictures Co. production, *Spring Silkworms* (*Chuncan*) (dir. Cheng Bugao, 1933), would have been sold to UFA in Germany had it not been for a Chinese student protest overseas.[37] *Sister Flowers* was eventually sold to Japan, which *Star Monthly* (Star Motion Pictures Co.'s house magazine) triumphantly pronounced as China's first foray into the Euro-American and Japanese film market, a significant progression from marketing to Southeast Asian colonies. It signaled Chinese cinema's moving beyond the defensive stance of "boycotting Japanese goods" (*dizhi rihuo*) to the assertive stance of "promoting domestic goods" (*tuixiao guohuo*).[38]

Thus, the film took on a political mission of exporting Chinese values and film culture to capitalist countries, thereby imaginarily reversing the nearly centurylong Western penetration into China. The triumphant discourses on the international as well as domestic success of *Sister Flowers* went in tandem with the high praise for Hu Die's on- and off-screen performance. Overall, both the film and the leading actress were seen as acoustic and visual vehicles for Chinese values that facilitated the construction and propagation of a positive Chinese national image on the international stage.

If *Sister Flowers* and Hu Die not only appealed to China's petty bourgeoisie sentiment (as criticized by some reviewers), but were also paraded to overseas Chinese and international audiences to establish a positive image of China and Chinese cinema, the acoustic spectacles in the Hong Kong re-versions were concerned with different issues and addressed different audiences. *The Sister Flowers from the South* features Cantonese opera singer Hu Dieying (1911–1989), who was both the leading actress and the producer of the film. Hu had had prior experience performing for Chinese communities in San Francisco and Honolulu. She also starred in one of the earliest Cantonese talkies, *Romance of the Songsters* (dir. Joseph Sunn), which was shot and premiered in San Francisco in 1933.[39] *The Sister Flowers from the South,* the debut production of Hu's own Hu Dieying Film Company, serves as Hu's star vehicle, featuring her direct address to the audience. The film opens with two close-up shots that precede the narrative, showing Hu Dieying smiling and nodding to her audience, beckoning the latter to enter her world. Within the diegesis, her Cantonese operatic performance also readily appeals to the regional sentiments of Cantonese audiences in southern China, Hong Kong, and overseas.[40]

To be sure, the Cantonese-based acoustic allure is not free from nationalist politics. Rather, Hu's diegetic operatic address to the audience not only bespeaks intense regionalism and translocalism, which are characteristic of Cantonese opera, but also appeals to nationalism through adding a specific twist to the repertoire opera piece titled "Wang Zhaojun Goes beyond the Pass" (*Zhaojun chusai* 昭君出塞). This operatic set piece narrates the legend of Wang Zhaojun, originally a court lady who refused to ingratiate herself with Emperor Yuan Di of the Han dynasty, and who volunteered to be married to a Hun chief in the year 33 BC in order to appease the barbarian minority. Wang's act has conventionally been praised as a heroic attempt to alleviate interethnic tensions and solidify the Han dynasty's authority. This is underscored in Hu Dieying's performance.

In the long, stand-alone singing sequence, Hu Dieying plays Da Die, who performs Wang Zhaojun to a crowd of social celebrities gathered for her foster father's birthday. The purpose of the party, according to Da Die's design, is to raise funds for China's anti-Japanese war. This patriotic agenda resonates with the conventional interpretation of her operatic persona, Wang Zhaojun. To reinforce Wang's patriotism, Da Die's performance adds a detail. When the Hun chief points out that the Han emperor is so inept that he resorts to trading off his woman for peace, Da Die's Wang Zhaojun repudiates the humiliation and states that she sides with the Han emperor and that all Han people are united against the barbarian minority (Figure 2.9).

Her lyrics further urge "our compatriots" to unite and behead the "treacherous enemy leader" in order to "revenge our homeland." Given the time of the film's production during China's war against Japan, we can understand the barbarian

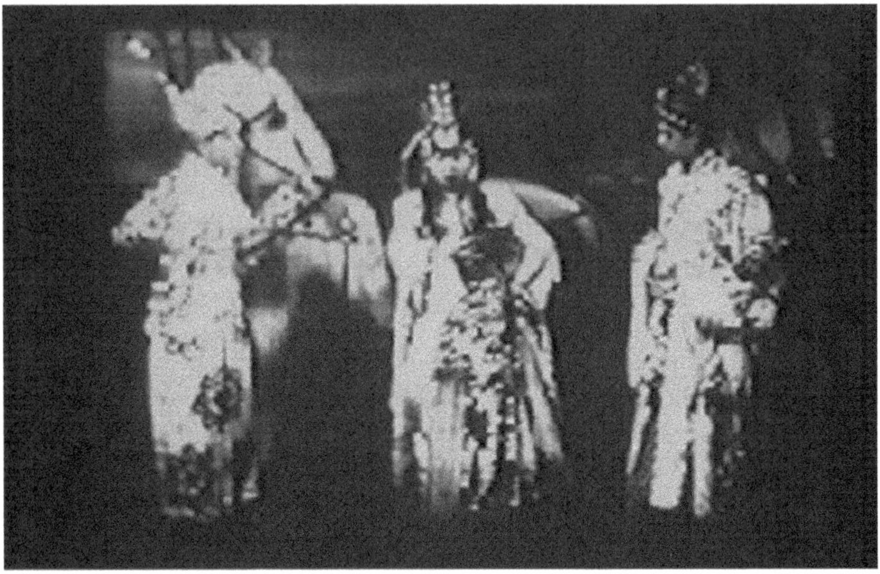

Figure 2.9 Hu Dieying's direct address to the audience through her character Da Die (middle), who plays Wang Zhaojun repudiating the Hun chief, in *The Sister Flowers from the South*

Hun's hostility to the central Han dynasty as an allegory for the Japanese invasion. In this sense, Da Die's Wang Zhaojun conveys a nationalist sentiment appropriate to late 1930s "national defense cinema" (*guofang dianying*).[41] It also foreshadows Da Die's eventual border-crossing to mainland China to participate in the anti-Japanese war toward the end of the film. The diegetic fund-raising in the singing interlude echoes actual wartime fund-raising campaigns launched by patriotic Cantonese artists both in Hong Kong and in California.[42]

However, the allegory of patriotism conveyed by Wang Zhaojun's story is easily ruptured, even reversed, by its multiple interpretations. Historically, poets have tended to describe Wang as a resentful exile, suffering from homesickness and homelessness simultaneously. This view has gone hand in hand with criticism of the Han emperor's incompetence to the extent that he had to trade a concubine for temporary truce with the invading minorities. These interpretations critique the male game (of war and negotiation) for rendering women disposable and creating their dilemma of being caught up in split allegiances. To an extent, this critique may constitute a poignant allusion to or allegory of Hong Kong's interstitial position as a colony ceded by the Qing dynasty to the British Empire in a truce. Like Wang Zhaojun, Hong Kong's value for its "mother" land depends on its exchange value, that is, its ability to be disposed of and transferred to a foreign power for appeasement, which in turn secures the motherland's survival.

On the extradiegetical level, Hu Dieying's re-version of the Wang Zhaojun legend also brackets the apparent nationalist message in its operatic mode of addressing the audience. First, Hu's audience appeal was deeply rooted in her star persona. During her 1927 tour in North America, she had already performed the "Wang Zhaojun" piece for overseas Chinese in San Francisco, which helped disseminate the traditional regional operatic culture across geographical borders. Her reprisal of the audio-visual spectacle in the 1939 film not only reminded the audience of her operatic background, but also reinforced her versatility as a border-crossing Cantonese opera star.

Furthermore, like Hu Die's performance of the lullaby in *Sister Flowers,* Hu Dieying's reenactment of Wang Zhaojun is captured in a long sequence that is stylistically separate from the narrative and consequently arrests the narrative flow. In this sequence, frontal, long, or medium shots are heavily used, with occasional close-ups on her face and cut-away shots to the guests' reactions. Such visual presentation evokes theatrical spectatorship and interpellates the film audience (via the party guests) as theatergoers. The operatic emphasis on costuming, body language, and vocal skills, which elicit a sense of fascination, resonates with what Tom Gunning describes as "aesthetic of attraction." According to Gunning, such aesthetics deviate from Hollywood's codified narrative cinema by privileging exhibitionism over voyeurism, the astonishing effect over narrative closure.[43] Given Hu Dieying's border-crossing star charisma and the central position of the "Wang Zhaojun" program in her repertoire, her operatic sequence addresses regional and transregional Cantonese audiences as both a pleasurable, stand-alone audio-visual attraction and a distraction from the historical expediency of the nationalist message. Unlike Hu Die's lullaby in *Sister Flowers,* which uses the new acoustic attraction to promote a positive Chinese national image to the international as well as domestic audience, Hu Dieying's operatic performance in *The Sister Flowers from the South* is ultimately oriented toward the local and diasporic Cantonese audience, which serves to reinforce a linguaculture-based regional and transregional consciousness.

The departure from the nationalist imperative becomes further developed in *The Happy Reunion,* a re-version of the twin sister scenario for yet another geopolitical situation, one that stood at the intersection of the local and the Western (as opposed to the interaction between Hong Kong and China in *The Sister Flowers from the South*) in early 1960s Hong Kong. Prefiguring late 1960s urban youth films, *The Happy Reunion* significantly expands the repertoire of song numbers by fully displaying the singing skills of the lead actress, He Lan, and the two supporting actors, Lan Tian (who plays the wealthy sister's fiancé, Jiaxiang) and Zheng Junmian (1917–1995) (the "Oriental Elvis" who plays the murderous cousin, Guoji). Contrary to the mostly static camerawork in the 1933 and 1939 films, which captures a highly theatrical indoors setting, the 1962 film deploys brisk camera movement, showcasing more dynamic singing sequences. He Lan's Westernized Cantonese songs are mostly performed in open space—the sea, the streets, or the mountain trail—parading Hong Kong's variegated landscape while showcasing the main actors' vocal performance. Additionally, instead of packing the vocal performance into one prolonged solo, the 1962 film features a series of song numbers performed by He Lan, sometimes solo, sometimes in a duet with Lan Tian or with Zheng Junmian.

Not only do the singing interludes punctuate the film at different moments, He Lan's songs also address different issues from those implied by Hu Die's lullaby and Hu Dieying's "Wang Zhaojun" opera. The lullaby eulogizes poor parents' love for their children—a motif running through Shanghai-made family ethics dramas, as already illustrated in Wu Yonggang's *The Goddess* and *Rouge Tears*. Hu Dieying's "Wang Zhaojun" opera seemingly espouses nationalism yet distracts from it and subsumes it to her star aura and operatic audio-visual pleasure. He Lan's vocal performance, in contrast, more dynamically integrates with the narrative development. As a result, her songs are expressive, improvisational, and situation-dependent. They ultimately contribute to justifying Hong Kong's modernization drive while glossing over class and gender conflicts.

He Lan's character, Lanfen, the wealthy sister, sings while yachting and hiking, which conveys a Westernized, urban lifestyle, inviting the local audience to enjoy Hong Kong's natural landscape and partake in modernity as an urbanized insider. Contrary to this, the twin sister, the rustic Lanfang, performs three numbers that highlight her cultural shock at the marvelous yet intimidating urban Hong Kong. The three singing interludes take place when she approaches urban Hong Kong on a boat, when she encounters TV culture in Mrs. Yu's home, and when she dances with Guoji, the murderous cousin, at the family party. In these singing sequences, Lanfang's perspective predominates, conveying her reaction to the urban environment. Thus, the audience is put in an outsider's position like that of Lanfang and is vicariously taken on a tour of early-1960s urban Hong Kong, experiencing simultaneous amazement and alienation. Consequently, her songs interpellate and educate viewers who share her status—newly arrived from rural Hong Kong (or some equivalent background)—in how to engage with contemporary urban Hong Kong.

Lanfang's first song number, "Beautiful Hong Kong" (Meili de Xianggang 美丽的香港), captures her initial encounter with the brave new world as she enters the harbor by boat. Various distance shots display urban scenery, alternating with Lanfang's reaction shots. The lyrics of her song catalog the beautiful bay, the skyscrapers, and the hustle and bustle of the street. Yet they also express her increasing self-consciousness about her rustic appearance. This sequence grants the local audience the pleasure of recognizing Hong Kong on the screen. For the nonlocal audience (including new immigrants), it helps to establish a discernible and desirable image of Hong Kong, thereby fostering a sense of modern Hong Kong subjectivity that beckons the outsider viewer to participate.

Lanfang's second song, "The World in the Mirror" (Jingli qiankun 镜里乾坤), caricatures the shocking clash between the local (represented by Lanfang) and the Western (represented by TV culture). In this sequence, Lanfang is mistaken for Lanfen and locked up in the latter's fashion-filled bedroom in the Yu residence. Accidentally, Lanfang turns on the TV set—a luxury item in early-1960s Hong Kong.[44] Her subsequent reaction to the moving images on the TV monitor, or what she calls "the big mirror," evokes the Shanghai audience's initial encounter with cinema at the end of the nineteenth century. According to an 1897 report titled "Watching American Shadow Plays" (Guan Meiguo yingxi ji), the Chinese viewers of the shorts "felt as though [they] were actually on the site, and they felt exhilarated. Suddenly the lights came on again and all the images vanished. . . . It was indeed a miraculous spectacle."[45] The same credulous naivety ("seeing is believing") and fascination with a new technology characterize Lanfang's reaction to "the world in the mirror."

When she sees Western soldiers charging toward enemies and planes dropping bombs, Lanfang breaks into singing about the thrilling horror as she mimics the charging, makes a terrified face, and covers her eyes.[46] She also sings about her admiration for a Western female singer, though she feels frustrated at not being able to understand the lyrics. When a Western couple dances, she imitates the motion while calling it "disgusting." Lanfang's simultaneous mimetic admiration and critical distance dramatize the impact of the plethora of urban stimuli, of which TV culture is emblematic. Once again, her reactions simultaneously mediate the cultural shock experienced by viewers who occupy the similar outsider or new immigrant position and demonstrate ways to negotiate and learn to desire modern Hong Kong.

In her last song, "Mad Singing, Hot Dancing" (Kuangge rewu 狂歌热舞), performed in duet with the cousin, played by Zheng Junmian—the "Oriental Elvis"—Lanfang mocks upper-class extravagance by breaching its protocols with her improper manners and comic prancing steps. Her innocuously mocking perspective allows the audience to laugh at Hong Kong's blind Westernization while continuing to desire its modernity.

Through elaborate camerawork and fast-paced editing in these singing interludes, *The Happy Reunion* eulogizes youth, energy, and speed, and ultimately construes Westernization as the desirable present and future for contemporary Hong Kong residents. It flaunts "the modern trappings middle-aged filmmakers thought the young audience would want," including "dancing parties, nightclubs, bars, campfire dances, B-B-Q outings, scenes from school life, sport cars, extravagant homes and yachts, Western fashions, dating, fighting, and musical scenes."[47] Targeting the expanding youth audience in Hong Kong and Southeast Asia,[48] the film foreshadows the craze of youth cinema (or *qingchun pian* 青春片, sometimes associated with youth problem films) that was to dominate mid-1960s Cantonese film culture.[49] The re-version that drastically repurposes the twin-sisters scenario contributes to producing a postwar Chinese film market beyond mainland China, which in turn allows Hong Kong cinema to emerge from its historical marginalization vis-à-vis Shanghai cinema and to survive its loss of the Chinese market after 1949.[50]

Contemporaneous with *The Happy Reunion,* yet produced under diametrically opposite geopolitics, the postrevolutionary *Stage Sisters* offers a drastically different acoustic allure and elicits a different structure of desire. Consistent with the narrative emphasis on collective political conscientization and reeducation, *Stage Sisters* transforms Shaoxing opera precisely for this political purpose. Performed by all-female troupes since the late 1920s in southeast China, Shaoxing opera in this film undergoes a twofold transformation: (1) cinematic adaptation of its formulaic melody and (2) thematic rewriting of the lyrics in accordance with the ideological agenda of the time.[51] As a result, the film shows the reformation of the female solo and the chorus performance from the pre-1949 middle- and lower-class entertainment to the post-1949 vehicle of ideological indoctrination of the masses. Furthermore, the chorus, representing the collective voice, increasingly supersedes the female solo as an expression of heightened collective political consciousness, which serves to interpellate and agitate the lower-class audience.[52] In other words, the acoustic allure and its political effect are achieved through downplaying the individualist female-star cult (contrary to the other three sisterhood films that underscore such a cult) and replacing it with the collective "people's voice," now articulated by the female chorus, or the community of "sisters."

Not only is the operatic performance coded differently in the "new" versus "old" China, the "stage" (including both the physical theater and the geographical, social setting of performance) also shifts with time. The film opens in the 1930s, with a long take panning over a vast rural landscape, landing at a crowded bazaar, then craning down to reveal a bare open-air stage surrounded by excited peasant viewers. As the "stage sisters," Chunhua and Yuehong, gain a reputation, they move to Shanghai and start to perform in a modern theater. Thus, exterior shots are replaced by interior shots, focusing on the stage sisters' increasing exposure to sexual and economic exploitation within the small world dictated by the theater manager. The meeting with Jiang Bo, the progressive female journalist, leads Chunhua to see the necessity of fighting for one's "own stage," that is, to obtain one's own space of performance and propaganda. In other words, they should not simply perform a show of their own choice; they should also systemically challenge and transform the current social stage characterized by imperialistic (especially American) exploitation. This is achieved with the founding of the "new" China, which retools Shaoxing opera to educate new Chinese citizens and revalorizes the rural stage as the base of education. As Chunhua returns to the countryside with the theater troupe after 1949 and is reunited with her "sisters," the film reaffirms the value of the open-air stage, accompanied by exterior shots that both recall and differ from the beginning of the film in that this time the rural space opens up the vista, promising a liberating future.

All four sisterhood films deploy musical interludes to complement and enhance the melodramatic effect derived from the sisters' recognition and reunion. Framed within the narrative, these interludes explicitly address their respective audiences with the purpose of entertaining, reshaping their viewing habits, and fostering a new affective basis of collective identification. If the first three films more or less highlight the spectacle quality of the leading actresses' acoustic performance, *Stage Sisters* heightens the utilitarian value of vocal performance (chorus as well as solo)—as a means for making a living in pre-1949 China, then as a vehicle of politicization after 1949.

Furthermore, while both *The Happy Reunion* and *Stage Sisters* privilege a regional musical culture and exterior shooting, they serve diametrically opposed agendas. The first disavows class disparity and promotes Western-style modernity and urbanity articulated in modern Cantonese popular music, whereas the latter foregrounds class difference and gender conflict as set out in *Sister Flowers* and finds resolution in the collective political conscientization articulated by the "new" Shaoxing opera actresses. Consequently, contrary to *The Happy Reunion*, where the twin sisters' accidental reunion illustrates the illusory homogenizing Westernization of Hong Kong in the early 1960s, *Stage Sisters* promotes the empowerment of the downtrodden, which would gesture toward a utopic community free from patriarchal injustice and class conflict in the future. In this utopic anticipation, the subaltern speech would no longer be "subaltern" but instead would have acquired its own stage and audience.

Unlike Hollywood musicals that necessarily disavow the issue of class (as Dyer argues),[53] the four sisterhood singsong dramas that mix melodrama with musical interludes adopt variant approaches to class conflict as well as gender hierarchy. The strategy of representing or depresenting class and gender tension indicates a distinct social vision and ideological underpinning, which correlates to each film's conditions of production, be it pre-1949 (semi)colonialism or post-1949 Cold War politics.

The Political Divide and the Depleted Utopia

In the 1930s, *Sister Flowers* and its leading actress, Hu Die, freely traveled to Hong Kong, and *The Sister Flowers from the South* partially followed the political sensibility of wartime China's "national defense cinema" by dispatching the elder sister, Da Die, on the mission of joining China's war of resistance. By the 1960s, owing to the establishment of the socialist system in mainland China and global Cold War politics, the China–Hong Kong linkage increasingly gave way to a divide. Correspondingly, their filmmaking pursued two opposite trajectories, as represented by the two 1960s sisterhood films. If the Shanghai-made *Stage Sisters* carefully follows postrevolutionary political discourse and foregrounds leftist class and gender ideology, the Hong Kong–made *The Happy Reunion* steers away from such politics and instead focuses on developing a localized Hong Kong subjectivity and modernity. Despite the opposite agendas, however, both 1960s films subscribe to the Cold War binary structure (of socialist politics versus capitalist modernity) in order to present an unambiguous ideological message. The clear-cut either/or binary structure inevitably entails an excluded term in each film, which is symptomatic of the films' ideological blind spots. These underlying ideological blind spots eventually delimit and undermine the films' utopic resolutions.

In *Stage Sisters,* the older Shaoxing opera actress and the domestic space are both ruled out for being incompatible with the collectivist ideology in the "new" China. More fundamentally, this revolutionary ideology excludes microlevel experiences or self-determinacy that are irreducible (albeit related) to the political macrostructure. This exclusion stems from the film's tortuous political circumstances. During the One Hundred Flowers Campaign (1956–1957), intellectuals and artists were encouraged by the Communist Party to exercise freedom of speech and voice their criticism.[54] This democratizing endeavor was soon cut short by the Anti-Rightist Campaign (1957), which labeled those who did speak up as Rightists who were to be persecuted. In 1960, the tide turned again when Premier Zhou Enlai gave a speech calling for reevaluation of the importance of the intelligentsia and encouraging artists to drop ultraleftist ideological constraints and strive for self-expression. Shortly thereafter, the central propaganda bureau issued new policies, encouraging artistic creation (including filmmaking) and granting more creative latitude to film studios and artists. Consequently, the period between 1960 and 1964 experienced a short "warm spring," when Chinese cinema actively explored new modes of expression that departed from the Soviet model or the ultraleftist ideology. Xie Jin's initial plan of reworking traditional Shaoxing opera in *Stage Sisters* was formulated in precisely this atmosphere.

The warm spring was short-lived, unfortunately. The year 1964, when the film was made, was already verging on a new round of political campaigns that would soon culminate in the Cultural Revolution. The ascending panpoliticization dictated heavy-handed intervention in the making of the film. Xie Jin, as director, originally planned to have the two stage sisters reunited in the "new" society, which would allow them to "perform Shaoxing opera with full devotion and to lead a life with a clear conscience."[55] This conclusion, however, was (mis)interpreted by ultraleftist dogmatists as reactionary and individualist, detracting from political movements. As a result, Xie was forced to change the ending to one where Chunhua encourages Yuehong to "become a revolutionary person and perform revolutionary plays." The fundamental difference between the two endings is that Xie Jin originally privileged the humanist idea of individual self-determinacy and artistic fulfillment enabled by the "new" society, whereas the imposed ending promotes a "new" society where every individual would be subsumed into the orthodox ideology. Under such circumstances, the transformation of Shaoxing opera was derailed from the original project of exploring new cinematic aesthetics and instead became a means of ultraleftist ideological inculcation that aimed to shore up the Socialist bloc behind the Iron Curtain.

Yet Xie Jin's hijacked project was still viewed as inadequate for political needs, and it was declared a "poisonous weed" by Shanghai's propaganda bureau, headed by Zhang Chunqiao (who was to become one of the Gang of Four).[56] Furthermore, it was used as a pretext for attacking Shanghai's art and cultural workers. Not only Xie Jin, the director, but Yuan Xuefen (1922–2011), one of the most prominent Shaoxing Opera experts, who served as the film's consultant, was also subjected to harsh condemnation. Xia Yan (1900–1995), a key figure in early- to mid-1930s leftist cinema culture who revised and endorsed the script of *Stage Sisters,* was also persecuted and imprisoned as the Cultural Revolution started. To add an uncanny twist, Shangguan Yunzhu (1920–1968), a popular film actress from the 1940s who played the aged Shaoxing opera actress in this film, duplicated her character's fate by committing suicide shortly after the Cultural Revolution started. Given its official condemnation as a "poisonous weed," the film was not theatrically released until after the Cultural Revolution. Since 1980, the film has acquired an extended afterlife with its showing in Hong Kong and then at a number of international film festivals, where it was highly acclaimed.[57]

The film's belated yet resounding international success does not so much signal the ultimate triumph of art over ideology or humanism over ultraleftism as it reconfirms the film's branding by its shifting political circumstances. Simultaneously enabled and delimited by the overdetermining yet rapidly shifting political discourses, the film manifests an inherent disjuncture between two desires: the humanist vision of renewing Shaoxing opera as a means of self-expression and the artistic endeavor of reworking the regional opera for the medium of cinema, on the one hand, and the dogmatic conversion of opera and film into a tool of panpoliticization, on the other. Whether the film was denounced as a "poisonous weed" or reclaimed as a rare artistic feat on the cusp of Cultural Revolution, its inherent disjuncture is disavowed.

In this sense, the imposed conclusion that chants a monolithic definition of the "new" society registers a vision that both anticipates and forecloses the future. Just as the ending of *Rouge Tears* serves to bare the ideological premises of the utopic vision of *The Goddess* (as discussed in Chapter 1), the dogmatic conclusion of *Stage Sisters* undermines the utopic potential of sisterhood by foregrounding its ideological constraints. In other words, the political aspiration for sisterhood as a trope for class and gender liberation becomes usurped as a pretext for eradicating different voices. Conversely, when the film resurfaced in the 1980s within and outside China, the reviews that emphasize the film's technical accomplishment also failed to address the utopic social vision that is both enabled and curtailed by the film's political environment.

Meanwhile, *The Happy Reunion,* made in Hong Kong, similarly demonstrates a depleted utopic thrust—through a different form of political overdetermination. If the 1939 re-version, by having the twin sisters pursue divergent futures, fulfills the dual goal of supporting the political agenda set out in the China-centered "national defense cinema" and developing a specific interest in local Cantonese linguacultural sentiment, the 1962 re-version presents a uniform vision of Hong Kong as modern, Westernized, and emphatically nonnationalistic. Paradoxically, however, the film that promotes youth leisure activities and urban modernity was made at a time that was rife with profound social contradictions, especially with regard to class polarization. The year 1962, when *The Happy Reunion* was made, witnessed the erection of Hong Kong City Hall—a symbol of new Hong Kong and the gateway to Western art and culture.[58] Yet the same year was also embroiled in Hong Kong's refugee crisis in May, resulting from severe famine in mainland China that triggered another wave of refugee influx into Hong Kong. This crisis led the colonial government to mount a modernization campaign.[59]

In this light, the film must be understood in relation to the disjuncture between Hong Kong's self-projection, the actual living situation of new immigrants, and the British colonial government's management of social contradictions. Furthermore, the colonial government's modernization project went in tandem with more strict censorship. China-made films showing the flag, the national anthem, or the national leaders of the People's Republic of China had been systematically censored since the 1950s. As of 1963, all films produced were required to have English subtitles, which allowed the censorship board to better control anticolonial and leftist messages. The self-projected image of modernity both on and off the screen is thus predicated upon controlling and disavowing radical geopolitics and erasing ideological differences.

In these terms, *The Happy Reunion*'s focus on youth and modernity to the exclusion of economic and political instability anticipates the colonial government's late 1960s endeavor to design a modern Hong Kong identity that would disassociate Hong Kong from mainland China.[60] This project sought to preempt any future occurrence of mainland-related social unrest, such as the 1967 riots that echoed the mainland's Cultural Revolution in calling attention to class issues and power disparity in colonial Hong Kong. Like the film, the government sought to manage Hong Kong's social problems in the late 1960s through displacing and concealing social contradictions.

The exclusion of real-life social tensions renders the film's utopia of harmony and abundance a delusive fait accompli, as suggested by the fairy tale ending of the rural sister's reunion with her wealthy family and the narrative promise of them "living happily ever after." Yet, just as the film concludes with a fait accompli, the ideological premise of colonial capitalism and colonial modernity also resurfaces when the rural sister is folded into the wealthy family as an inferior copy of her wealthy sister to become conditionally and probationally urban. Thus, the teleology of modernization is reinforced on the condition that the class hierarchy is properly managed, naturalized, and thereby occluded.

The simultaneous inclusion and exclusion, homogenization and differentiation in *The Happy Reunion* echoes the underlying structure of *Stage Sisters,* both having been made in the Cold War context, albeit from diametrically opposite perspectives. Given the Cold War dichotomy of capitalism versus socialism, individualist self-determinacy versus collectivist anonymity, and the attendant politics of mutual border reinforcement, both 1960s re-versions privilege internal homogeneity and ideological purity. The location-specific collective consciousness inscribed in the two films also conforms to such politics. To that extent, whether it is class-based women's solidarity or apparently classless, youthful modernity, both films encourage the audience's identification with the current social system as the best option developed from previous trial and error.

Conclusion: Split Twins—Negative Utopia—Negotiated Subjectivity

The four sisterhood singsong dramas examined in this chapter interweave Shanghai and Hong Kong from the (semi)colonial to the postwar and Cold War eras. In the process of producing sisterhood, family reunion, and domestic and social harmony under different circumstances, these films develop variant strategies of negotiating and representing the social contradictions of class, gender, and associated urban-rural tensions. These representational strategies in turn produce and address their respective audiences, thereby carving out their markets. Specifically, the films address the audience on two registers: the melodrama of recognition and reunion, and the acoustic allure of singing interludes. These registers of audience address effectively construct collective desire for a certain social relationship in response to the films' respective geopolitics.

Yet each utopic projection of a desirable social relationship simultaneously bears and bares its own ideological premise. The virtual impossibility of anticipation without self-deconstruction, according to Fredric Jameson, makes utopia inherently "negative." It demonstrates "our utter *incapacity to imagine such a future*—our imprisonment in a non-utopian present without historicity or futurity—so as to reveal the ideological closure of the system in which we are somehow trapped and confined."[61] If the utopic thrust in each of the four sisterhood films is indeed "negative," that is, delimited and undermined by its closed ideological premise, then we must reassess the films' utopic value not in terms of what is positively utopic about it but rather in terms of how one utopic gesture differs from another and in what ways such differential values contribute to exposing and critiquing the ideological blind spot of both its own and its predecessors' utopic gesture(s). In other words, by juxtaposing the different utopic gestures proffered by the four re-versions and by comparing their logic of inclusion and exclusion, I hope to have illuminated their geopolitical and ideological conditions of production, leading to a better understanding of their allegorical power.

In the previous chapter on maternal melodrama remakes, I emphasized two representational difficulties derived from Shanghai's colonial modernity and director Wu Yonggang's China-centered, humanist, male intellectual stance. The first representational difficulty concerns the crisis of figuring a subaltern woman's abject sexuality and anticipatory vision. The second representational difficulty has to do with the Shanghai–Hong Kong hierarchy in the early twentieth century, which leads to the marginalization of Hong Kong's (and southern China's) locality, even when the latter constitutes an important condition of the remake's production and reception. If Wu's maternal melodrama remake presents a somewhat monolithic perspective that privileges the geopolitical location of Shanghai and the male humanist stance, the sisterhood re-versions I analyze in this chapter offer divergent location-specific visions that compete with and critique each other. Just as the sisters who grow up in different environments both diverge from and converge with each other, the re-versions imprinted by different geopolitics also display the unfolding interactions and contentions between Shanghai and Hong Kong at different historical conjunctures. These interactions and contentions, in turn, provide the stage for multiple location-specific subject positions to play out against each other.

The development of location-specific collective subject positions here largely hinges upon domestication or localization of what are perceived as external and foreign elements (such as the Hong Kong filmmakers' domestication of the Shanghai predecessor). In the next chapter, where I study a set of fantasy musical comedies that traverse Hollywood, Shanghai, and Hong Kong from the 1930s to the 1950s, I emphasize the opposite direction of re-versioning that results from the Self-Other encounter: that is, the direction of foreignization, or self-foreignization, which plays a crucial role in the (re)formation of southern China's and Hong Kong's subject positions in the shifting geopolitical terrain.

CHAPTER 3

The Love Parade Goes On

"Western-Costume Cantonese Opera Film" and the Foreignizing Remake

No man is a genius unless he can deliver honest entertainment.
—Ernst Lubitsch[1]

Cantonese opera's strengths and weaknesses are the same—adaptability and chameleonlike changeability.
—Mai Xiaoxia[2]

When Ma Shizeng (1900–1964), a well-known Cantonese opera master, traveled to San Francisco in 1931, he brought a volume titled *Qianli zhuangyou ji* (Writings for My Long Journey to the United States), which he had compiled in preparation for this American trip. This volume contains his essays on how to reform Cantonese opera and how to mobilize opera as a vehicle of mass education and for building Sino-American friendship. It also includes excerpts of one of his opera scripts, *Xuangong yanshi* (literally, "Passionate Romance in the Jade Palace") (1931), a quasi-clone translation of Ernst Lubitsch's first talkie produced by Paramount—a musical comedy titled *The Love Parade* (1929).

What prompted Ma's operatic translation of *The Love Parade;* and why did he choose to bring this play to his potential audience in America? These questions must be considered in the larger context of power disparity in the Sino-US mutual perception. As I shall argue in this chapter, Sino-US interactions resulted in Ma's deployment of the "foreign" perspective in his translated play. What then are the ramifications of the "foreign" perspective, even becoming foreign, in the opera/film adaptations undertaken by Ma and other Cantonese opera masters and filmmakers? In this chapter, my discussion of the "foreign" draws on Lawrence Venuti's notion of "foreignizing translation." Unlike the "domesticating translation" that seeks to transpose the foreign into the self (assuming transparency, compatibility, and one-to-one correspondence between the source film and the target film), "foreignizing translation" posits translation as "a violent rewriting of the foreign text [or source text], a strategic intervention into the target-language culture, at once dependent on and abusive of domestic values."[3] This notion offers a fruitful lens for my study of the ways in which the "foreign" contributes to formulating Cantonese (and later on Hong Kong) cinema and the correlated linguacultural subject positioning from the 1930s to the 1950s. As demonstrated in the Chapter 2, this is also a period when the Hong Kong–centered nexus became an increasingly important linguacultural and regional anchor for Chinese-language cinema.

My study in this chapter is based on Ma's Cantonese opera adaptation and two film remakes, all derived from Ernst Lubitsch's *The Love Parade* (1929). These operatic adaptation and film remakes faithfully reproduce certain aspects of Lubitsch's musical comedy, especially the fantastic palatial setting. Thus, they constitute a hybrid fantasy-musical comedy, more specifically known as "Western-costume Cantonese opera/films" (*xizhuang ju* 西装剧) in their times.[4] This remaking trajectory started in 1930 in southern China and Shanghai, and lasted until the late 1950s in Hong Kong. Upon its release in Shanghai in 1930, *The Love Parade* was quickly adapted into two "Western-Costume Cantonese operas" (*xizhuang ju*), starring Xue Juexian (1904–1956) and Ma Shizeng respectively, both leading Cantonese opera artists. The Cantonese film version, again starring Xue Juexian, made in Shanghai, followed in 1934. In 1957, it was reprised in Hong Kong by veteran Cantonese film director Zuo Ji (1916–1997), followed by a sequel in 1958, shot in Eastman color. All these Cantonese opera and film versions are titled *Xuangong yanshi.* The 1957 version was officially translated as *My Kingdom for a Husband,* and the 1958 sequel was translated as *My Kingdom for a Honeymoon.* The Cantonese song numbers from these versions continue to be influential and were a key component in the Cantonese opera repertoire until the 1970s.

In studying the train of Cantonese operatic adaptations and filmic remakes of *The Love Parade* from 1930s Shanghai to 1950s Hong Kong, I emphasize that the self-foreign border, which is crucial to the construction of Cantonese cinema and the southern Chinese–Hong Kong subject positioning, is not just a line to be either crossed or reinforced. Rather, I understand it as a zone that stages and unfolds the continuous contact, confrontation, fascination, and osmosis between the colonized local Self and the colonial foreign Other. I describe this perpetual state of in-between vacillation as "trans"—a deliberately awkward use of the prefix that mirrors the awkward yet productive shuttling situation. In this "trans" state, the foreign perspective does not become domesticated into willy-nilly hybridity, nor does the local/regional Self get erased and completely colonized by the foreign

Other. Rather, the foreign perspective remains an external yet interactive factor that helps to reconfigure the local/regional Self in relation yet not in subordination to the foreign influence. Thus, the key to understanding the gradual (re)formulation of the peripheral Cantonese cinema and subject positioning is to maintain a dual vision in the border zone of trans.

I. Setting the Stage: The Convergence of Broadway, Palace Fantasy, and Cantonese Opera

In December of 1926, four months after the American screening of Warner Brothers' earliest Vitaphone experiments, a wave of sound hit the shores of East China. By 1930, Hollywood's partial musicals and "all-talking, all-singing, all-dancing" musicals (many adapted from Broadway shows) flooded Shanghai's movie theaters. This influx included *Showboat* (dir. Harry Pollard, 1929), *Chasing Rainbows* (dir. Charles Reisner, 1930), *New Movietone Follies of 1930* (dir. Benjamin Stoloff, 1930), and *Lord Byron of Broadway* (dir. Harry Beaumont, 1930). Among them, *The Love Parade,* Ernst Lubitsch's first talkie produced by Paramount, was the inaugural film shown at Mingxing Daxiyuan 明星大戏院 (Star Theater), which opened on October 29, 1930. According to an advertisement in *Shen bao* 申报 (a major Shanghai newspaper), the Paramount sound comedy (with Maurice Chevalier receiving the top billing) was screened with detailed Chinese translation in the brand-new theater wired with sound technology, and each viewer could receive a bonus opening-night souvenir brochure (Figure 3.1).[5] In the same year, *The Love Parade* became the first Movietone film shown at the Zhonghua Huayuan 中华画院 (China Movie Theater) in Guangzhou (Canton), which instantly sparkled a local craze for talkies.[6]

The widespread popularity of *The Love Parade* catalyzed immediate Cantonese operatic adaptations, unlike other border-crossing remakes I have studied that lag years, even decades, after the initial contact. The end of 1930 witnessed the birth of *Xuangong yanshi,* starring Xue Juexian cross-dressing as Louise—the queen of the fictional country of Sylvania.[7] This was soon followed by another Cantonese opera adaptation starring Ma Shizeng, which resulted in the fierce competition between the two major Cantonese opera masters, historically known as *Xue Ma zhizheng* 薛马之争 (Xue versus Ma). Their competition precipitated active transformation and rejuvenation of Cantonese opera. The reform of Cantonese opera in the 1930s also involved Ma's operatic reworking of *Thief of Bagdad* (dir. Raoul Walsh, 1925) into *Zei wangzi* (The Thief Prince, early 1930s) and Xue's operatic adaptation of *The Grand Duchess and the Waiter* (dir. Malcolm St. Clair, 1926) into *Baijin long* (The Golden Dragon, 1930).[8]

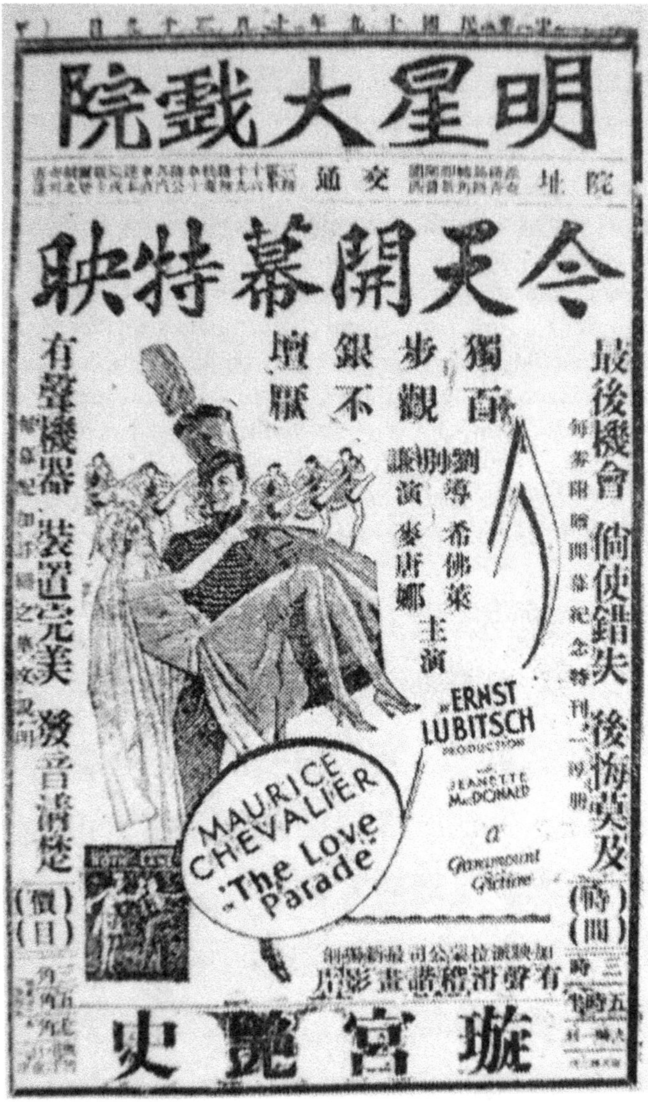

Figure 3.1 *Shen bao* advertisement for *The Love Parade,* screened at the Star Theater in October 1930

Riding on the wave of successful Western-costume Cantonese operas in Shanghai, southern China, and Southeast Asia (among the Cantonese communities), and taking advantage of the newly available sound technology, Cantonese film adaptations quickly came into being. Both *The Golden Dragon* and *The Thief Prince* also acquired film versions in 1933 and 1939 respectively, featuring their original leading actors. Following the successful opera *Baijin long,* the film version of the same title (dir. Tang Xiaodan, 1933) was produced by Xue Juexian's Nanfang

Yingpian Youxian Gongsi 南方影片有限公司 (Southern Motion Picture Company, Ltd.) (registered in 1932 during Xue's sojourn in Shanghai) in collaboration with Shanghai's Tianyi (Unique) Film Production. The film, starring Xue and his wife, Tang Xueqing (replacing the female impersonator in the opera version), and boasting extravagant sets, was another instant hit with Cantonese communities within and outside China (Figure 3.2).[9]

The film's overseas as well as domestic box office success convinced Tianyi's owner, the Shaw family, to branch out into Hong Kong. Tianyi Production—Hong Kong Branch (Tianyi Gangchang 天一港厂) was thus set up in 1934, dedicated to producing Cantonese films in order to expand the company's market share in Southeast Asia. Mirroring *Baijin long*'s trajectory (from a Hollywood film to a Cantonese opera to a Cantonese film), the 1934 Cantonese film version of *Xuangong yanshi* that quickly followed the opera (which was adapted from Lubitsch's film) became another runaway success. Xue Juexian's straddling of the stage and the screen in both *Baijin long* and *Xuangong yanshi* also pioneered the path of intermedia or amphibious performance for other Cantonese opera actors.

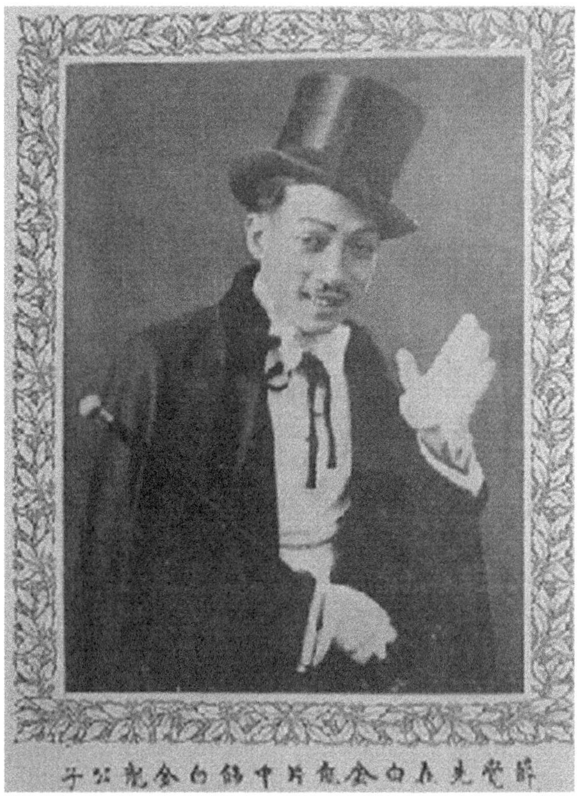

Figure 3.2 Xue Juexian playing the prince in Western costume in *Baijin long* (The Golden Dragon) (1933) (*Lingxing er zhounian jinian zhuankan* [1933], n.p.)

The spate of Cantonese operatic adaptations of Hollywood fantasy period dramas (both silent and talkie) at the turn of the 1930s signals an important phenomenon, namely, the meeting of Western audiovisual spectacle (especially the fantastical mise-en-scène, special effects, and sound technology) with Cantonese opera that traditionally privileges stylized acting and hypothetical settings. Mai Xiaoxia, a renowned Cantonese opera historian and film director, compares Cantonese opera (as well as other Chinese traditional regional operas) favorably with Western theater by maintaining that the former has a *xieyi* quality; that is, it is capable of implying an idea through suggestive performance on a bare stage.[10] This suggestive performance involves a rich repertoire of body language and gestures that, by conventionalized association, convey specific meanings, situations, and sentiments to the initiated audience.

According to Mai's theory, Cantonese opera has little use for modern audiovisual technology embodied by cinema. However, their imbrication became possible and formative for two main reasons. First, their encounter happened at a historical moment when Cantonese opera was poised for change and regeneration, partially owing to the pressure of cinema's (especially talkies) emergence as a major form of entertainment. Second, the Chinese regional opera and Hollywood's early 1930s fantasy films share an uncanny affinity, namely, heavy dependence on stagy mise-en-scène, a relative lack of camera movement, and a plethora of song numbers.

Debate regarding the reform of Cantonese opera (and Chinese opera overall) started in the 1920s. Ouyang Yuqian (1889–1962), a well-known Peking opera playwright, actor, film scriptwriter, and active opera reformer, expressed reservations about the unprincipled malleability of Cantonese opera in the late 1920s. According to him, the unsystematic reform of Cantonese opera led to half-baked realism in acting and costuming. Such awkwardness made it too crude to be new and too anomalous to be old.[11]

Meanwhile, both Ma Shizeng and Xue Juexian actively promoted Cantonese opera reform. In preparation for his 1931 trip to San Francisco, Ma Shizeng compiled his book *Qianli zhuangyou ji* to educate the overseas Chinese about Cantonese opera. In this book, Ma argues that opera artists must reform and regenerate the local opera in the face of the fierce competition between theater and cinema as well as the increased Sino-West communication that had led to radical changes in China.[12] On returning from America in 1933, Ma, inspired by American cinema and opera, proposed six initial steps to reform Cantonese opera. These measures include using practical, physical settings (as opposed to the traditional bare stage) and phasing out stylized acting (*tu'an shi biaoyan* 图案式表演), which he deemed particularly unsuitable for contemporary drama.[13] Ma did emphasize that, as a patriot, one should preserve the indigenous moral culture and that Western (or, for that matter, northern Chinese) techniques could work only if properly assimilated.[14] Assimilation, however, does not necessarily lead to a seamless convergence, as I shall demonstrate with examples of Western-costume Cantonese operas and their film versions, such as *Baijin long* and *Xuangong yanshi.*

Similarly, Xue Juexian expounded opera reform in the pamphlet he prepared for Cantonese communities before his trip to Southeast Asia. He described his mission as merging southern and northern Chinese operas, combining Chinese and Western music in order to "make Chinese opera into the world's public opera," thereby "strengthening the Chinese nation and human civilization."[15] In 1938, he proclaimed that his opera troupe's performance synthesized "the essence of Cantonese opera, the body language of the northern opera schools, the martial arts of Peking opera, the beautiful style of Mei Lanfang [the best-known Peking opera actor who specialized in female roles], the facial expressions of film acting, the social concerns of spoken drama, and, finally, the setting of drama."[16]

Compared with Ma and Xue, Mai Xiaoxia, who privileged the *xieyi* style of Chinese opera, adopted a more cautious perspective on opera reform. He saw Cantonese opera's chameleon adaptability as both its strength and its weakness (see the epigraph at the beginning of the chapter).[17] In his treatise on how to revive Chinese opera (including Cantonese opera), Mai argued that the originally superior *xieyi*, or suggestive, art form had recently been vanquished by "the Hollywood crusade," just as China was subdued by the West. Thus, reform was unavoidable. In his prescription for reviving Chinese opera, he urged opera workers from the south and the north (representing Cantonese and Peking operas) to synergize and to turn to films for inspiration. He also advocated a complete revolution in theater structure, setting and lighting, music composition, subject selection, and format of presentation. Specifically, he praised the effective amalgamation of different forms of presentation in Xue's *Baijin long,* which took the form of spoken drama in act 3, yet switched to Westernized opera in act 7.[18] However, he objected to drastic changes that would jettison tradition and disregard the audience's viewing habits. He suggested that the poor reception of Ma Shizeng's new opera, produced after his return from America, stemmed precisely from Ma's overly hasty abandonment of stylized acting, which conflicted with the audience's traditional viewing habits.[19]

Despite their different approaches to opera reform, opera critics and artists concurred that Chinese opera was being edged out by Hollywood cinema (especially early musicals and talkies) and that opera reform needed to learn from its Western film rival in terms of setting, lighting, makeup, and acting. In other words, they perceived and (re)conceptualized Cantonese opera in reference to its Western rival. Such compulsive cross-referencing echoes what Benedict Anderson calls the "spectre of comparison" or the "restless double-consciousness" produced by the telescope that forces a perspective that is simultaneously far away and close up.[20]

Interestingly, the context in which Anderson theorizes the "spectre of comparison" is not dissimilar to early-twentieth-century China and Hong Kong.

Anderson references the colonial era Filipino novelist and national hero, José Rizal, who returned to Manila in the 1880s after a long sojourn in Europe only to find that he could no longer experience Manila without thinking of Berlin or vice versa.[21] The fact that Rizal, the colonial subject shuttling between the European metropolis and the peripheral colony, acquired the "incurable vision" of *el demonio de las comparaciones,* or the "spectre of comparison," powerfully prefigures Cantonese opera masters like Xue and Ma. These figures toured Southeast Asia and America in the 1930s, fully aware of China's subordination to and inescapable interactions with colonial forces, yet seeking to revive Cantonese opera (deemed the essence of Chinese art and culture) by introducing a Western/foreign perspective. Through the pamphlets they compiled, Ma and Xue systematically formulated their proposals of opera reform for the overseas Cantonese communities in Southeast Asia and America as well as those in China and Hong Kong. The "spectre of comparison" allows them to deploy the dual vision (with the inherent foreign perspective) in order to best educate diverse audiences about their reconceptualization of Cantonese opera from geopolitically subordinated China. Their comparative lens is inherently foreignizing (as defined by Venuti) to the extent that it derives from their interaction with the widely disseminated audiences in southern China, Hong Kong, and overseas, where being perceived as foreign and perceiving others as foreign constitutes the everyday experience.

The built-in foreign perspective is precisely what links Xue, Ma, and their Western-costume Cantonese opera/films with Ernst Lubitsch and his first talkie, *The Love Parade.* One might say that Xue's and Ma's operatic and film adaptations of *The Love Parade* inherit Lubitsch's foreign perspective as a means of negotiating China's subaltern position in the world system.

The Foreign Perspective in *The Love Parade*: From the Diegetic Foreigner to the Extradiegetic Audience

In early-twentieth-century Shanghai, many film workers were initiated into filmmaking through repeatedly watching Western (especially Hollywood) films and meticulously analyzing their cinematography, lighting, and story telling strategies. Among the most influential Western film directors were Ernst Lubitsch, Charlie Chaplin, Frank Borzage, and Frank Capra. Lubitsch, in particular, not only inspired film directors such as Hong Shen (1894–1955), Zhu Shilin (1899–1967), and Sang Hu (1916–2004), but also attracted the attention of leftist film critics like Xia Yan (1900–1995) and Shu Yan (1914–1999).[22]

Originally a German filmmaker, Lubitsch came to Hollywood in 1922 at the behest of Mary Pickford. As Leo Braudy points out, unlike many other European émigré directors in Hollywood, Lubitsch showed no apparent angst over being a foreigner.[23] Instead, he danced well with the Hollywood studio system and produced commercially successful films, most of which were shown in Shanghai (as well as other treaty port cities) thanks to Hollywood's post–World War I global hegemony. Ironically, his international success led European leftist critics to bemoan his fantasy films for trivializing history and politics.[24] In China, similarly, praise and emulation of his masterfully subtle techniques were dogged by anxiety with his films' capitalist mode of production and insinuations. According to one critic, *The Love Parade* sprang from capitalism's second phase, the heist of capitalism, and it functioned as capitalist spiritual opium, diametrically opposed to the Soviet cinema that was being produced under an emerging socialism. In this review, the critic wondered, "Who would want revolution after watching a film [like *The Love Parade*]?"[25] To further provoke readers, he predicted two possible futures for Chinese cinema: either the doom of becoming a second and secondary Hollywood or the genuine future of developing a cinema for the people.[26]

Over a decade later, anxiety persisted with the ongoing popularity of *The Love Parade*'s two leading stars, Maurice Chevalier and Jeanette MacDonald, fondly known to the Chinese audience as the "king" and "queen" of singing (*sheng wang* 声王 and *ge hou* 歌后). In 1943, the Chinese Film Association addressed an open letter to Euro-America, complaining that Western films' excessive emphasis on romance and luxury had led Chinese youth astray, the symptom being women aspiring to MacDonald's flippant beauty and Garbo's seductive appeal, and men desperately imitating Chevalier and Gilbert.[27] To counterbalance the debilitating trend, the letter encouraged the West to produce a more didactic cinema that would nevertheless retain its entertainment value—a better model for a China-oriented cinema (*Zhongguo benwei de dianying* 中国本位的电影).[28]

However, Lubitsch's films were also lauded and emulated for being witty, nuanced, and liberal. According to one Chinese commentator, Lubitsch's opulent style and apparent moral lapse were quintessential to his European flair. His *So This Is Paris* (1926) was considered superior to *We Moderns* (dir. John Francis Dillon, 1925) because it unapologetically painted a picture of the unrestrained lifestyle of Parisian men and women, while the latter criminalized the modern girl only to deliver an inept moral message. "So we know how useless the paper crown of morality is!" concluded the commentator.[29] For director Sang Hu, whose comedy of urban marriage was deeply influenced by Lubitsch, Lubitsch was undoubtedly a pure "artist of dollars" (*jinyuan yishujia* 金元艺术家) who disregarded "ideology" (*yishi* 意识) and "didacticism" (*shuojiao* 说教), and focused exclusively on giving the mass audience their money's worth through entertainment.

Yet, despite the absolute capitalist materialism, Sang argued, Lubitsch's unique oeuvre was pure pleasure, thanks to his flawless skills and unrestrained wit.[30]

The divided reception of Lubitsch, "admir[ing] Lubitsch's style and condemn[ing] what he is saying in that style,"[31] constitutes a classic case of the form/content split. Given China's geopolitical subordination to Western capitalist countries, this bifurcated reception seems natural, even necessary. One could easily argue that Chinese filmmakers should jettison Lubitsch's "bad" content while borrowing his "good" form in order to simultaneously resist Western cultural imperialism and develop their own craft. Nevertheless, the implicit assumption of a clear-cut form/content division not only obscures the politics of the form per se, but also fails to consider a fundamental linkage between Lubitsch's *The Love Parade* and the Cantonese operatic and filmic adaptations. This connection consists in neither the content nor the form exclusively but rather in the foreign perspective as a mode of presentation and audience address that underpins both the content and the form.

In Lubitsch's works, the foreign perspective comes not so much from his German émigré background as from his ironic dual vision (which adds a witty twist to Anderson's "spectre of comparison"). His interest in operetta, according to Braudy, enables him to "light heartedly inflate manners and passions into extremes that can be portrayed simultaneously at full tilt and with a genially mocking eye."[32] I would suggest that the dual register (of indulgence and distance) is not inherent in the form of operetta but rather marks the "Lubitsch touch." This enigmatic touch has been glossed in various ways. Herman G. Weinberg compares it to the raisin at the bottom of the Russian drink called kvass—a small detail that flavors the whole drink, or film in this case.[33] The "touch" that is so infectious in Lubitsch's films is precisely his simultaneous indulgence in and ironic distance from his characters' microcosm. As Braudy argues, Lubitsch employs the actor's perspective and the director's perspective at the same time, which allows him to "embrace the audience as a co-conspirator of interpretation, *an accomplice to the director's and the camera's knowingness.*"[34] His knowing wink at the audience entices the audience to enjoy the film as a show, that is, to derive pleasure by assuming the dual position of resonating with the film from within, while staying outside and being able to mock the contrived nature of the spectacle. Because of this, Braudy sees the "Lubitsch touch" as a form of "epistemological subversion" and "a demonstration of the theater of behavior that defy Leftist criticism of his triviality."[35]

Such subversive mockery underpins *The Love Parade,* Lubitsch's first talkie and fantasy-musical comedy, adapted from a play, *The Prince Consort,* and produced by Paramount with a total cost of US$600,000. The title not only echoes one of the song numbers, "My Love Parade," but also underscores "love" as a "parade"—a rigidly coded and elaborately staged fanfare for the foreign, external gaze (both within the diegesis and in the movie theater). The goal of the parade, of self-exhibition, is financial gain. This satiric and distanciating framing of an ultimately materialist transaction (in the name of "love") starts with the narrative's setting in a fictitious country, Sylvania, helmed by Queen Louise (played by Broadway actress Jeanette MacDonald), for whom the ministers are anxious to find a spouse so that the royal image will be positive enough to attract loans from foreign countries. At this point, Sylvania's military attaché in Paris, Alfred (played by Maurice Chevalier), is sent back to be punished for womanizing. Alfred's meeting with the queen sparks instant mutual attraction, which leads to their night banquet and then their wedding. Yet, the royal marriage soon disintegrates owing to Alfred's discontent with his subservient status as the prince consort—the queen's appendage. After dramatic scenes of contention punctuated by the queen's copious sobbing, the royal couple reunites after agreeing to reverse their roles: the queen will become "Louise" and Alfred will become "my king."

Throughout the entire film, the fantastic setting not only frames the narrative but is in its turn framed by an external foreign gaze, which implies elaborated layers of spectatorial positions. The film's opening, interspersed with miniature shots of the Eiffel Tower, Montmarte, Paris, and the queen's castle, instantly positions the audience at an engaged distance. By playing with the necessarily imperfect yet intricate optical illusion, the miniature shots invite the audience to gaze into the fantasy world as outsiders, from a distance. This distance is further borne out in the framing of the queen's castle. It appears first and foremost as an object of exhibition scrutinized by a group of tourists, who are driven in to marvel at the $110 million artifact yet care nothing about its history.

Not only the fantastic setting, but the driving force of the film—the royal couple's courtship and wedding—is also staged for the external or foreign perspective at multiple levels. The queen's morning bath, love parade, wedding, and quarrel with the prince consort are all presented from the perspective of the omnipresent observing and eavesdropping supporting characters, including ministers and ladies-in-waiting at the queen's night banquet (Figure 3.3), foreign ambassadors at the wedding, the diegetic audience who are watching an opera with the royal couple (yet who seems to be more interested in the royal couple than the opera performance) (Figure 3.4), and, finally, the royal couple's servants, Jacques and Lulu. It is through the mediation of these diegetic spectators that the film audience comes to experience the film as a *parade* of love. The wide range of gazing and eavesdropping positions plays with the various distances between the love parade and the spectators, resulting in constant readjustment of the focus and affect of spectatorial engagement.

Yet the most intimate yet also satiric foreign gaze comes from within, that is, the prince consort, Alfred. Alfred's sojourn in Paris before returning to Sylvania

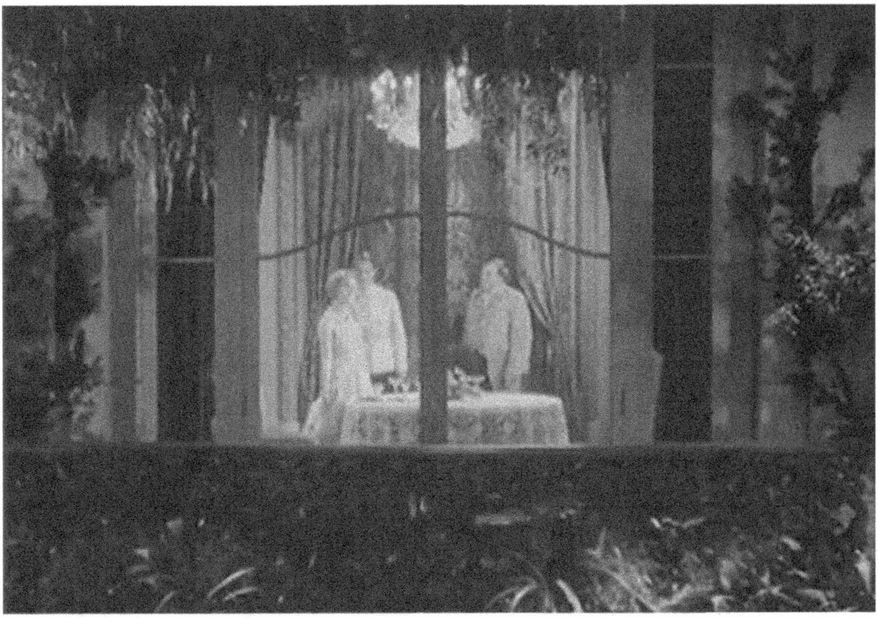

Figure 3.3 The night banquet/royal courtship witnessed by servants in long shot in *The Love Parade*

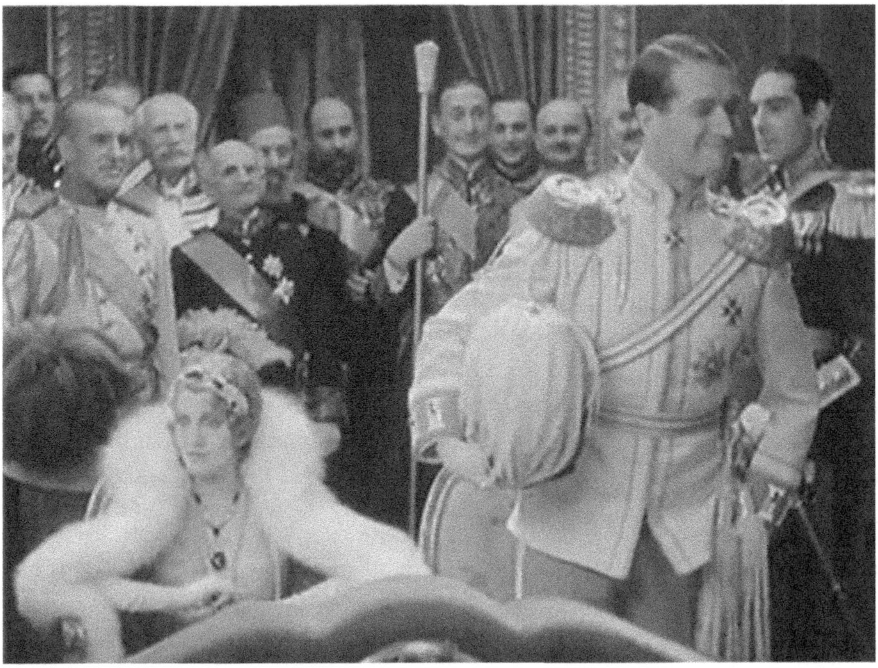

Figure 3.4 The royal couple striving to project an image of harmony for the public gaze in the opera house

makes him a quasi-foreigner in his homeland, especially when he speaks French to protest the queen's rigid court protocols. Significantly, his curse in French is left untranslated, alienating the English-speaking characters and the audience. This decision introduces an ironic distance at the semiotic and sonic levels, while visualizing Alfred the quasi-foreigner's sly tactic of resistance that is recognizable to the audience without understanding his French. Alfred's recalcitrant foreign perspective parallels the position of Maurice Chevalier, who plays the role. A French actor hailing from Paris, Chevalier's heavy French accent and cabaret singing stylistically offset Jeanette MacDonald's Broadway soprano voice and American accent. The two leading actors' stylistic incongruity is successfully translated into the ironic dynamic between a "European rake" and a "nice American girl."[36] The convergence of the diegetic royal contention and the extradiegetic contrastive casting underscores the significance of the inside outsider's perspective.

Such elaborated layering of multiple spectatorial positions, ranging from the internal outsider Alfred, the court staff, the foreign diplomats, and the movie audience, satirically frames the royal marriage as a public image deployed to secure loans from foreign countries. While the investment of the foreign gaze does successfully generate commercial revenue, it also simultaneously mocks the materialist premise of the "love parade." Such dual operation also underpins Lubitsch's own lavishly produced fantasia–musical comedy, which simultaneously boosted box office revenues in the midst of the America Depression and satirized money-driven show biz. The audio-visual, commercial, and satiric pleasures are delivered all at once as a result of the frame-within-a-frame effect and the persistent foreign perspective. In this layered structure of spectatorial positions, the audience indulges in the luscious audio-visual presentation and comic gags, while seeing through and mocking the farcical high society mannerisms and the commercial drive of the movie industry.

Stylistically, the dual vision of the "foreign" perspective is produced through Alfred's occasional direct address to the camera and the repetitive use of medium and long shots. These shots frame the characters in a window, a door, a symmetrical architectural space, or appearing and disappearing through draperies as if entering or exiting the stage. The closing shot of the film tellingly evokes the live stage experience by showing Alfred closing the window curtain, blocking the audience from his rejuvenated "love parade" with Louise, and thus decisively announcing the end of the film/show.

Such an ending, which resolves the war of the sexes between a "European rake" and a "nice American girl" through the taming of the American girl, who is reduced to King Alfred's "love parade," seems to posit an anti-utopia by blatantly justifying and reinscribing patriarchal sexism. Understood as such, the film lends itself to feminist as well as leftist criticism. Yet the film's built-in, comic or satiric foreign perspective (in the narrative, the aesthetic style, the structure, and the filmmaking process) drives a wedge into the smooth ideological suturing process, forcing the audience to constantly step back and question the surface presentation. Indeed, the audience is required to continually vacillate between identification and distanciation, or to occupy a spectatorial position that simultaneously engages and disengages with what Braudy calls "the entire social world, from emotions to politics, as a set of costumes and manners."[37] Thus, the narrative resolution does not so much propose an anti-utopia as question/mock the possibility of utopia by showing that any serious engagement inevitably flips into farce. The film's comic suspension of utopia (different from Jameson's "negative utopia" discussed in Chapter 2) is correlated with the audience's ironic, (dis)engaged outsider perspective, which foregrounds the performative and pretentious nature of show biz or any display-oriented visual representation.

In colluding with the audience as an engaged critical "foreigner," the film raises the issue of audience address. For Paul Willemen, a film's mode of addressing the audience determines its national status. He writes, "The issue of national cinema is . . . primarily a question of address, rather than a matter of filmmakers' citizenship or even of the production finance's country of origin." "From a historical critical perspective, the fundamental question to ask of a film is: *in which direction does this particular bundle of discourse seek to move its viewers or readers?*"[38] *The Love Parade* is structured from a built-in foreign perspective, and it travels to and interacts with an actual foreign (Chinese in this case) audience, triggering foreign operatic and filmic adaptations and remakes. To that extent, I argue that *The Love Parade* addresses or "moves" the audience by placing them at a foreign and defamiliarizing distance, which encourages satire. This process in turn complicates the film's American origin in that its audience address destabilizes the origin and opens it up for border-crossing traversing and critical negotiation.

Unsurprisingly, the foreign quality inscribed in *The Love Parade* makes it particularly appealing to the Chinese audience, as evidenced in the appreciative reviews of Lubtisch's European flair (also embodied in Maurice Chevalier). When the film was transposed into Cantonese operatic and filmic versions, the foreign perspective continued to structure and drive the narrative and the audio-visual presentation. If *The Love Parade* deliberately leaves Alfred's French curse and dialog untranslated in order to distance the English-speaking audience and force it to occupy a (dis)engaged foreign(izing) perspective, then the Cantonese versions similarly deploy the defamiliarizing mode of audience address with the result of destabilizing and redefining the "local" art form and "local" subject positioning in relation to the hegemonic foreign perception and implantation.

Looking Foreign and Sounding Local: Foreignizing Translation in *Xuangong yanshi*

The Cantonese versions deploy the defamiliarizing "foreign" perspective on both formal and narrative levels. The production of the "local" is predicated on precisely the implanted foreignness and the resultant incongruity and inequity as well as pleasure. As Mary Farquhar and Chris Berry suggest, the transnational consists in "the connection of difference" rather than unproblematic synergy and assimilation.[39]

I have previously noted that Chinese reception of Lubitsch was inherently comparative. Whether lauded for superb skills and a sophisticated style or criticized for corruptive sensuous materialism, Lubitsch in China was mobilized to build a local cinema. In other words, Lubitsch's films represented the filmic Other that simultaneously provided a positive or a negative model for Chinese cinema to define and construct itself against. This comparative gaze, associated with the colonial subjects' "spectre of comparison," is paradigmatic of Chinese cinema's continuous negotiation with Western cinema. It foregrounds the role of the foreign difference in constituting local cinema and subject positioning. Chinese cinema is therefore always already a Self constructed in interaction with the foreign Other. As such, it is defined through constant "connection of difference" and self-foreignization.

Lawrence Venuti's theorization of "foreignizing translation" is instructive here. If "domesticating translation" emphasizes assimilation and commensurability, thus erasing the violent transformation inherent in the translation process, "foreignizing translation" constitutes not only "a violent rewriting of the foreign text [or source text]," but also "a strategic intervention into the target-language culture" by abusing the "domestic values."[40] My emphasis here is on the latter, that is, what is considered to be local or domestic is subjected to foreign rendering and thus becomes foreignized, yet without being reduced to a replica of the "foreign." The conjugation of "foreignization" and "translation" suggests precisely the delicate and polyvalent Self-Other negotiation in the zone of trans, or border-crossing encounter. It is manifested in the split of the audio and visual modes of audience address in the various versions of *Xuangong yanshi*.

These versions include Xue Juexian's and Ma Shizeng's Cantonese operas in 1930 and 1931; the first film version produced by Shanghai's Tianyi Film Production in 1934, starring Xue Juexian; and the 1957 film version and its 1958 sequel, both produced by Motion Pictures and General Investment (renamed Cathay in 1965).[41] In the 1970s, the Hong Kong record industry released new versions of the song numbers performed by the younger generation of Cantonese opera artists.[42] In adapting the Hollywood musicals into Cantonese *xizhuang ju* (Western-costume opera/film), Xue Juexian and Ma Shizeng not only pioneered the new genre of Cantonese opera and film, but also theorized their motives, methods, and goals of reform in the pamphlets they compiled for their trips to America and Southeast Asia respectively.

Despite their discursive emphasis on incorporating Western elements in order to rejuvenate Chinese art and civilization on the world stage, their practice suggests that their heavy borrowings from Hollywood films as well as northern Chinese opera traditions went far beyond simply rejuvenating any presumed notion of Chinese art and civilization. The title *Xuangong yanshi,* literally meaning "Passionate Romance in the Jade Palace," already cues an exoticizing gaze at a fantastical scenario.[43] Indeed, the new genre of Western-costume Cantonese opera/film encapsulates a jarring, even violent amalgamation of the Cantonese singing (which itself commingles northern and southeastern Chinese folk melodies as well as Western conventions of vocal performance), fantastic narrative, and outlandish mise-en-scène. Such foreignized Cantonese opera and film versions depart from the realism of here-and-now and effectively address Cantonese-speaking audiences with their drastically different experiences of dislocation in a variety of geopolitical locations including Southeast Asia, North America, and Shanghai as well as southern China and Hong Kong.

Dwelling in diverse environments and assimilated into their adoptive countries to different degrees, the diasporic Cantonese audiences were also exposed to the rising cinema culture (armed with the most recent sound technology), which made them especially susceptible to novelty and change. Furthermore, one might argue that these Cantonese audiences' diasporic experiences made them quasi-foreigners in ways not dissimilar to Alfred in *The Love Parade* or Chevalier in Hollywood. Unsurprisingly, therefore, Xue's and Ma's Westernized operatic adaptations in 1930 and 1931 resonated with these audiences' experiences of dislocation and foreignization.

One major foreign aspect of the Western-costume opera is the implantation of novel music. Both Xue and Ma incorporated Western as well as northern Chinese musical instruments, including violin, electric guitar, banjo, saxophone, as well as lute, drum, and zither.[44] In Xue Juexian's version, his performance of the song number "Xuangong yeyan" 璇宫夜宴 ("Banquet in the Jade Palace," corresponding to "My Love Parade" in Lubitsch's film) is accompanied by only three instruments: the violin, *yangqin* (扬琴, the Chinese hammered dulcimer originating from Persia), and *dongxiao* (洞箫, a traditional Chinese vertical bamboo flute). Led by the violin, the song was recorded by Pathé in Hong Kong and has become a standard piece in the Cantonese opera repertoire.[45]

In addition to music, the narrative of *Xuangong yanshi* also has a heavy Western flavor. Ma Shizeng's opera script is virtually a replica of *The Love Parade* in Cantonese. It directly transliterates the characters' names and inherits not only the plot, but also a number of comic details. Examples include the queen's initial plan to punish Alfred by making him grow a beard and Alfred's protest against rigid court hierarchy by eating apples and leaving a pile of apple cores (in lieu of the breakfast that the servants refuse to serve without the queen's permission).[46] The mise-en-scène, likewise, is saturated with newfangled Western props, encouraging the audience to feast on such visual displays as a chocolate pistol, wine glasses, oil paintings, a luxurious sofa, and Western aristocratic fashion.[47]

The commercial success of Xue's and Ma's operatic versions of *Xuangong yanshi* led to the first film version in 1934. Like the film version of *Baijin long* (dir. Tang Xiaodan, 1933), *Xuangong yanshi* was again produced by Shanghai's Tianyi Film Production, starring Xue Juexian and his wife, Tang Xueqing. The narrative again closely reproduces that of *The Love Parade,* with Paris becoming Donglin 东邻 (East Neighboring Country) and Sylvania converted to Xueguo 雪国 (Country of Snow). As in Lubitsch's film, the contentious royal romance is mirrored in the physical and vocal comedy of the servants and the dogs who belong to the queen and Alfred. It also features four songs, "Bieyi Donglin" 别矣东邻 (Goodbye, East Neighboring Country), "Mengli qingren" 梦里情人 (Dream Lover), "Xuangong yeyan" 璇宫夜宴 (Banquet in the Jade Palace), and "Donglin jiuhua" 东邻旧话 (Memories of East Neighboring Country), with the first two corresponding with "Paris, Stay the Same" and "Dream Lover" in Lubitsch's film. To cater to the audience's desire for novelty and exciting spectacles, the film enhances both comic and modern Western attractions. The fake pistol with which one of Alfred's lovers in Donglin attempts to commit suicide—to avoid the anger of her cuckolded husband—turns out to be not just a toy (as in *The Love Parade*), but also one made of chocolate, which Alfred happily chews on. Furthermore, Alfred describes his carefree life in Donglin not just in terms of unrestrained womanizing, but also by exhaustively bragging about his activities of car cruising, wining and dining, and the modern comforts of climate control. Saturated with these embellishments, *Xuangong yanshi* does not localize or domesticate Lubitsch's musical comedy; rather, it inherits and plays up the foreign, fantastic dimension in order to cater to a multilocal Cantonese market.

The outlandish quality is amply demonstrated in a full-page advertisement of the film printed in Singapore. In addition to stressing the fantastic plot, romantic acting, melodious singing, and infectious comedy, the advertisement states: "Xue Juexian's handsome Count Alfred will surely shock Maurice Chevalier, and Tang Xueqing's flirtatious queen will dumbfound Jeanette MacDonald." Equipped with multiple attractions, the "all-Cantonese talking and singing romantic masterpiece" is a must-see for both those who have seen *The Love Parade* and the opera *Xuangong yanshi,* and those who have not seen either, claims the advertisement.[48]

The heavy dose of novelty (in music, narrative, and mise-en-scène) combined with Cantonese dialog and singing in the 1934 film version of *Xuangong yanshi* can be ascribed to its transnational loop of production, reception, and renewed production. Along with *Baijin long*, the first Cantonese film shot in Shanghai, Xue's *Xuangong yanshi* signals an interesting phenomenon of the long-distance filmic circuit. That is, the film was made in one dialect (the Shanghai dialect) region yet targeted primarily at audiences in other regions (namely, Cantonese audiences in southern China and overseas). In the larger historical context, the discrepancy between a film's sites of production and exhibition underpins the formation of Chinese cinema, which began by serving as a market saturated with Pathé and then Hollywood cinema and developed through addressing audiences who were widely disseminated and spoke different dialects. In other words, Chinese cinema, from its inception, was predicated on the transnational and long-distance loop of production, reception, and renewed production prompted by films from elsewhere. This long-distance loop continues to drive the 1957 Hong Kong remake of *Xuangong yanshi* (officially translated as *My Kingdom for a Husband*) and its 1958 Eastman color sequel, *My Kingdom for a Honeymoon*.

The 1957 remake and its sequel were produced by Loke Wan Tho's Motion Pictures and General Investment. Loke Wan Tho (1915–1964), son of a wealthy Chinese entrepreneur family in Malaysia-Singapore, started buying and building cinemas in Singapore and Malaysia in the mid-1940s, right after World War II, which precipitated fierce competition with Shaw Brothers Company Ltd.—Tianyi's distribution arm in Southeast Asia. To guarantee a sufficient film supply for their cinema networks, both Loke and Shaw Brothers expanded their film acquisition and started setting up film production companies in the 1950s, first in Southeast Asia, then in Hong Kong. In 1951, Loke founded the International Films Distribution Agency (Guoji Yingpian Faxing Gongsi 国际影片发行公司) and established a Hong Kong branch in 1953. In the same year, he launched Cathay-Keris Films in Singapore to produce Malay-language films. In 1954, Guoji started film production. By 1955, Loke had acquired Hong Kong's best equipped Yung Hwa Motion Picture Industries Ltd. (Yonghua Yingye Gongsi 永华影业公司), which specialized in Mandarin film production but was on the verge of bankruptcy. In the following year, he merged Yung Hwa and Guoji into Motion Pictures and General Investment (Guoji Dianying Maoye Youxian Gongsi 国际电影懋业有限公司, or Dianmao 电懋)—a company that integrated production, distribution, and exhibition in the Hollywood style.[49]

Whereas Motion Pictures and General Investment specialized in Mandarin films that flaunt Western fashions and modernity, catering mainly to a contemporary urban, upper-middle-class audience, it also contained a Cantonese film production section. Even before the establishment of Motion Pictures and General

Investment, Loke's International Films Distribution Agency had already launched its film production with a Cantonese melodrama, *My Wife, My Wife* (*Yu zhi qi*) (dir. Zuo Ji, 1955). Even though Cantonese films tended to be marginalized in Motion Pictures and General Investment's oeuvre, their output in the 1950s far outnumbered that of Mandarin films. Unlike Mandarin films, whose market shrank drastically with the official closing of the China–Hong Kong border in 1951 (resulting in the loss of the mainland Chinese market), Cantonese cinema continued to thrive in the 1950s with its expanding distribution in Hong Kong and Southeast Asia. Under such circumstances, the Cantonese film production sections of in Motion Pictures and General Investment and Shaw Brothers played an important role in building postwar Cantonese cinema in Hong Kong.

Zuo Ji, a veteran Cantonese film director who remade *Xuangong yanshi* for Motion Pictures and General Investment, explored a wide spectrum of genres including melodrama, martial arts, comedy, and musicals. He also directed the first Cantonese film, *My Wife, My Wife* (1955), for Loke's International Films Distribution Agency, and continued to make over ten Cantonese films for Loke's Motion Pictures and General Investment in the late 1950s. More importantly, he seemed to take much interest in remaking films. In addition to *My Kingdom for a Husband* (1957), he remade MGM's *Love Me or Leave Me* (dir. Charles Vidor, 1955) into *Pipa yuan* (The Sorrowful Lute) (1957), which he remade again in 1965 into *Zhenzhu lei* (Tears of Pearl). In 1958, he remade MGM's *Scaramouche* (dir. George Sidney, 1952) into *Lijin cangsang yi meiren* (True Love), in which Cantonese singing and fantastic Western mise-en-scène again occupy prominent positions. Furthermore, in both *My Kingdom for a Husband* and *True Love,* he casts Zhang Ying (1919–1984) and Luo Yanqing (1929–) as the two leads, the former being a popular young Cantonese film actor, the latter being a Cantonese actress who got her start in Cantonese opera and then ventured into martial arts films in the 1950s.

Arising from the transnational feedback loop of Chinese cinema, Zuo Ji's 1950s reinvention of the 1930s Western-costume Cantonese opera/film in Hong Kong continues to adhere to the built-in foreign perspective as illustrated by *My Kingdom for a Husband.* Its Cantonese singing follows the Xue Juexian style. Yet, it is already a quasi-foreign experience, for male lead Zhang Ying's vocal performance is dubbed by Jin Yongtang (靳永棠). The use of dubbing produces an implicit split and stitching between bodily performance and vocal skills, which cater to the diverging tastes of audiences, with the older generation attached to "authentic" Cantonese opera, while the emerging postwar generation preferred younger screen idols like Zhang Ying, who did not necessarily have training in Cantonese opera. Cantonese opera in this case is not just foreignized through the accompaniment of Western musical instruments (as in Xue's and Ma's

Xuangong yanshi versions in the 1930s). It is further divested of the physical anchor and its correlated body language, and is therefore corporeally alienated or foreignized.

The "foreign" perspective becomes especially prominent at the narrative and visual levels, producing significant ramifications for postwar Cantonese cinema and subject positioning that are increasingly anchored in the Hong Kong–centered nexus. As in *The Love Parade,* the key diegetic foreign perspective in *My Kingdom for a Husband* at the narrative level is embodied by Ali, the prince consort (played by Zhang Ying), an accomplished musician (different from the dandy Alfred in the previous versions). At the opening of the film, we learn that Ali is from the Snow Country,[50] and sojourning in the country of romance, Champs (Xiangchi 香池, literally, "the Fragrant Pond"). Although Ali does not speak a foreign language as Alfred does in *The Love Parade,* his foreign experience makes him an internal "foreigner" back in Snow Country, and he constantly refers to Champs as a positive Other (evoking Anderson's compulsive "spectre of comparison"). Ali points out three differences between the foreign Champs and his homeland, Snow Country. During the evening banquet sequence in the "Jade Palace" where the romance begins, Ali questions the court hierarchy in his homeland by referring to the harmonious and democratic relationship between the king and his subjects in Champs. This comparative perspective immediately prompts the Snow Country's Queen Luoyi (played by Luo Yanqing) to invite him (a subject) to sit down for a mutual toast.

Ali's second intervention has to do with gender relationships. Countering the queen's accusation of his womanizing and debauchery, he explains, "In Champs, men and women are free to associate with each other. It is considered normal rather than promiscuous." This foreign perspective allows Ali to not only restore his reputation, but also redefine himself as an open-minded "teacher" of the queen. After all, unlike in *The Love Parade,* which opens with Alfred caught flirting with a married woman (a detail reproduced with great humor in the 1930s Cantonese operatic and filmic versions), in the 1957 remake, Ali is shown firmly rejecting his seductresses. His musician status further clinches his cultural capital as a polished, liberal, and upright cultural hero, while the raucous physical comedy is largely displaced onto his servant Jack and the queen's maid Lulu, played by the overweight Cantonese comedians Liang Xingbo (1908–1981) and Tan Lanqing (1908–1981).

Following the scenario of "taming" the queen, the 1957 remake injects a further twist—Ali's successful correction of the class bias in Snow Country. In *The Love Parade,* the royal courtship, contention, and reconciliation are mirrored in their servants' relationships in ways reminiscent of Shakespeare's world of comedy. The servants' romance never amounts to an independent plot line because it simply serves to manifest and complement the royal coupling, which occupies the higher position in the Great Chain of Being (the medieval model of the cosmos based on the harmonious coexistence of hierarchical ranks). In *My Kingdom for a Husband,* however, the queen's maid Lulu and Ali's servant Jack become increasingly independent, with the help of Ali, the liberal-minded musician. Initially dominated by the queen, the maid is encouraged by Ali to pursue her own happiness outside the royal court as a commoner (Figure 3.5). The song "Let's Be Common," performed by the servants in *The Love Parade,* becomes a real possibility only in the 1957 remake.

More importantly, when the queen dogmatically refuses to attend the servants' wedding since the royal family must not mingle with ordinary subjects, Ali leaves the "Jade Palace" and honors the servants' wedding invitation. The queen's ultimate education takes place when she steps off the throne and ventures out of the luxurious palace into her subjects' lives. When she appears at the servants' wedding party in an attempt to retrieve Ali, she is perceived as actively connecting with her subjects. Her compliance with their expectation leads to the film's narrative resolution: a double honeymoon with the royal and the commoner couples sharing the same vehicle.

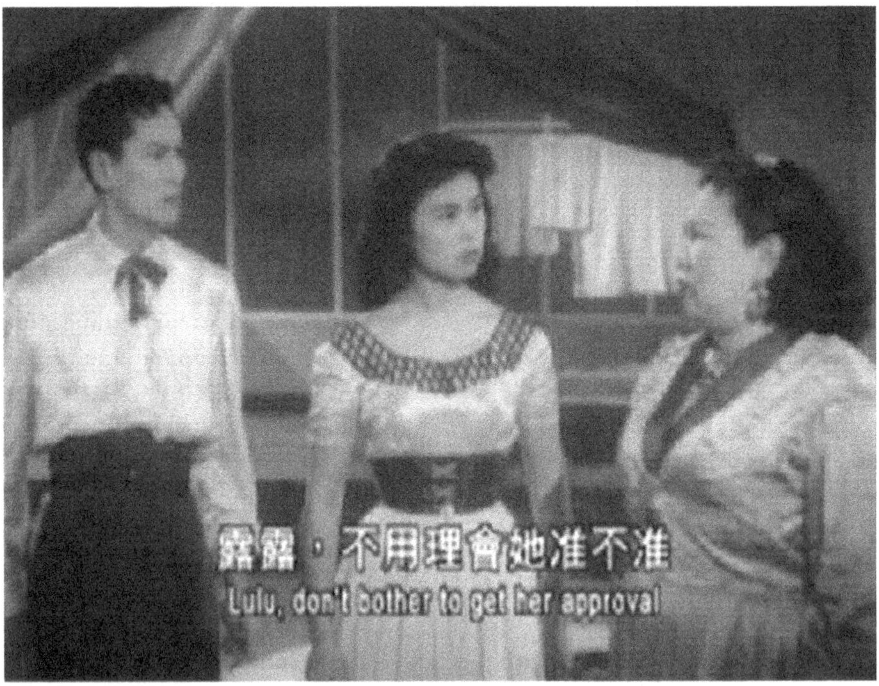

Figure 3.5 Staging the encounter between Ali (left), the queen (middle), and the maid Lulu (right) in *My Kingdom for a Husband*

The royal couple's abandonment of the "Jade Palace" at the end of the remake significantly departs from the reinstatement of kingship at the end of *The Love Parade*. Like the frustrated Alfred, the internal foreigner Ali refuses to assume a submissive position vis-à-vis the queen. Yet, unlike Alfred, who articulates his foreignness through his French language and dandyish flippancy, Ali expresses his liberal "foreign" perspective by introducing rudimentary democratic practices transplanted from Champs. By channeling his discontent with the microcosmic hierarchy within the palace to redressing larger social inequities, Ali ultimately remedies the gender and class contradictions outside the palace. As the queen becomes "Yi Mei" (伊妹, or Sister Luoyi) and Ali remains Ali, the Hong Kong remake suggests the relinquishment of royal power rather than just a power shift from the woman to the man.

In this light, the English title of the film, *My Kingdom for a Husband*, becomes doubly poignant. It plays with and twists the Chinese legend of a king giving up his country for a beauty (a case of love conquering all) or a king indulging in sensuous pleasure and as a result weakening his country and eventually losing it (a cautionary story). This legend is reworked in the remake, first through a gender reversal and then through an ideological shift. It is not the king but the queen who has to decide what to lose for what purpose. And what she gains in this film is not simply the ability to become a spoiled wife in a happy marriage (as in *The Love Parade*), but also a certain understanding of modern democratic politics, even if democracy here is illustrated in the most simplistic terms. As she gives up state power, she learns a new mode of statecraft, which is to regain the state metaphorically.

The message of political reform at the narrative level is driven by Ali's utopic vision, drawn from his foreign experience in Champs. It signals a major departure from Lubitsch's film and the 1930s Cantonese operatic and filmic versions. This implantation of a borrowed, foreign utopic vision arguably relates to Hong Kong's political position in the postwar world system. In his study of the film's director, Zuo Ji, Hong Kong film critic Lee Cheuk-to describes Zuo as a *metteur-en-scène* who specializes in didactic, formulaic family drama but is incapable of serious social engagement.[51] Whereas Lee's observation seems to be justified by Zuo's predilection for the operatic format that is different and oftentimes disengaged from the mode of realism, he fails to recognize Zuo's ability to reinvent and foreignize the formula, which in turn implies a political commentary. Ali's straight-faced didactic demand for modern political democracy through his comparison of Snow Country and Champs conveys an earnest political commentary that converges with Hong Kong's modernization drive at the turn of the 1960s (as we saw in the 1962 film *The Happy Reunion* in the Chapter 2). When this film is shown to Cantonese audiences in Southeast Asia and North America, the message potentially encourages the diasporic viewers to align with Hong Kong as an aspiring modern region that distinguishes itself from mainland China behind the Iron Curtain, while desiring the West as its own ultimate destination.

Nevertheless, the utopic drive toward modernity and democracy entails a homogenizing and teleological ideology since it privileges a single standard (Western democracy). The logical result of Ali's political reform is that Snow Country will become Champs, which would paradoxically render the "spectre of comparison" and its dual vision irrelevant, thereby rendering further improvement and self-reconstitution impossible. The problem with reifying a single standard is that it fails to account for the persistent underlying incommensurability between the Self and the Other in the translational processes. That is, it fails to acknowledge the undesirability as well as the impossibility of erasing the differences between Hong Kong and the West.

If the narrative disavows the Self-Other incommensurability, the film's ostensibly apolitical fantastic visuality foregrounds it, leading to the remake's "foreignizing translation." The narrative and the visuality constitute the film's two modes of audience address with divergent ramifications. The first mode addresses the audience on the didactic and semiotic level, positing a complete political makeover. The second mode addresses the audience through fantastic exoticization that suspends the principle of realism and undermines the rhetoric of political reform. With the second mode of address, Zuo Ji accomplishes a distanciating effect comparable with what the "Lubitsch touch" achieves through ironic framing and the mocking spectatorial perspective. As I argue below, it is precisely through Zuo's distanciating framing and foreignizing visual presentation that the remake points to a way of becoming local by partaking in the global flow (as opposed to becoming unanimously Westernized or completely domesticating the foreign).

The film's overwhelmingly fantastic quality is confirmed by a non-Cantonese viewer unfamiliar with the genre of Western-costume Cantonese opera/film, who described the film as "a dream, a lingering beautiful dream."[52] Indeed, the foreignizing visual presentation (as suggested by the mise-en-scène and props) that already characterizes Xue Juexian's and Ma Shizing's operatic and filmic versions in the 1930s now becomes even more prominent in *My Kingdom for a Husband.* The audience is invited to feast on a modernist, angular architectural style, art deco paintings with a primitive theme, and a bathtub that occupies the center background in the queen's boudoir, reproducing and reminding the audience of the sensuous bath scene from *The Love Parade* (Figures 3.6, 3.7).

Unlike the narrative inculcation of rudimentary democracy that meets little resistance in the diegesis (yet goes unnoticed in the theater, as indicated by the above quoted viewer who completely misses the political message of the film), the fantastic visuality simultaneously seduces and befuddles the audience. As a contemporary commentator points out, the "Jade Palace" evokes the palace of the

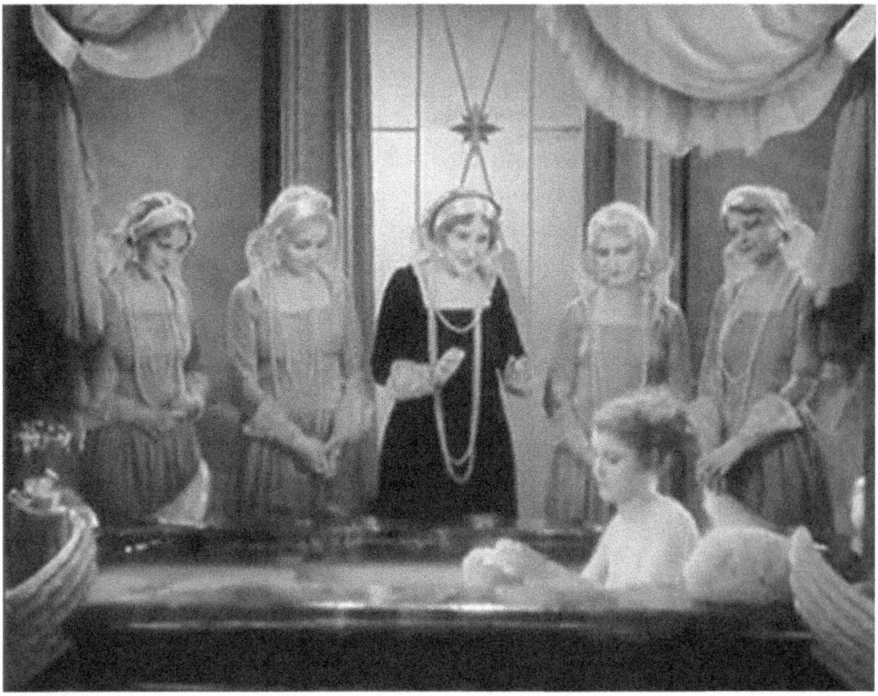

Figure 3.6 Queen Louise bathing under the gaze of the court ladies in *The Love Parade*

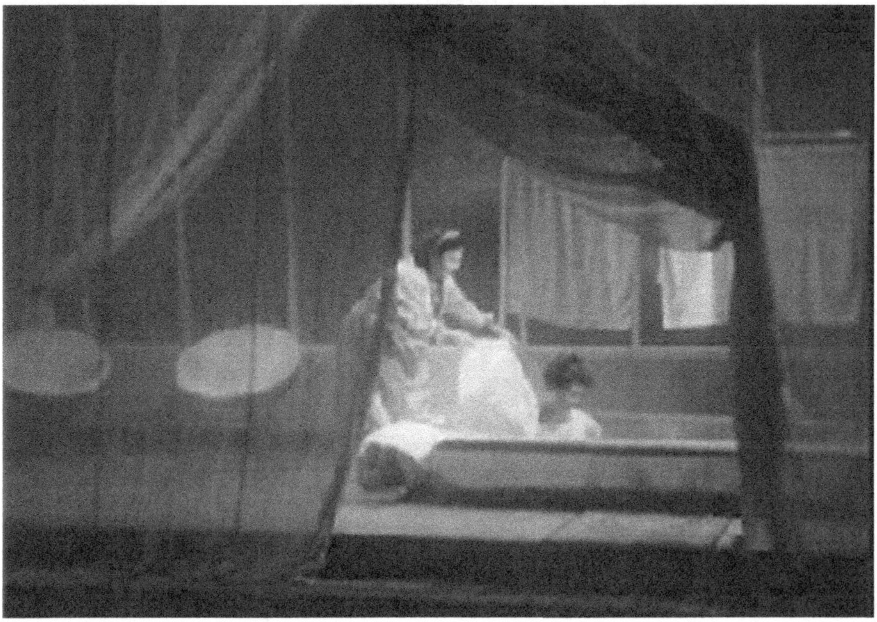

Figure 3.7 Queen Luoyi bathing in a look-alike bathtub, framed by gauze curtains, in *My Kingdom for a Husband*

Roman Empire, yet also resembles the cartoon version of an opera house. The costuming of the royal couple and the servant couple are nondescript. Luo Yanqing in her long dress looks like a queen but also not too different from a song-and-dance actress. Zhang Ying as the musician Ali could be a native Romeo and a gentleman at a masked ball, all at once. To enhance the bizarre and incongruent look, Ali's servant, Jack, wears a suit made of pajama material and cut like pajamas. The queen's maid, Lulu, wears dresses that merge the classic and the modern, the foreign and the local (Figure 3.8). All of these aesthetic touches suggest that the visual presentation of the film is characterized by symbolism, not realism.[53]

To be sure, the fantastic mise-en-scène serves a commercial purpose. The film, billed as a "grand musical comedy," or *gechang da xiju* 歌唱大喜剧, was considered foreign to the audience's viewing habits. According to a reviewer of *My Kingdom for a Husband,* the audience is conventionally attracted to tear-jerking films (*kuqing xi* 苦情戏, literally, "bitter sentiments films") that dramatize doomed romance and therefore may find it hard to sympathize with characters in a comedy. To address this potential problem, the film tries to entice the audience by "soaking them in honey," or indulging them in the exotic romance enacted in a newfangled mise-en-scène by a top-notch cast.[54] In addition, the film publicity

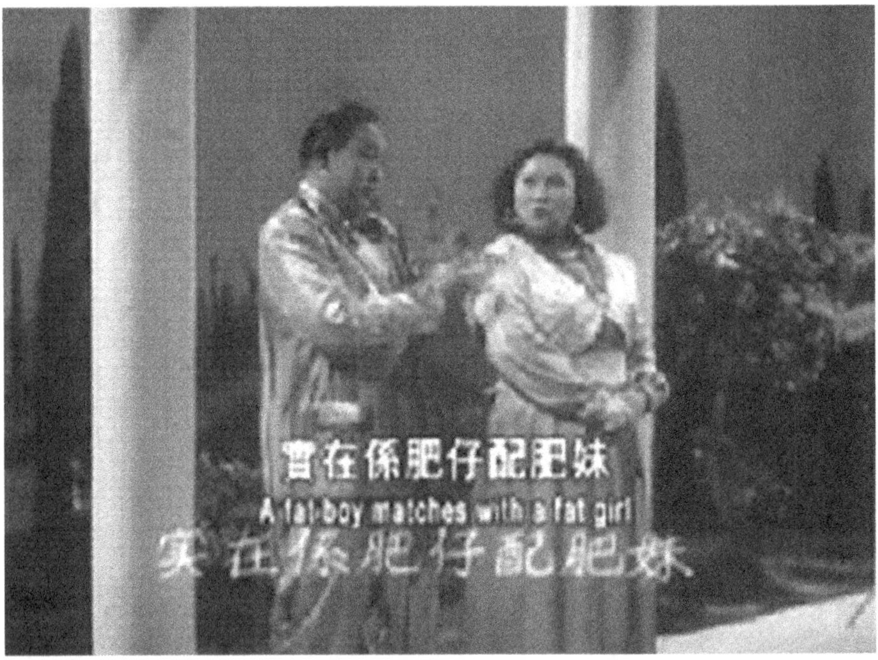

Figure 3.8 Jack and Lulu serenading and flirting in nondescript costumes in *My Kingdom for a Husband*

emphasized sensual experience by using Kodak color and wide-screen film stills to trick the audience into expecting the newest technology (when the film was actually shot in black and white with regular aspect ratio). In addition to the formal and technological allure, the production company, Motion Pictures and General Investment, also publicized the film through a different medium by recording sections of the film's sound track, adding voice-over narration, and distributing it to Rediffusion for radio broadcasting.[55]

Aside from the commercial intentions, the film's emphasis on visual novelty at the diegetic and extradiegetic levels, juxtaposed with the seemingly traditional Cantonese singing, simultaneously shocks and attracts the audience, thus underscoring the importance of fashioning the local through implanting the foreign. This process becomes more compelling when we explore two issues: (1) how contemporary audiences responded to and made sense of the film's incongruous and foreignizing modes of address and (2) what the foreignizing modes of address can tell us about the self-positioning of postwar Hong Kong (and Cantonese) cinema, which had lost the mainland market yet was reemerging in the Cold War climate thanks to the vibrant Hong Kong–Taiwan–Southeast Asia nexus and commerce.

Whereas the shortage of documentation does not permit us to systematically reconstruct audience reception of the film in the 1950s, we can heuristically compare two writers' memories of their childhood experiences with *The Love Parade* and Western-costume Cantonese opera/films like *My Kingdom for a Husband.* Chen Shibai recalls *The Love Parade* as one of the most sensational Western talkies in Hong Kong. Although no translation was provided, those who did not know much English (like him) still enjoyed the film immensely. He highlights two moments in particular. The first concerns Jeanette MacDonald's undressing in the bathing scene. When the camera cuts from her bare shoulders to her ankles as the dress drops, some viewers impulsively stood up with the hope of seeing more. The second moment has to do with MacDonald's performance of the "March of the Grenadiers," which is corrupted into multiple Cantonese versions with completely rewritten lyrics.[56] Interestingly, Chen attributes the ebullient cinema (and other popular) culture of the 1930s Hong Kong to its peaceful society under British colonial governance (in contrast to China's increasing subjection to Japanese invasion in the same period).

If Chen Shibai's childhood memory of *The Love Parade* focuses on the Hollywood film's sensational foreignness and its local appropriation or corruption, Chen Guanzhong, a Hong Kong writer, describes the audience's acculturated reception of the foreignizing Western-costume Cantonese opera/films in the 1950s. As he puts it, in these films, Cantonese opera stars readily "pass" as Europeans, Arabs, and Indians, then suddenly break into Cantonese song; the audience (including Chen himself) found the jarring incongruity hilarious and amusing.[57] Indeed,

Chen sees such incongruity as the essence of a Hong Kong culture that constantly bastardizes (*zazhong* 杂种) and localizes imports, leading the audience to readily enjoy hybridized forms of entertainment as a form of canon in its own right (*zhengguo* 正果).

The two accounts mark two different phases in Hong Kong's negotiation with Western cultural (cinema) products, from sensationalized encounter and reception to self-foreignizing film production (in the form of Western-costume opera/films). Chen Guanzhong's emphasis on the canonization of bastardized cultural products usefully underscores Hong Kong's interstitial existence and heterogeneous cultural makeup. However, he fails to clarify who gets bastardized (the West or Hong Kong) and what exactly is the relationship between localization and bastardization. Consequently, his account risks fetishizing sheer mixture. To unpack the cultural politics of such mixture or "bastardization" in relation to the formation of postwar Hong Kong (and Cantonese) cinema and subject positioning, I highlight the process of "trans," the awkward and obstinate interstitial zone characterized by crossing, incongruity, *and* blockage in the processes of cross-Pacific and transregional Chinese filmic commerce.

The zone of "trans" produces what Mary Farquhar and Chris Berry describe as "the connection of difference" rather than of homogeneity.[58] It negates the teleology of complete domestication or foreignization, and instead privileges constant vacillation between foreign and local/regional positions in the interstitial zone of contact. As such, the status of "trans" foregrounds the unavoidable mutual penetration and irreducible mutual irreconcilability between the foreign Other and the local/regional Self, which result in defamiliarizing self-foreignization rather than complete homogenization (be it Westernization or domestication). This "trans" process is amply illustrated in the audio-visual presentation of *My Kingdom for a Husband*.

By offering the audience the sensorial and affective experience of the foreign (visual exotica) and the (trans)local (Cantonese opera) as being different yet inevitably connected, mutually penetrating yet hardly integrated, the film's audio-visual presentation necessitates the audience's constant vacillation between different positions, driven by the persistent "spectre of comparison." As such, it appeals to the dispersed (diasporic) Cantonese audiences in two ways: confirming their sense of belonging based on a popular brand of hometown culture—Cantonese opera—and teasing and satisfying their curiosity for Occidental novelties by parading exotic settings and costumes. This foreignizing mode of audience address differs drastically from Motion Pictures and General Investment's staple productions in the 1950s and 1960s, namely, urban-themed, Mandarin song-and-dance films, which tend to be set in modern-day Hong Kong, flaunting unified (instead of incongruent) audio-visual modernity modeled on Hollywood musicals, and appeal more exclusively to the urban youth audience.[59]

It also significantly differs from a new-millennium Chinese-language film characterized by audio-visual incongruity. I refer to Ang Lee's Mandarin Chinese blockbuster *Crouching Tiger, Hidden Dragon* (2000). In her study of Sinophone visual culture under globalization, Shu-mei Shih proposes that the Sinophone visual form more readily travels across boundaries, whereas the linguistic particularities, indicated in the multiple Chinese dialects, tend to remain local and thus underscore the heterogeneity and untranslatability of Chineseness. In this light, Shih ascribes the drastically different reception of *Crouching Tiger, Hidden Dragon* by Western and Chinese-speaking audiences to the film's divergent visual and linguistic modes of audience address.[60] Whereas the readily portable visual presentation appeals to the Western audience, the heavily accented Mandarin Chinese spoken by two of the leading actors (Chow Yun-fat from Hong Kong and Michelle Yeoh from Malaysia, both speakers of Cantonese) instantly alienates the Mandarin Chinese speakers, who dismiss Lee's martial arts film as unauthentic.

The audio-visual discrepancy in the Western-costume Cantonese opera/films made in 1930s Shanghai and 1950s Hong Kong operates in markedly different ways. The linguistic particularity in these opera/films is emphatically not local, nor does it coincide with national boundaries. Thus, it does not necessarily serve as a marker of national or regional authenticity. In fact, the Cantonese dialect travels with the widely disseminated Cantonese population throughout the long history of migration. Consequently, Cantonese cinema is both subnational and supranational; that is, it is both marginalized by the discursive emphasis on Mandarin national cinema and effectively transcends national confines (if not national politics). Counterpoised to the simultaneously specific and transnational Cantonese linguaculture is these films' liberal display of sumptuous and fantastic visual attractions, which seem to proffer a universally legible imaginary of abundance. Yet, a crucial difference from the portable visuality of *Crouching Tiger, Hidden Dragon* is that instead of marketing "Chinese" iconography to Western audiences in the self-Orientalist fashion, the Western-costume Cantonese opera/films parade Occidentalist imagery and graft it onto the Cantonese-speaking cast, targeting transnational Cantonese audiences. In this sense, the Occidentalist display does not presume instant visual legibility but rather instigates self-foreignization that solicits a new mode of visual literacy as well as subject positioning on the part of the disseminated Cantonese audiences.

Such discrepant audio-visual address (self-recentering on the one hand, self-foreignizing on the other) propagates the Western allure while retaining its foreignness to and incongruence with the Cantonese (trans)regional culture. This is particularly important since the Western costume opera/films target audiences who are already constantly experiencing split interests and desires as a result of diasporic movements. These films' bifurcated modes of address simulate the diasporic audience's everyday experiences, helping them reenact and balance multiple anchors of affiliation in the migrating processes. As such, the films help to constitute the audience's diasporic identity by enabling their self-(re-)recognition. Such self-(re-)recognition hinges on "espacement" that defines identity and subject positioning in terms of alterity, or becoming different through interacting with the foreign Other. "Espacement" is opposed to conventional understanding of identity as reiterating a reified category.[61]

As Kwai-cheung Lo argues in the context of contemporary Hong Kong popular culture (including cinema), the kernel of the local (or regional) is "self-estrangement," and the nonlocal "can provide a viewpoint from which the local can identify itself as something other than itself."[62] In other words, the "foreign" must remain the "foreign" (rather than becoming domesticated) in order to constitute the "Self." Conversely, the local/regional Self necessarily undergoes constant slippage and reconfiguration without becoming completely assimilated by the foreign. The audio-visual discrepancy in *My Kingdom for a Husband* both produces and appeals to the dialectical tension between (trans)local and foreign attachments. As such, it is not only a border-crossing, but more specifically a foreignizing remake that allows its audiences to continue experimenting with and performing their plebian, in-transit, diasporic positions through film spectatorial experiences.

Foreignizing Remaking

The examples of Western-costume Cantonese opera/films illuminate a new way of conceptualizing the local-foreign negotiation in border-crossing film remaking under global colonialism and capitalism. Walter Mignolo highlights "bilanguaging" (the clashing of languages) as a condition for postcolonial border thinking. It registers deeply entrenched border politics while debunking the essentialist understanding of the border.[63] In the case of cinema—a medium not exclusively based on language—bilanguaging should be expanded to include bicoding or multicoding, as illustrated in the dual modes of audience address in the various versions of *Xuangong yanshi*, especially *My Kingdom for a Husband*. Bi-/multicoding stems from the border zone of "trans"—a contested and fluctuating interface that both necessitates cross-flow and obstructs fair exchange as well as complete hybridization. Thus, bi-/multicoding resists easy assimilation or translation by stressing that any translation and transaction in the border zone necessarily involves what Venuti calls "foreignizing translation."[64] Instead of completely domesticating the foreign or completely foreignizing the Self, both of which end up virtually disavowing the intractable difference, "foreignizing translation" originates from and underscores the persistent incommensurability as well as the osmosis and vacillation between the foreign Other and the local Self.

Foreignizing translation, as embodied in "the Western-costume Cantonese opera/films" made in 1930s Shanghai and 1950s Hong Kong, gives rise to what Fredric Jameson describes as "oppositions preserved in the very condition of that precarious (and maybe even fictive) synthesis."[65] He compares this condition with the result of genetic transfer:

> In this new postmodern process what happens is evidently that a single characteristic fragment is selected from one gene and inserted into another one—more or less the way a virus is implanted in a cell. This results in a new—dare we call it an artificial?—gene, which is neither the parent cell nor the donor, but which in its realization or embodiment (in the ear of corn, say) is indistinguishable from either of those, and detectable only later on, in its afterlife and its impact on the ecosystem.[66]

Whereas the Western-costume Cantonese opera/film is easily distinguishable from both "the parent cell" (Cantonese opera films) and the "donor" (Hollywood fantasy musicals), Jameson's idea of grafting the "characteristic fragment" of one gene onto another one vividly captures the intractable incongruity inherent in the precarious transplantation. And similar to the new artificial gene's "afterlife" and "impact" on the future ecosystem, foreignizing translation has far-reaching ramifications for the reconfiguration of Hong Kong–made Cantonese cinema from the mid-twentieth century to the new millennium. The grafting of the foreign gene means that the foreign is not to be prioritized as the homogenizing frame of reference, but is rather deployed as a perspective that instigates self-difference and reconstruction without erasing the demarcations of the regional Self. This foreign perspective, correlated with the "spectre of comparison," urges us to understand cross-Pacific film remaking not simply in terms of what can be assimilated or how to assimilate but rather in terms of what "characteristic fragments" are kept and flaunted as "foreign," with what implications.

The self-foreignizing Cantonese remakes of Lubitsch's fantasy–musical comedy *The Love Parade* indicate that the formation of peripheral regional cinema and collective subject positioning in 1930s Shanghai and 1950s Hong Kong is intertwined with cultural politics across borders. It is through negotiating the border politics and the attendant "spectre of comparison" that the remakes adopt a foreign perspective. By mobilizing ambivalent modes of address, they produce destabilization and espacement, thereby enacting the process of unthinking and defamiliarizing any type of reification, be it Sino-centrism or Euro-American-centrism. The foreignizing remaking studied in this chapter thus stages the tension between deterritorialization (looking foreign) and reterritorialization (sounding local) that undergirds the (re)formation of Cantonese cinema (as a peripheral yet key component of Chinese-language cinema). This tension further contributes to shaping (through destabilizing) Cantonese subject positioning that becomes increasingly anchored in Hong Kong as it vacillates between the local, regional, national, and supranational realms from the 1930s to the Cold War era.

In the next chapter, I tackle the "spectre of comparison" in temporality by studying a set of phantom films made in Hollywood and remade in Shanghai and Hong Kong. In parallel with the local/regional Self being constituted by the foreign Other (as I have argued in this chapter), my study of the phantom films addresses how trauma in the historical past intertwines with the present so as to make the present a veritable remake and afterlife of the past. Furthermore, this present is not only determined by historical trauma, but also redeems the past by endowing it with an afterlife. In other words, the spectre of the past shadows the present just as the present reinspires (in the etymological sense of breathing life back into) the past—all in a comparative process that shuttles back and forth between the past and the present/future.

CHAPTER 4

Mr. Phantom Goes to the East

History and Its Afterlife from Hollywood to Shanghai and Hong Kong

Glut your eyes on my accursed ugliness.
—Phantom Eric to his female protégé, Christine, in *The Phantom of the Opera,* 1925

Friend, I've waited for you for ten years. You're the ideal in my mind.
—Phantom Song Dangping to his male protégé, Sun Xiao'ou, in *Song at Midnight,* 1937

This is sheer trading! You teach me how to play Romeo only to make me into your double.
—Wei Qing, Phantom's male protégé, to Phantom Song Danping in *The Phantom Lover,* 1995

Lon Chaney (1883–1930), Jin Shan (1911–1982), and Leslie Cheung (1956–2003)—three actors from drastically different cultural and historical backgrounds—intersect at one point: at the height of their careers, they all played the disfigured and horrific phantom originating from *The Phantom of the Opera.* Springing from a 1909–1910 French gothic mystery novel by Gaston Leroux (1868–1927), the phantom figure has inspired numerous film remakes in various national/regional and linguistic contexts as well as multiple opera versions (the most famous being Andrew Lloyd Webber's 1986 musical). In Shanghai, Hong Kong, and Beijing, four film remakes (two of which also spawned a sequel) and one thirty-episode TV drama have been produced. They share the Chinese title *Yeban gesheng,* respectively translated into *Song at Midnight* (1937, sequel in 1941, Shanghai), *Mid-Nightmare* (1962, sequel in 1963, Hong Kong), *Song at Midnight* (1985, Shanghai), *The Phantom Lover* (1995, Hong Kong), and *Song at Midnight* (2005, Beijing). The film versions constitute an important genealogy of Chinese horror film (or *kongbu pian* 恐怖片). During the century-long remaking process, the disfigured and disavowed phantom is revived, refigured, and ultimately canonized as a romantic yet tragic hero.

In this chapter, I focus on the phantom's three filmic manifestations and then briefly consider the TV drama. These versions register major historical, political, and technological shifts, and express variegated visions of the future. Technologically, they represent different phases of sound recording and color usage. They also emerge from important historical and political conjunctures throughout the twentieth century. *The Phantom of the Opera* (dir. Rupert Julian, 1925, Universal Studios) was made after World War I, when Hollywood achieved worldwide dominance, while European cinema declined owing to war damage. *Song at Midnight* (dir. Maxu Weibang 1937, New China Film Company, Shanghai) stemmed from semicolonial China's national crisis and was released on the eve of the Second Sino-Japanese War, which erupted in July 1937. Finally, *The Phantom Lover* (dir. Ronny Yu, 1995, Mandarin Films and Sil-Metropole, Hong Kong) arose amidst the Hong Kong people's collective anxiety surrounding Hong Kong's impending 1997 handover to China, which would end Hong Kong's century-long status as a British colony. Ten years later, the new-millennium TV drama produced in Beijing features the phantom's new historical makeover that registers Hong Kong's postcolonial interactions with mainland China and China's participation in globalization.

Understood in relation to the precarious geopolitical circumstances in 1930s Shanghai and 1990s Hong Kong, the 1937 and 1995 remakes exemplify what I am calling "subaltern remaking" that subverts and revitalizes the predecessor film(s) all at once, thereby reconfiguring the power structure across the Sino-American and China–Hong Kong borders. My task in this chapter is to develop the concept of "subaltern remaking" by analyzing two aspects of the phantom films: (1) their deployment of the disfigured phantom and (2) the phantom's interactions with his student. I believe that the masked and disfigured phantom in the Shanghai and Hong Kong remakes embodies a repressed and traumatized past that continues to haunt the present. This past can be allegorically related to Shanghai's and Hong Kong's subaltern positions in the world system of colonialism. Thus, the difficulty of representing the disfigured phantom within the diegesis serves as an analogy for the difficult encounter with the historical trauma (and its impact on the present) in the filmmaking processes. The challenge of audio-visualizing and embodying the phantom through available sound recording and color technologies significantly shapes each film's aesthetic style.

Furthermore, the phantom's relationship with his student, as depicted in the remakes, allegorizes the ways in which the present/student inherits, resists, and/or reinvents the past/phantom. The phantom-student dynamic also serves as a trope for understanding border-crossing film interaction and remaking. To remake a film, especially from a subaltern and peripheral perspective, is to adopt the position of the student, whose very existence is simultaneously enabled and constrained by the powerful "teacher," or the predecessor film. In this sense, the difficulty of representing the phantom parallels the difficulty of carrying on a dialog with a predecessor film from a dominant industry. As a cinematic rejoinder, the "student" film must strategically position itself vis-à-vis the "teacher" film. Its strategic self-positioning speaks volumes about the negotiation of the dominant-subaltern disparity in the colonial and postcolonial contexts.

Not only does the "student" film negotiate the power structure, it also potentially reshuffles it. By showing how the student's interaction and interference with the phantom teacher eventually brings about a tentative redemption for the past trauma, I delineate the ways in which the subaltern "student" remake gestures toward a utopic vision of the future diegetically, historically, politically, and metacinematically. This vision implicitly correlates with the attempts to configure a subaltern national or regional cinema and the attendant subject positioning through the Hollywood–Shanghai–Hong Kong triangular film remaking under different historical and political circumstances.

Unveiling the Phantom

All three phantom films I study share the same basic narrative: a disfigured phantom haunts a theater (either in the underground catacomb of the Paris Opera House in Universal's silent classic or in the attic of a dilapidated theater in the Shanghai and Hong Kong remakes). The haunting suggests the phantom's strong desire to communicate with and command the present world through a young person he has selected as his student/protégé. In every version, the hidden phantom coaches his student in vocal performance and enables his or her stage success. Meanwhile, the phantom also demands love (in the Universal version) and obedience (in the Chinese remakes) from his protégé, which provokes drastically different reactions from the latter. These reactions in turn lead to endings that suggest distinct visions of the future.

In *The Phantom of the Opera,* Christine Daae, a young opera understudy, is selected by the phantom Eric as his protégé. She admires her invisible "master" for his "angelic voice," yet eventually unmasks him only to reveal his grotesque skull face. Terrified by this revelation, she flees and, after much suspense, is eventually reunited with her aristocratic fiancé. Chased by an angry mob, the phantom confronts the mob with a menacing grin on his disfigured face before jumping into a river.[1] The film concludes with an image of Christine on her honeymoon with her aristocratic husband.

The 1937 Shanghai remake, *Song at Midnight,* reaches a similar climax when the mob chases the phantom up a tower, from which he leaps to his death into the torrential river below.[2] The difference, however, is that his elimination is not celebrated as the end of evil; rather, it is mourned by his male student and by the phantom's mentally deranged lover. In the 1995 Hong Kong remake, *The Phantom Lover,* the ending switches from the phantom's elimination to his ultimate vindication when his torturer from ten years ago is finally exposed and properly punished in public. This film then concludes with the phantom's reunion with his deranged lover.

In all three films, the phantom's disfigurement and reclusion pose a challenge in his visualization or figuration as the physical source/presence of his singing voice. This challenge is further compounded in Universal's silent version, where the phantom is not audible to the audience. The difficulty of audio-visualizing the phantom points to the larger problematic of representing the historical trauma and humanizing the abject Other that is embodied in the phantom. This representational conundrum is exploited in the silent version's publicity to enhance the film's shock value. According to Robert Birchard, early publicity photos tended to leave out or white out the face of the phantom, played by Lon Chaney, the reputed "man of a thousand faces."[3] The underlying challenge of visualizing the phantom and making him an audio-visual unity continues in the two Chinese remakes, despite their more sophisticated filming technologies. As I shall argue, the persisting difficulty is reflected in the lingering silent-film aesthetics and the use of dubbed singing in *Song at Midnight,* and the casting choice and the romantic turn in *The Phantom Lover.* These technical, aesthetic, and narrative shifts in the making and remaking of the phantom figure correlate with China's (semi)colonial and postcolonial circumstances; meanwhile, they also contribute to shaping subaltern collective subject positions.

To make the phantom a palpable audio-visual unity, he must be unveiled or "de-acousmatized." As Michel Chion explains in the context of *The Testament of Dr. Mabuse* (dir. Fritz Lang, 1933), de-acousmatization means to assign a disembodied voice to a "visible and circumscribed body" that actually produces the voice.[4] Before de-acousmatization, the disembodied voice, or what Chion calls the "filmic acousmetre," wanders "along the surface, at once inside and outside, seeking a place to settle." It occupies "the borderlands that are neither the interior of the filmic stage nor the proscenium—a place that has no name."[5] The disembodied phantom is precisely the "filmic acousmetre" that wanders in the nameless borderlands and impersonates the sedimented history of the repressed past. By embodying the repressed past, the phantom represents the uncanny, or "the inverted form of the familiar . . . the return of something familiar and old—established in the mind that has been estranged only by the process of repression."[6]

To de-acousmatize the phantom, or to make him an audio-visual unity, therefore, means to excavate and redress the past. This is the job of the phantom's selected student. The degree to which the student fulfills this task determines the teacher-student power relationship and the possibility of a utopic future.

In Universal's silent version of *The Phantom of the Opera,* the phantom Eric is represented in split modes. For the characters (including Christine), the phantom is the filmic acousmetre par excellence. Emitting from behind Christine's dressing mirror, the acousmetre is omnipresent, omniscient, ubiquitous, panoptic, and "usually malevolent, occasionally tutelary," as Chion describes.[7] Contrary to Christine, who is enraptured by the disembodied "angelic" and "imperial" voice, the audience of the silent film does not hear the acousmetre but only sees a gesticulating shadow projected on the wall.[8] This figure is hidden from Christine until she is lured through the mirror into the catacomb. For Mary Ann Doane, the separation of "an actor's speech from the image of his/her body" produces an "uncanny" effect that ruptures the illusion of audio-visual unity.[9] Facing the uncanny audio-visual split and the domineering shadow, the viewer tends to perform a "fetishistic act," according to Dennis Giles. This act ensures the power of the acousmetre by establishing a defensive vision that prevents the shadow's revelation, thus protecting the viewer from encountering "a horrible spectacle."[10] The viewer's defensive vision, I would argue, hinges upon a delicate balance between scopophilia (the desire to see more) and scopophobia (the fear of unobstructed vision).

When Christine's scopophilia overpowers her scopophobia, she breaches precisely this balance inherent in the "fetishistic act." Lured into the catacomb, wanting to see behind the mask despite the phantom's warning, "Look not at my mask but at my devotion to music," Christine eventually de-acousmatizes the phantom and exposes the "horrible spectacle." In a *New York Times* review, movie critic Mordaunt Hall recounts how a woman in the movie-theater audience "stifled a scream" at the "repellant sight," when Christine snatches off the phantom's mask from behind as he plays "Don Juan Triumphant" on the piano.[11] When the unmasked phantom turns around to face Christine, forcing her to look at his skull-like face with its hollowed eyes, up-turned nose, and gaping mouth with long teeth, Christine retreats in fear. In response to the phantom's sadomasochistic order: "Glut your eyes on my accursed ugliness," she does the opposite—covering her eyes. As her blocked vision structurally duplicates the female viewer's stifled scream, the phantom mirrors her terror and abhorrence when he stumbles back and covers his ghastly face (Figures 4.1, 4.2).

Linda Williams suggests that the unmasking sequence underscores the identification and sympathy between the woman and the monster—"the two objects of the cinematic spectacle who encounter one another in this look."[12] I would like to add a third party—the (female) audience. The female viewer's stifled scream

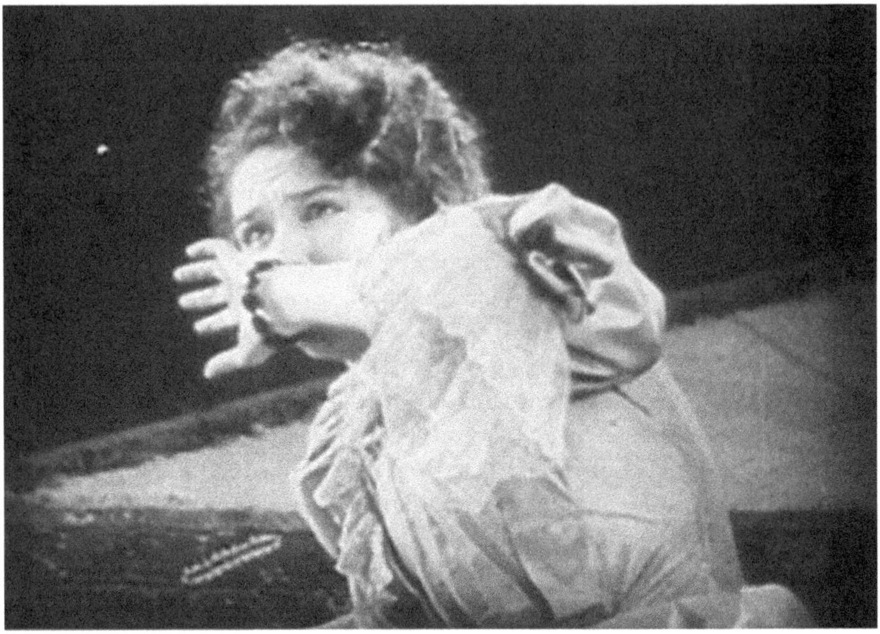

Figure 4.1 Overwhelmed by the "horrible spectacle" she has unveiled, Christine tries to block the vision in *The Phantom of the Opera*

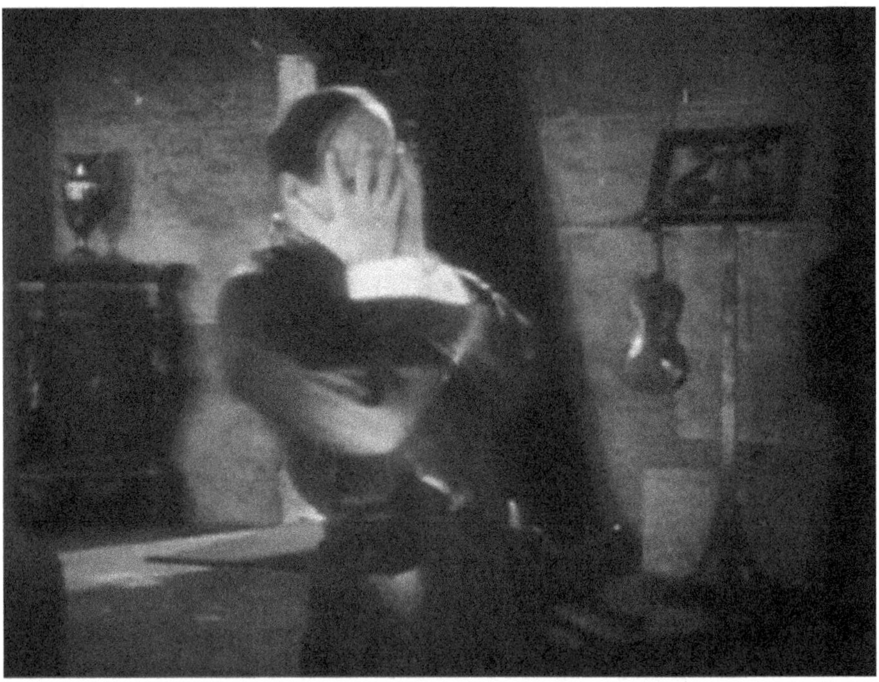

Figure 4.2 Mirroring Christine's abhorrence, the phantom covers his face and blocks his vision

(as Hall recounts) suggests precisely the convergence between the monster, the woman, and the (female) audience, who relay, remediate, and reinforce each other's shock-and-block reactions. Their mutually mirroring reactions suggest the analogously traumatic experience of being exposed as monstrous and being forced to face the exposed monstrosity. In other words, de-acousmatization and the resultant unobstructed visibility of horror do not simply strip the phantom of his power, as Chion argues;[13] rather they make the phantom, his student, and the (female) viewer equally vulnerable and disempowered.

To reestablish equilibrium in the context of the film, the dehumanizing "spectacle of horror" must be cleansed rather than scrutinized. The film's ending fulfills the act of disavowal. As the phantom leaps to his death in the engulfing Seine, followed by Christine's domestication into an aristocratic housewife, the viewer, gendered feminine in Hall's review, also recovers from the shock, ever more convinced of the "no trespassing, no deviating" message imparted by the film's cautionary tale. The concluding disavowal of the desire to audio-visualize the phantom, which has driven the entire film in the first place, leads to further repression of the phantom's history. Indeed, the film contains only one intertitle that describes the catacomb as a torture zone where the phantom used to be imprisoned during the Second Revolution in France. Instead of delving into the traumatic history, the film does just the opposite: releasing Christine, along with the viewer, from the gaze of the skull face, from the task of excavating and engaging with the spectre of past, and consequently from the challenge of self-rerecognition through understanding the past. To extend Chion's contention that de-acousmatization disempowers the filmic acousmetre, not only is the phantom disempowered and eventually destroyed, but, more important, such disempowerment and repression derive from the film's ideological exclusion of the past, the monstrous, and the abject.

From De-acousmatizing the Phantom to Deciphering Historical Trauma

The exorcism of the past as seen in the Hollywood silent film *The Phantom of the Opera* is reversed in the 1937 Shanghai and 1995 Hong Kong remakes. *Song at Midnight* (1937) recontextualizes the narrative of the silent horror-romance, setting the story in China of the 1910s to the mid-1920s. This period was one of chaos in China, owing to domestic warlord strife and Sino-Western contentions that started with the 1840 Opium War. Within the film, the tumultuous 1920s are used to allegorize Japan's escalating invasion in the 1930s, which constitutes the sociopolitical background for the production of the 1937 remake. In other words, China's political subordination following its defeat in the 1840 Opium War resulted in the ongoing national crisis that was looming large at the film's premiere on February 20, 1937, barely five months before the outbreak of the Second Sino-Japanese War.

The long-term semicolonial conditions and aggravating national crisis find expression in the film's extended flashback sequences (evoked by the phantom, Song Danping), which bring the student and the audience to engage with what has been repressed. Thus, unlike *The Phantom of the Opera,* the phantom's de-acousmatization in *Song at Midnight* restores his humanity and enhances his power by revealing himself as a witness of the past and an embodiment of history's demand for redemption. The revelation and continuation of the phantom's historical legacy depend on the student's negotiation with his powerful master. Indeed, as I argue below, the student's doubling of his phantom teacher within the diegesis constitutes a veritable remaking process that parallels the extradiegetic filmic remaking and the reshaping of China's subaltern/student subject positioning vis-à-vis the imperial Other(s).

To understand how the student in *Song at Midnight* remakes the phantom teacher's legacy through doubling, one must first examine how the phantom is audio-visualized, both diegetically and extradiegetically. *Song at Midnight,* the first important horror film in Chinese film history, unapologetically wields the power of horror. The director, Maxu Weibang (1901–1961), known as the "Lon Chaney of China," had been exploring corporeal plasticity and metamorphosis in his earlier films, including *The Stranger on the Love Scene* (*Qingchang guairen,* 1926) and *The Cry of the Apes in a Deserted Valley* (*Konggu yuansheng,* 1930). This preoccupation with metamorphosis continues in *Song at Midnight,* as manifested in the phantom's ingenious facial makeup.[14] However, unlike Universal's publicity photos of *The Phantom of the Opera* that white out Lon Chaney's monstrous makeup in order to create suspense and enhance the excessive horror, the poster of *Song at Midnight* readily divulges and exaggerates the phantom's horrific visage by showing a giant disfigured man with eyeballs made of light bulbs. This poster, designed by S. K. Chang, founder of Xinhua Yingye Gongsi (New China Film Company), which produced the film, was erected on the street and was rumored to have scared a child to death. The subsequent warning—"Children under six years old are not admitted"—further piqued the audience's interest. The film ran continuously for thirty-four days at the Jincheng Daxiyuan 金城大戏院 (Lyric Theatre).

The horror does not simply indicate a technical, aesthetic, and commercial gimmick crafted by Maxu Weibang and S. K. Chang. Rather, it also inscribes a political allegory coproduced by Maxu and left-leaning artists and critics. Tian Han (1898–1968), a romanticist who became a Communist in 1932, played an active role in promoting left-leaning films in the 1930s. He not only revised Maxu's script, but also wrote the lyrics for the three songs in the film. In his comments inserted in the shooting script used by Maxu Weibang, Tian Han specifically suggested rewrites that would make the film transcend its predominant horror interest (Figure 4.3).[15] The allegorical political dimension injected into the script resonates with China's semicolonial conditions since 1840 but does not translate the conditions into a monolithic political treatise. Indeed, the film's success has to do with its multiple appeals that are reflected in the dramatic narrative (which mixes horror, romance, and revolution) and the idiosyncratic style (that combines song numbers and sound effects with the silent aesthetics drawn from German expressionism). The hybrid quality stems from China's destabilized geopolitical situation, Chinese cinema's influence by a wide spectrum of foreign film practices, and the cinema medium's participation in education, entertainment, political instigation, and artistic pursuits.[16] All of these contribute to the fragmented audio-visual representation of the phantom, which necessitates an allegorical reading.

Song at Midnight, released in 1937, when the transition to the talkie era was almost complete in China,[17] unsurprisingly benefited from sound-recording technology, which enabled the production of the filmic acousmetre, or the phantom's disembodied voice. The film's title, compared with *A Ghostly Shadow in the Opera House* (*Gechang meiying* 歌场魅影, the Chinese translation of *The Phantom of*

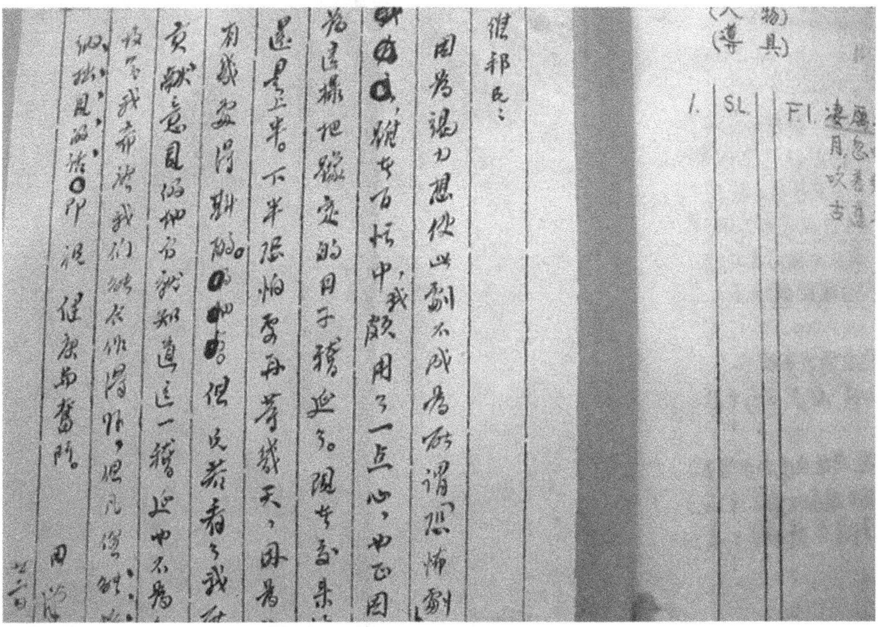

Figure 4.3 Excerpts of Tian Han's suggestions inserted in the shooting script used by Maxu Weibang, advising Maxu to transcend "the so-called horror drama" (courtesy of *Guiqu Shanzhuang's Blog*)

the Opera), encapsulates the very shift from the visual image (a "shadow") to the acoustic experience ("song" and singing). Nevertheless, from the very beginning, the film sets up an ambivalent relationship between the disembodied singing of the theme song, "Song at Midnight" (*Yeban gesheng* 夜半歌声), and the giant shadow cast on a wall. By layering the singing over the gesticulating shadow (borrowed from *The Phantom of the Opera* and German expressionist cinema) (Figures 4.4, 4.5), the audio-visual montage does not so much produce the illusion of synchronization or unity as underscore the disjuncture akin to the effect of a puppet play in which the voice and the puppet are emphatically split.

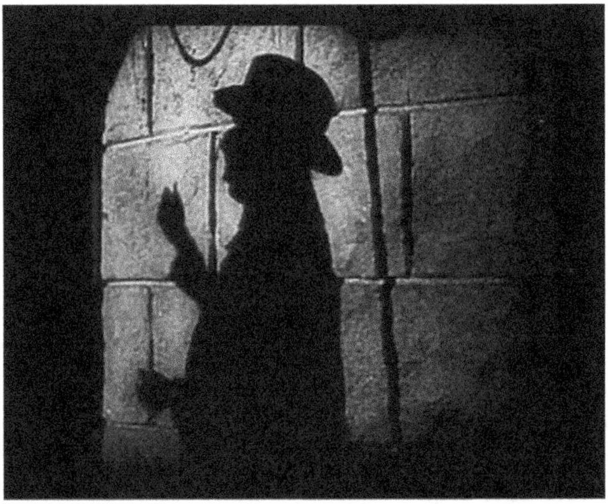

Figure 4.4 Phantom Eric's silent gesticulating shadow on the wall, as seen by the audience in *The Phantom of the Opera*

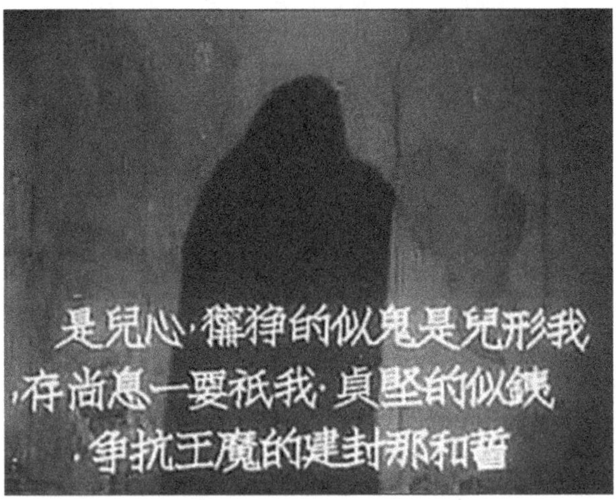

Figure 4.5 Phantom Song Danping's vocal performance grafted onto a moving shadow on the wall, as seen by the audience in *Song at Midnight*

The effect of splitting and doubling in the phantom's figuration is reinforced by the fact that the singing voice in actuality did not belong to the phantom's actor, Jin Shan (191–1982), but rather to Sheng Jialun (1910–1957), a musician, book collector, and gourmet. According to Tang Yu (1912–), a veteran editor of multiple Shanghai film magazines, "Song at Midnight" was Sheng's only vocal performance, which was distributed by Pathé Gramophone Company in Shanghai. This song, along with two other songs in the film, "Love on the Yellow River" (Huanghe zhi lian 黄河之恋) and "Hot Blood" (Rexue 热血), became instant hits that captivated audiences as far away as diasporic Chinese in Southeast Asia. In retrospect, Sheng's not-so-standard pronunciation makes his rendition inimitable.[18]

Whereas Tang Yu sees dubbing as a common practice in 1930s Chinese filmmaking, film historian Zhang Zhen productively argues that dubbing in this case is indicative of the "ambiguity in the relationship between the original and the copied voice" both on and off the screen, which makes the film "an exemplary case for reflecting on the complexity of film history at the closing of the silent era and the golden age."[19] In my focus on the translational strategies and the attendant cultural politics of cross-Pacific remaking, I argue that Sheng Jialun's extradiegetic dubbing and doubling of the phantom's singing voice interestingly mirror the phantom's diegetic vocal coaching of his student, Sun Xiao'ou. These layers of dubbing, doubling, ventriloquism, splitting, and remediation serve two functions: (1) to register the difficulty of audio-visualizing the phantom, who embodies repressed historical trauma and (2) to simulate intersubjective, intergenerational, and interfilmic negotiation and transmission, while negotiating their differences and incommensurability. To articulate and redress the historical trauma that he embodies through monstrosity, the phantom must find a new voice to communicate with the present-day audience. Vocal doubling facilitates precisely the goal of linking the past with the present, that is, rendering the phantom representable and comprehensible to the present.

The phantom's quest for a double is first manifested when he both overpowers and empowers Sun Xiao'ou, a young male actor who comes to the phantom's dilapidated theater with the traveling Angel Troupe. While practicing the song "Love on the Yellow River," which couches an anti–foreign invasion message in a love story, Sun repeatedly fails at the tenor line. In a long shot that frames Sun lowering his head in contemplation, we see a giant cloaked shadow projected on the wall behind him, literally overshadowing and dwarfing him. As Sun raises his head, the shadow jerks out of frame, while an acousmatic voice rises in the void, singing the tenor line that Sun has trouble with. Surprised, Sun looks around for the source of the singing, only to see the grotesque hunchbacked theater janitor who points to an old poster that shows the name Song Danping—a famous stage actor presumably dead for ten years. Still in shock, Sun nevertheless takes the cue and follows the acousmatic tutelage line by line. The coaching helps Sun improve his singing, which draws an audience for his troupe.

The phantom's power over Sun further increases when he de-acousmatizes himself. Unlike Christine's abrupt unmasking of her phantom master in *The Phantom of the Opera,* the phantom in *Song at Midnight* reveals his own disfigured face in an almost sadomasochist manner, imposing himself upon Sun in an extreme close-up shot. The self-de-acousmatization not only produces an aesthetic of disgust,[20] but also makes him what Doane calls a "phantasmatic body" that anchors the audio-visual unity. Such audio-visual unity serves to corroborate the phantom's narration of his traumatic past.

Aided by flashback sequences and two old photos showing his younger self, he reveals his true identity to Sun: He was originally named Jin Zhijian and was a young revolutionary leader in the 1910s, when China was fragmented and embroiled in warlord strife. When the revolution failed, he was forced into hiding. Donning a new identity as a stage actor under the name of Song Danping, he played the heroic lead in revolutionary operettas, including the famous *Hot Blood.* Meanwhile, he fell in love with Li Xiaoxia, the daughter of a local wealthy, conservative family. This infuriated Mr. Tang, a powerful official and Li's jealous suitor, who engineered Song's disfiguration with sulfuric acid. Seeing his disfigured face in the mirror, Song announced his own death and retreated into the attic of the abandoned theater, becoming an acousmatic singing voice that continued to console the now mentally deranged Li.

Upon meeting Sun, the phantom proclaims, "My body has always belonged to her [Li] and to you all." Furthermore, the phantom hails Sun as a "friend" and "the ideal in my mind," for whom he has waited for ten years. The phantom's quasi-homoerotic desire for Sun combined with his narration of repressed pasts as a revolutionary leader, a progressive actor, and a devoted lover underscores the intertwining of personal and collective passions and traumas. His personal trauma revolves around his romance with Li, which is truncated by conservative forces. This trauma in turn echoes the collective subaltern experiences that encompass class struggle (between the poor and the wealthy), political contention (between progressives and conservatives), and national crisis (China's subjection to Japanese and Western colonial forces). Etched into his disfigured visage, the collective trauma makes the phantom an authoritative embodiment of the past. His demand on Sun accordingly becomes a historical mandate upon the present. As his student, successor, selected double, even Platonic companion, Sun is encumbered to continue the phantom's revolutionary mission of fighting against sociopolitical inequities.

Yet, to the extent that the collective political mission is intertwined with the phantom's personal suffering, the transmission and execution of this political

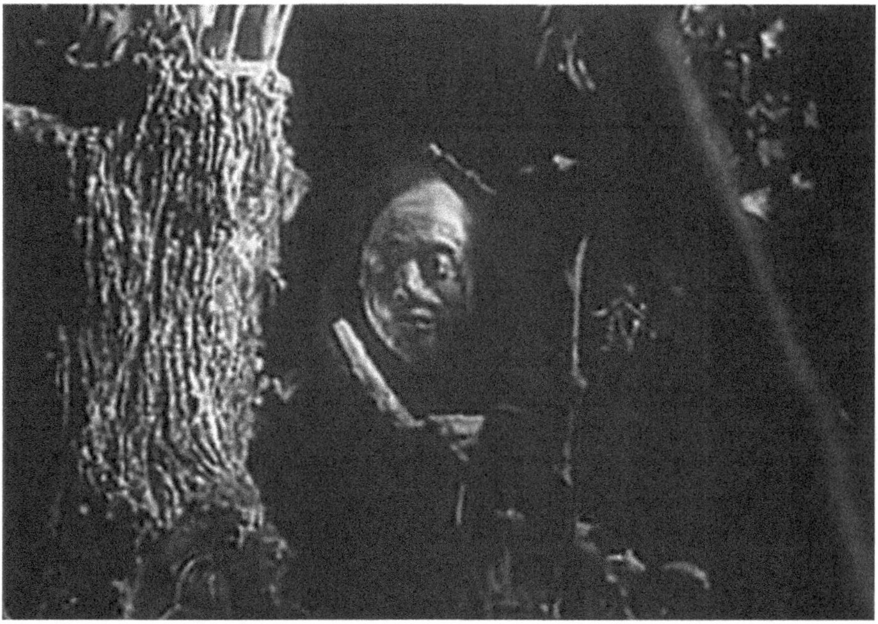

Figure 4.6 The camera cuts away to a dark corner, showing the phantom supervising Sun's rendezvous with Li Xiaoxia, orchestrated by himself

mission are necessarily routed through the redemption of the phantom's personal trauma. At the phantom's order, Sun substitutes for him and reenacts his "Song at Midnight" for the demented Li. In this key doubling sequence, Sun dons the black cape that the phantom used to wear and performs the song for Li in her dilapidated garden. Li approaches him under the delusion that he is her lover, and they have a "rendezvous" under Song's monitoring gaze. As the camera cuts from the couple to a dark corner, we see Song hiding behind bushes, nodding in agreement with Sun's off-screen encouragement to Li, "Song Danping [the phantom's stage name] is never away from you. . . . You should cheer up and pursue the meaning of your own life." Here, Sun's off-screen emphasis on Song's omnipresence echoes the phantom's supervising gaze (Figure 4.6). By endorsing and symbolically ventriloquizing Sun, the phantom both reinforces his supreme power over his student and passes his power to the latter. This power permeates collective politics and personal romance, as it does the heterosexual relationship and homosocial/homoerotic doubling.

If Sun's reenactment of "Song at Midnight" redeems the phantom's personal trauma, then it takes another doubling to regenerate Song's revolutionary mission. In this doubling, Sun reprises the phantom Song Danping's progressive operetta, *Hot Blood,* and is billed as "Song Danping Reborn" in the poster. Opening with a rebellious question, "Who would live under slavery? Who would toil like cattle?" the Western-costume operetta, in a mise-en-scène that evokes medieval Europe, vigorously espouses liberty, freedom, and equality. It eulogizes the human history of resistance that allegorically resonates with the French Revolution, China's 1911 revolution, and battles against warlords, feudal dictators, and Japanese aggressors. Sun's revival of the political play also instigates the repetition of the past violence. Mr. Tang, who disfigured Song ten years earlier, reappears at Sun's show and seeks to destroy Sun. The phantom comes to the rescue and kills Tang, but in the process he exposes himself to the fanatic crowd. Cornered into a tower that the crowd then sets on fire, the phantom leaps into the torrential river below.

Unlike his counterpart's most welcome eradication in *The Phantom of the Opera,* the Chinese phantom is mourned by Sun and Li. As they stand at the river, set against a sublime landscape of fiery clouds in a long profile shot, the last stanza of the phantom's "Song at Midnight" rises in the nondiegetic soundscape. As death re-acousmatizes the phantom's singing as a cosmic, disembodied voice, the lyrics of romance that revolve around an interlocutory relationship between "I" and "you" (or "my girl") now take on a new meaning. The cosmic acousmetre is interpellating Li, Sun, and all film viewers as his "girl"—the loyal listeners who are subjected to his acoustic charisma and will carry on his unfinished mission.

Orthodox criticism after 1949, represented by Cheng Jihua et al., has condemned the film for privileging the phantom's petty bourgeois individualist heroism and romance, which contradict the spirit of the "national defense film" (*guofang dianying*)—an explicitly resistant cinema that was not made until 1938, following the eruption of the Second Sino-Japanese War and the fall of Shanghai and Nanjing.[21] Instead of measuring the film with a prescriptive yardstick for how revolution or resistance should be depicted, I argue that it is important to understand the film in its intertextual and contextual circumstances, and to unpack the political ramifications of the phantom's amorous enchantment for his symbolically feminized followers (including his student Sun).

Song at Midnight departs from Universal's silent classic, *The Phantom of the Opera,* by localizing the narrative in China's subaltern geopolitics and national crisis. Prior to the eruption of the resistance war on July 1, 1937, the governing Nationalist Party forbade any explicit references to the "Japanese" invasion.[22] *Song at Midnight* premiered on February 20, 1937; therefore, its resistance message is necessarily allegorical. That is, a figure is deployed in the place of something that cannot be directly portrayed. The proxy figure in this case is commitment to the frustrated personal romance in the place of collective resistance against oppression. Such a refiguring process does not pretend that the two terms are exchangeable, replaceable, or that the proxy figure becomes disposable once the unrepresentable is successfully conveyed. Rather, it creates polysemy, even distraction, by engaging with the disjuncture as well as linkage between personal romance and collective resistance. Such an allegorical approach is already seen in Wu Yonggang's negotiation with the problematic of figuring abject female sexuality, as we saw in Chapter 1. His strategy in *The Goddess* is to hint at low-class illegal streetwalking through the figure of the noble mother. In *Song at Midnight,* the allegorical principle underpins the figuration of the phantom, the narrative structure, and the intergenerational doubling.

As I have discussed earlier, the phantom is difficult to figure because he embodies the repressed past. His self-account and self-de-acousmatization enhance his power, without, however, revealing the specifics of the revolutionary work he used to participate in. Nor does his revolutionary operetta, *Hot Blood,* address specific Chinese problems. Contrary to the cryptic "revolution," the narrative of the phantom's frustrated romance is much more fleshed out, even if it rehearses a stereotypical story of the progressive younger generation's rebellion against the domineering older, conservative generation. The romance serves to refigure and allegorize the politics of resistance, while also boosting the film's commercial appeal and even threatening to overshadow the political message (as Braester suggests).[23]

The same allegorical narrative strategy is also deployed in two of the film's songs, "Love on the Yellow River" and "Song at Midnight." Along with "Hot Blood," they were written by Tian Han, a romanticist-turned-Communist, and composed by the French-educated musician Xian Xinghai (1905–1945), who later became canonized as a people's musician.[24] Both songs allude to the national crisis through the figure of truncated romance. The allegorical strategy deployed in both the film and the songs confirms the prevalent imperative to romanticize politics and, conversely, to politicize romance.

By this logic, the intergenerational transmission between the phantom and his selected protégé/double is by no means a political transaction in the orthodox sense. Sun's first doubling job is to stand in for the phantom in order to comfort the latter's demented girlfriend, Li. And the film ends with Sun and Li standing shoulder to shoulder, mourning the phantom's death. These intergenerational arrangements raise a question regarding the nature of Sun's inheritance. Has he inherited the phantom's political mission, his girlfriend, or both?

The yoking together of romance and revolution in the figuration of the phantom, the narrative strategy, and the intergenerational transmission should not be simplistically understood as the film's failure to be radical, as the orthodox ideological criticism argues. On the contrary, the individual romance repressed by "feudal devils" (*fengjian de mowang,* according to the theme song, "Song at Midnight") offers a powerful affective structural analogy with China in crisis. In both the individual and collective domains, the feeling of emergency finds expression in the horror aesthetics that teeters between concealment and revelation, dominance and submission, unity and fragmentation, frustration and fulfillment. In other words, the polysemic layering of romance onto revolution underscores their shared sublime monstrosity that is ingrained in and allegorical of the geopolitics of China on the eve of war.

As the first major Chinese horror film that effectively combines commercial, artistic, and political appeal, *Song at Midnight* spawned a sequel in 1941, again directed by Maxu Weibang. In 1962 and 1963, Maxu's disciple Yuan Qiufeng "inherited" the horror tradition and did a remake and a sequel, *Mid-Nightmare,* for Hong Kong's Shaw Brothers. In 1985, not long after the Cultural Revolution, at the height of cultural reflection and literary, artistic experimentation, a fourth-generation director, Yang Yanjin (1945–), again remade the film with a striking modernist sensibility.[25]

From Deciphering History to Decolonizing the Future: Emergence of a Peripheral Postcolonial Subject Position

Fast-forwarding ten years to 1995—the eve of Hong Kong's 1997 handover to mainland China—the phantom film experienced yet another major makeover as *The Phantom Lover.* Directed by Hong Kong's Ronny Yu (1950–), this film subtly stages Hong Kong's renegotiation with the now postsocialist China with an eye to strategizing its anticipated post–United Kingdom position. Here, mainland China is engaged with as an important site where Maxu's film was made, Yu's remake was shot, and Hong Kong is to find its new "motherland" (if only reluctantly) and its future market (with great eagerness). It figures as the Other (formulated during the Cold War) that is approximating the Hong Kong Self (or even taking over the Self in the era of postcolonialism and globalization). In this light, the diegetic teacher-student doubling becomes a particularly poignant metaphor for extradiegetic tensions between the predecessor film and the remake, the mainland and Hong Kong, the center and the periphery, the dominant and the subaltern. By maneuvering the teacher-student relationship and refiguring the correlated utopic vision, Yu's 1995 Hong Kong remake positions itself alternatively as the rebellious student or the sophisticated teacher vis-à-vis China—the Other that is increasingly intertwined with the Self.

To assert its Hong Kong origin and originality (compared to the 1937 version), director Ronny Yu introduces two major changes in his 1995 remake. The first is a thematic shift from national crisis/resistance and romance to art and romance. The film style also switches from sublime monstrosity to uncompromising beauty. According to Yu and Leslie Cheung, the executive producer of the film and the leading actor who plays the phantom singer, the remake deliberately avoids the 1937 political message of resistance (to Japanese aggression) and instead focuses on the "unconditional love" between a talented artist and a beautiful woman in a bygone era.[26] In this nostalgic retrospective portrayal of a beautiful love story, the "bygone" era (the phantom's prime) is painted in luscious, vibrant colors of red, gold, and purple, in sharp contrast to the washed-out and sepia present (the phantom's ruined world that the student enters).

The second important change in Yu's remake is that the song numbers are completely rewritten. The traveling troupe's repertoire song, "Hot Blood," evokes its 1937 predecessor of the same title. But in the 1995 remake the song has become a farce and a box office flop because it mechanically shouts slogans that allude to the vacuous politics of resistance. Antithetical to the anemic "Hot Blood" is the phantom's masterpiece, "Romeo and Juliet," composed and performed by Leslie Cheung and his phantom character. The popularity of "Romeo and Juliet" with the diegetic audience, in sharp contrast to the appalling reception of "Hot Blood," asserts the appeal of apparently apolitical art and star charisma, the expensive production, the unconditional romance, and the beautiful melody. These qualities are embodied in the film's big production value, technical sophistication, romantic sentiments that erase all traces of national politics, and, finally, the charismatic leading actor, Leslie Cheung—Hong Kong's top-ranking megastar.

Yet it is precisely in the film's star economy, aesthetic supremacy, and depoliticizing turn that one detects the emergence of a postcolonial Hong Kong subject position in the intersection between globalization and China's postsocialism. Negotiating with the future motherland—mainland China—on the one hand, and with late-twentieth-century Hollywood, on the other, the film manifests the dual drive to become both re-Sinicized (so as to tap into the mainland Chinese culture, market, and other resources) and global (so as to come in sync with Hollywood technology). As such, it performs the protean subject positioning of a regional cinema that has historically been subjected and sensitive to—while also constitutive of—twentieth-century political, economic, cultural, political, and filmic circumstances. Such negotiation is manifested in the film's production (which draws on multilocal resources), its audience targeting, and its strategic treatment of the teacher-student relationship.

The film, set in 1936 Beijing, marks a major collaboration with the mainland Chinese film industry. It cast Huang Lei—a Beijing-based actor—as the student, and it was filmed in the back lot of Beijing Film Studio. To market the film in mainland China, the film was recorded in sync in Mandarin Chinese. The film also marshals then top-notch technology (Panavision and DTS, or Digital Theater Systems) and a crew that worked across the border.[27] By mobilizing multilocal resources, the Hong Kong film capitalizes on globalization and expanded market potential. It also indicates the Hong Kong film director's attempt to increase interactions with China in preparation for Hong Kong's post-1997 film development. Such strategic negotiations and realignments are subtly conveyed through the film's maneuver of the teacher-student doubling, both diegetically and extradiegetically. As I argue below, the teacher-student doubling in Yu's 1995 remake unfolds through a series of dialectic reversals, each reversal problematizing the previous order/hierarchy by reorienting and resignifying it, leading toward continuous reshuffling of the power structure.

At the outset, the casting of Leslie Cheung, the Hong Kong megastar, as the teacher, against Huang Lei, the then-minor mainland Chinese actor, as the student, already establishes the teacher's authoritative position. This power structure is further reinforced in the shooting process. Cheung not only served as the executive producer of the film and played the phantom-teacher, but also composed and performed the opera *Romeo and Juliet*. To play the phantom's double and student, Huang Lei listened to Cheung's recorded singing and imitated it in the actual shooting process, just as his student character, named Wei Qing, imitates the phantom Song Danping's singing in the diegesis. The phantom's power over the student is fully established when he offers to help by coaching the latter in performing his opera *Romeo and Juliet*. In a moment evoking the 1937 version, the student Wei Qing has trouble with the tenor lines on the stage. As he falters halfway through the second stanza, the camera first holds on him bending over the dead "Juliet," closes up on his bewildered look, then follows his look, and finally cuts to a profile shot of the cloaked phantom, hidden backstage, emotionally projecting the tenor lines (Figure 4.7).

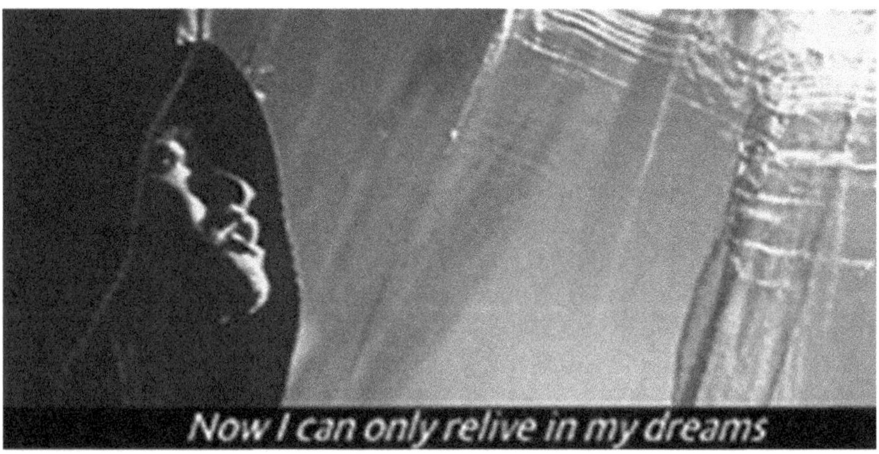

Figure 4.7 A profile shot showing Leslie Cheung's phantom character projecting his tenor voice from the backstage in *The Phantom Lover*

The splicing of Song's infectious singing with Wei's acting body produces an effect similar to that of the scene from Maxu's 1937 version where the phantom monitors the student's rendezvous with Li Xiaoxia from behind the bushes and endorses the student's revolutionary rhetoric. The common effect is that the student becomes a double of the phantom, being dubbed, ventriloquized, and usurped by the phantom's literal or symbolic voice.

As in *Song at Midnight,* in Yu's remake, the teacher-student hierarchy culminates at the moment of the phantom's self-de-acousmatization, which is triggered by Wei's initial resistance to the phantom's control over him. When the phantom-teacher asks Wei to stand in for himself in order to mediate his truncated romance with his mentally deranged girlfriend, Du Yunyan, Wei protests, "This is sheer trading; you teach me to play Romeo only to make me into your double." Wei's resistance, however, is temporarily quelled when the phantom asserts his supreme power through de-acousmatization. In a close reiteration of the equivalent scene from the 1937 version, Cheung's phantom reveals his disfigured face and pounces on Huang's student out of a dark corner. The phantom then recounts his narrow escape from fire and sulfuric acid ten years earlier in an extended, richly colored flashback sequence.

Here the Hong Kong remake departs from the 1937 Shanghai remake. In the Hong Kong version, the phantom's thwarted artistic and romantic ambitions are devoid of collective politics and are instead saturated with intense individualist sentiment. Yet, the individualist drive adumbrates collective political unconscious that can be discerned through relating the film to the ghost genre that surged in 1980s Hong Kong. A key example is Stanley Kwan's *Rouge* (*Yanzhi kou*) (1987), which contains a scene that prefigures Song's self-de-acousmatization and violent imposition upon Wei. In this scene, a frustrated female ghost, still dressed in her beautiful 1930s *qipao,* corners a present-day male journalist on the trolley, asking for help in locating her lover, who should have died in their double suicide half a century ago but who she suspects is still alive since she is not able to find him in the nether world. The task of locating a missing man from half a century ago leads the present-day journalist and his girlfriend, who have previously lived in collective amnesia, to excavate and rerecognize trivial and mundane past incidents that have been long forgotten. Made after the 1984 Sino-British Joint Declaration that stipulates Hong Kong's 1997 handover to China, *Rouge* has been read as a key allegorical text that concerns the impending "disappearance" of Hong Kong's history and identity,[28] and that implicitly calls for collective excavation and reconstruction of what is disappearing.

The imperative to redress the past in order to rebuild the present underlies the 1980s resurgence of the ghost genre in Hong Kong. Furthermore, it offers an important context for understanding the phantom's sadomasochistic self-de-acousmatization and violent imposition on his student in Yu's 1995 remake. Instead of seeing the phantom's enhanced power simply as his egoistic assertion, I ascribe his power to his implicit embodiment of Hong Kong's historical urge for self-rerecognition in the anticipated post–United Kingdom or postcolonial era. Pressured by such power, the student abandons his previous protest and agrees to become the phantom's prosthetic body in order to comfort the latter's demented girlfriend. Interestingly, his doubling of the phantom, signaling the phantom's supreme power, paradoxically leads to the reversal of the teacher-student power relationship.

To double the phantom and to communicate with the past he represents, the student must embody the phantom's voice. His creative intervention results in rewriting and regenerating the past, rather than in simply resuming it. Here the teacher-student hierarchy gets reversed. On behalf of the phantom, the student, Wei, takes a letter to the phantom's demented girlfriend, Du, who, in her delirium, believes that the phantom has returned. When Du asks him to read the message aloud to her, Wei opens the letter only to see a blank sheet of paper. As the phantom's double, he improvises a poem that expresses the phantom's everlasting love for her.

On the surface, his authentic-sounding letter makes him a faithful conduit for the phantom's voice. Nevertheless, his very act of improvising a poem by mimicking the phantom's voice evokes what Harold Bloom describes as "apophrades," or the return of the dead. According to Bloom, this is the last phase in a strong successor poet's negotiation with the influence of a prior poet. A poet at this stage "holds his own poem so open again to the precursor's work that at first we might believe the wheel has come full circle, and that we are back in the later poet's flooded apprenticeship." However, "the new poem's achievement makes it seem to us, not as though the precursor were writing it, but as though the later poet himself had written the precursor's characteristic work."[29] Wei's improvised poem indicates precisely such a reversal of authorship: instead of the phantom giving orders and dubbing Wei's singing, it is Wei who now reverse ventriloquizes his teacher, in an uncannily subversive way.

Like the strategy of excessive mimesis discussed in Chapter 1, reverse ventriloquism challenges the authority and authenticity of the "original" (the cult of the phantom in this case) by exposing the "original" as a reproducible construct partially deriving from public discourses, including the audience's participation in mythmaking. The hierarchy between the "original" teacher and the "copy" student becomes even more destabilized when the student self-consciously undertakes what I call "performative reiteration." This process takes place when Wei briefly adopts the phantom's lover identity and reciprocates Du's kissing and embrace. On witnessing the scene, the phantom chastises Wei: "I asked you to pretend to be me [*jiaban wo*] but not to pretend so earnestly [*ban de namo renzhen*]." Wei's performative reiteration threatens the phantom's authority precisely because it trespasses and negates the distance that is necessary to maintain the existing teacher-student power structure.

Wei's subversive reverse ventriloquism and performative reiteration differ from Homi Bhabha's postcolonial tactic of mimicry[30] in that his doubling does not simply subvert, but also fulfills and revitalizes the "original." Song's "original" letter, a blank sheet of paper, aptly inscribes his self-imposed absence. It becomes materialized and meaningful only when Wei improvises a letter and reverse ventriloquizes Song. Similarly, only when Wei dethrones the phantom through performative reiteration does the latter dare to face and acknowledge his own trauma. In the end, the phantom emerges from the backstage area, shows his disfigured face to the audience, and exposes those who disfigured him ten years ago. Standing as the witness and bearer of the past trauma, Song instigates the public demand for justice. Following his successful comeback, the disfigured phantom reunites with Du, and they embark on the journey to their future life together. The film completes a circle of fulfillment, opening with a crane shot of carriages bringing in Wei's traveling troupe and concluding with another crane shot of a carriage riding into the background, carrying away the eternally romantic couple (Song and Du).

Saccharine as the ending seems, it enables the refiguration of Song's disfigured face for the present-day public. If, as Walter Benjamin argues, the potential in the "prehistory" can be materialized or fructified in its "afterlife" through a form of translation, then it is the student's interventional performative reiteration that converts the phantom's repressed and truncated prehistory into a redeemed and fulfilled afterlife in his public reappearance and resumed life as a human. The textual unfolding of the shifting teacher-student relationship (characterized by both hierarchy and coimplication) offers a template for us to understand peripheral film remaking and the correlated postcolonial subject position of Hong Kong. This postcolonial subject position is simultaneously subaltern (per Hong Kong's colonial status) and empowered owing to Hong Kong's advantageous position in mobilizing border-crossing resources in its negotiation between China's postsocialism and global capitalism in the late twentieth century.

Hong Kong's shuttling position is borne out in the film's extradiegetic orchestration of the teacher-student dynamic. As discussed earlier, the casting of Hong Kong megastar Leslie Cheung as the phantom teacher, opposite the Beijing actor Huang Lei as the student, already signals the Hong Kong remake's claim for the "teacher" position. Furthermore, the casting of Cheung completely reorients the politics of monstrosity in *Song at Midnight* (1937). Unlike the actor Jin Shan, whose face is completely obliterated by his disfigured phantom character, the celebrity Cheung dominates his character (Figures 4.8, 4.9). His good looks, fetishized by fans, make complete disfiguration impossible.[31]

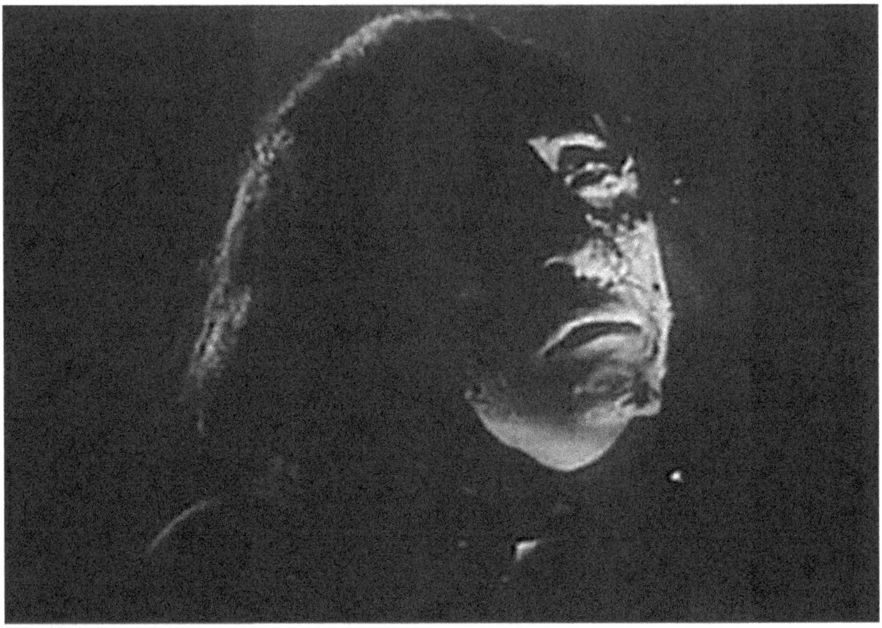

Figure 4.8 Jin Shan's completely disfigured face (in the fashion of Lon Chaney's phantom character) in the 1937 Shanghai version, *Song at Midnight*

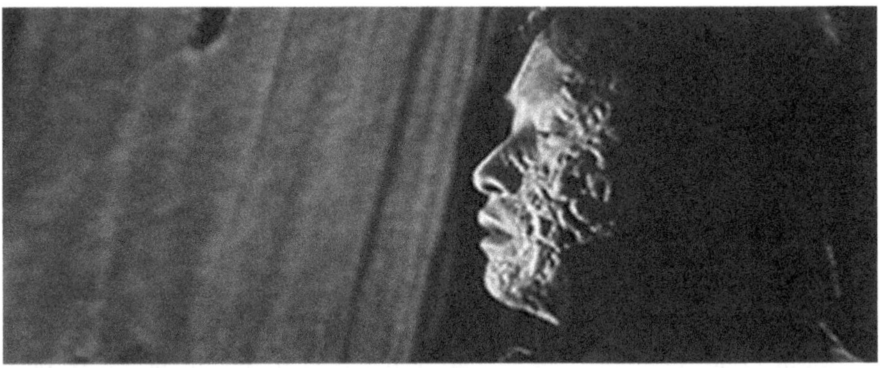

Figure 4.9 Close-up on the half-blistered face of Leslie Cheung's phantom in *The Phantom Lover*

Still, Cheung did attempt to stress the spirit of horror. In an interview, Cheung explained that the phantom role allowed him to act out his own fear of disfiguration (not by people who hate him but by his fanatic fans),[32] and that it also let him test the limits of his audience with his disfiguration. Yet, even while he was stressing the importance of disfiguration, Cheung stuck his flawless face into the interviewer's camera, as if to reinforce his inviolable charm by daring the audience to imagine how disfiguration would transform his star face. If Jin Shan's hideous makeup adheres to the aesthetic of disgust by conjuring a phantom figure that stimulates "a Metzian disavowal," then Cheung's indelible star face deflects horror and disgust by inviting "a Barthean fascination."[33]

In addition to endowing the phantom with an indelible iconic "Hong Kong" face, Cheung also suggested that his portrayal of the phantom is the superior one. Sidestepping Jin Shan, Cheung stressed his own affinity with the phantom. Both were committed to art and unconditional love, according to Cheung. Indeed, the fact that Cheung authored and performed *Romeo and Juliet* in the remake, contrary to Jin Shan's dubbed singing (provided by Sheng Jialun), produces the preposterous illusion that Jin Shan occupies the student position (in terms of artistic skill), despite his anterior position and teacher status in the 1937 film. Cheung's claim for superiority thus entails the reversal of the predecessor-successor, teacher-student order. And this reversal allows the Hong Kong remake to valorize itself as the superior rendition of the phantom prototype, thereby transcending the Oedipal competition with the Shanghai version.

In addition to striving to supplant the 1937 version, the Hong Kong remake also effectively engages with its contemporary interlocutors—postsocialist China and global Hollywood. Such engagement again hinges upon maneuvering the teacher-student relationship through textual-contextual mutual inflection. Vis-à-vis China, the casting of Cheung as the teacher and the fact that Huang Lei imitated Cheung's singing in the filming process allow the remake to claim the "teacher" position. Yet, when Huang's student in the film ends up subverting the authority of Cheung's teacher, the Hong Kong remake accordingly appropriates the student position as the self-empowered latecomer, thus successfully maintaining its agency.

As Huang imitates Cheung's vocal performance, Cheung also adopts Huang's language—Mandarin Chinese, the official language of mainland China.[34] This seems to position Cheung (and the Hong Kong remake) in the student position, while elevating Huang (and China) to the symbolic "teacher" position. Such reshuffling apparently restores the hierarchical order of mainland China's "teacher" film vis-à-vis colonial Hong Kong's "student" film. Yet the implications of adopting Mandarin Chinese are far more complex. In terms of marketing, shooting the film in Mandarin Chinese was a business strategy that facilitated the film's entrance into the expansive Chinese market—a move that would become increasingly important after Hong Kong's 1997 handover. Geopolitically, adopting the student position allows Cheung (and the Hong Kong remake) to lay claim to the student's subversive power that is developed in the film diegesis. Translated to the extradiegetic level, the student's subversive power fractures the authority of China as the purported origin of Chinese cinema and as Hong Kong's would-be motherland.

Thus, by alternately posing as the teacher (with superior artistic skills vis-à-vis Jin Shan and Huang Lei) and as the student (with subversive power vis-à-vis China-centered history and authority), the Hong Kong remake highlights the osmosis and mutual inflection between the teacher and the student's identities. Such flexible self-positioning enables the Hong Kong remake to benefit from interactions with its Chinese interlocutor.

Besides China, the remake also engages with Hollywood—Hong Kong cinema's century-long inspiration, rival, and collaborator. Whereas the crew of *The Phantom Lover* makes no mention of Lon Chaney's *The Phantom of the Opera,* which is probably deemed too arcane and overshadowed by the Shanghai-made *Song at Midnight,* the remake does aspire to a contemporary Hollywood style of technical sophistication. To emulate Hollywood, director Yu employed DTS (Digital Theater Systems) in sound recording for the first time in Hong Kong cinema. Yu reasoned that the new technique would convince Hong Kong film critics that Hong Kong was capable of high-quality filmmaking on a par with that of Hollywood and that the Hong Kong audience should proudly view homemade cinema.

Yu's endeavor undoubtedly and unsurprisingly reifies Hollywood's authority. It is also evocative of a similar situation that the Chinese film industry encountered in the early twentieth century. In both cases, the predominance of Western (especially American) cinema forces the local industry to simultaneously collaborate and compete with the external pressures.[35] The fact that the 1937 *Song at Midnight* draws heavily upon *The Phantom of the Opera* as well as German Expressionist cinema is ample evidence of the unequal dialogic field that engenders (and circumscribes) early-twentieth-century Chinese cinema. The attempt to "revive national cinema" (*fuxing guopian*), as promoted by 1930s Shanghai's major film studio, United China Photoplay and Publishing Service (Lianhua, which produced *The Goddess*), emerged precisely in reaction against Hollywood's hegemony as well as the more commercially driven Shanghai film studios.[36]

The early-twentieth-century anticolonial impulse is apparently absent in contemporary Hong Kong cinema (as illustrated by *The Phantom Lover*), which seeks to compete with Hollywood by following its rules of the game and thereby risks colluding with and reinforcing Hollywood hegemony. However, the desire for transnational appeal and technical sophistication, as demonstrated in *The Phantom Lover*'s aesthetic turn, responds to a different geopolitical situation. Here, Hong Kong cinema (along with Hong Kong's regional subject positioning) straddles anticipated postcolonialism and global capitalism, and occupies a site that is both subaltern and empowered. On the one hand, the 1984 Sino-British Joint Declaration makes Hong Kong a silenced, subaltern pawn on the Sino-British political chessboard. Rey Chow, one of the most influential voices on this issue, contends that Hong Kong, unlike other colonies, cannot entertain an illusion of reclaiming a "native" culture or identity; rather, it is inevitably transferred from the current colonizer to a future colonizer and thus registers "a postcoloniality that is a forced return (without the consent of the colony's residents) to a 'mother country,' itself as imperialistic as the previous colonizer."[37]

On the other hand, however, the 1997 handover by no means suggests that Hong Kong is simply passively absorbed into and subjected to the mainland Chinese dictatorship. With Deng Xiaoping's open policy and economic reform launched in the late 1970s, China's economics, politics, and material culture have undergone drastic transformation, leading to what some scholars have termed the "postsocialist" turn,[38] which has since reshaped China into an active player in globalization. Yet, compared to Hong Kong, which developed a more mature capitalist system as a British colony, China symbolically occupies the late-coming "student" position in the scheme of globalization, especially global capitalism.

Thus, for some Hong Kong–based critics, Hong Kong's 1997 handover could become an opportunity for Hong Kong to expand its capitalist economy and corporate culture in China. For these critics, Hong Kong's imaginary northward advance (*beijin xiangxiang*) signals exploitation of mainland China's cheap labor, natural resources, and market. The result would be Hong Kong's quasi-colonization of China, contrary to Rey Chow's prediction of Hong Kong's recolonization by China.[39] Although it is questionable to what extent Hong Kong's capitalist economy and culture can indeed colonize China (especially when the seat of governance remains in Beijing), the critique of Hong Kong's "imaginary of northward advance" makes us vigilant of the macrogeopolitical conditions of globalization, which empowers postcolonial Hong Kong as a regional economic and cultural center, even if it is politically subordinated to the central Chinese government.

As a result of the permeating global flow or, more specifically, globalization of the capitalist economy, the colonial era hierarchy and the Cold War opposition between China and Hong Kong collapse into what Appadurai describes as "an altogether new condition of neighborliness," comprising concatenated, media-induced "communities with 'no sense of place.'"[40] In other words, the geopolitical borders are no longer defined exclusively in terms of opposing national or regional economic-cultural-political systems, which entail explicit confrontation or exploitation of one party by another. Rather, the borders now exist as less tangible, more permeable (albeit intractable) demarcations of differences *and* connections that facilitate cultural and economic cross-flows under globalization while reconfiguring the persistent underlying power disparities. Thus, the new "neighborliness" has two qualities, according to Appadurai. On the one hand, the increased mass media coproduction engenders "fantasies (or nightmares) of electronic propinquity."

On the other hand, the power disparities, manifested in the border-crossing redivision of labor and resources, produce "rhizomic, even schizophrenic" neighboring communities.

Ronny Yu's 1995 remake, *The Phantom Lover,* is enabled precisely by global capitalism (with its expanded market and labor resources), which produces "rhizomic, even schizophrenic" neighborliness by mobilizing and reconfiguring axes of power structure and border politics. By alternatively appropriating the authoritative "teacher" position and the subversive "student" position diegetically and extradiegetically, the remake formulates a flexible and situation-specific approach to the resources and obstacles presented by its anticipated handover to the postsocialist and globalizing China. As such, it projects a regional subject position that is simultaneously subaltern and empowered, differentiated from and neighborly with its Chinese and Hollywood interlocutors/neighbors.

Rebirthing the Phantom in the Pan-Chinese Matrix

The triangulated transposition of the phantom film between Hollywood, Shanghai, and Hong Kong throughout the twentieth century charts out a border-crossing feedback loop that encompasses production, distribution, consumption, *and* reproduction. In the continuous cross-Pacific circulation, the dialogic field is never a neutral space but is rather rifted with economic, political, and cultural imbalances and contentions. These tensions become especially pronounced in geopolitical interfaces, or what Mary L. Pratt calls contact zones. In China, such contact zones are exemplified by Shanghai and Hong Kong, which are sutured into the global economic, cultural, and political system, yet oftentimes as peripheral spaces. Within such contact zones, flexible peripheral and subaltern strategies of film remaking are developed to negotiate the dominant forces and engender alternative collective subject positions.

Song at Midnight and *The Phantom Lover* illustrate two subaltern remaking strategies born out of their respective historical conjunctures. In *Song at Midnight,* the strategy is domestication and contextualization on two levels. First, the remake recontextualizes the 1925 Universal Pictures' horror romance in accordance with the political situation of semicolonization and deepening national crisis in 1930s China. The remake's imprinting by China's geohistorical politics is further manifested in the diegesis when the student character is sutured and domesticated as the phantom teacher's willing double, faithfully mediating the latter's unfulfilled desire and ambition. In this scenario, the horrific is transvalued into the sublime, and the utopic vision of collective politics becomes figurable through the teacher-student resonance and intergenerational inheritance.

Contrary to the domesticating strategy that emphasizes alignment and unity, *The Phantom Lover* develops the teacher-student dissonance as well as resonance. The role of the student is an external force that keeps a distance from the position of authority. By refusing to become assimilated and domesticated, or by insisting on remaining foreign (in a manner reminiscent of the "foreginizing translation" discussed in Chapter 3), the external force embodied by the student catalyzes an "afterlife" for the teacher's repressed "prehistory." Extradiegetically, the "student" film (i.e., the remake) not only revives the predecessor film(s), but also mobilizes all available resources for its own formation and authority in the late-twentieth-century power structure.

The Phantom Lover signals an emerging model of film and media production in response to the shifting Hong Kong–China relationship toward the end of the twentieth century. This is the trend of Hong Kong–China coproduction that became increasingly prominent between 1989 and 1995 (and was to steadily acquire more momentum in the new millennium) thanks to the prospering of Hong Kong cinema during this period and to the new policies issued in 1993–1994 by China's Bureau of Radio, Film, and Television. These new regulations put an end to the state-monopolized film distribution system and facilitated further marketization of the mainland film industry. China–Hong Kong coproduction reached a peak in 1992, when over fifty coproduced films were made (equivalent to one-third of the total output of China-made films), and in 1993, when thirteen out of eighteen films made by Beijing Film Studio were coproduced.[41]

The production of *The Phantom Lover* in 1995 by Hong Kong's Mandarin Films Ltd. (Dongfang Dianying Chuping Youxian Gongsi 东方电影出品有限公司) followed the two-pronged strategy of (1) mobilizing Chinese resources to reduce the costs of filmmaking and (2) harnessing the Chinese market to increase box office revenues. The ability to collaborate with the Chinese film industry was to emerge as a crucial move not only for the successful survival and revival of Hong Kong cinema after 1997; it also contributes to restructuring the China–Hong Kong power relationship while reconfiguring the production and consumption of Chinese-language cinema. By aligning Hong Kong and mainland resources, collaboration and cross-over reception converge with the global flow. This convergence in turn facilitates a cinematic, pan-Chinese subject position that addresses transregional and transnational viewers by manufacturing easily legible Chinese icons for polylocal circulation and exchange. In this sense, the external Hong Kong intervention (as a student, successor, foreignizing translator, and reinventor) brings the domesticated "phantom" in the 1937 Shanghai film (back) onto the global stage. As such, it engenders an "afterlife" for the "prehistory" of the 1937 phantom in a different geopolitical context.

The border-crossing rebirth of the "phantom" continues with another remake ten years later, now repackaged as a thirty-episode TV drama *Song at Midnight* and directed by none other than Huang Lei, who played the student in the 1995 version. With the express intent to pay tribute to Leslie Cheung, who committed suicide on April 1, 2003, the "student"-turned-director signals a new spin on the teacher-student dynamic that drives the phantom narrative and the remaking process. Furthermore, the making of the TV drama marks yet another new development of the Chinese-language media culture resulting from the Closer Economic Partnership Arrangement (CEPA)—the first regional trade agreement between China and Hong Kong signed in June 2003 and implemented in 2004.

This arrangement aims to promote further trade liberalization by reducing or eliminating tariff and nontariff barriers between the two sides. In the domain of China–Hong Kong filmic interactions, not only do Hong Kong's audio-visual distributing companies obtain more access to the Chinese market, China–Hong Kong coproduced films are now categorized as domestic films and are therefore exempted from China's foreign film quota restriction. This new trade agreement grants Hong Kong cinema a competitive edge over Hollywood productions, despite the remaining difficulties related to the different censorship systems on the two sides. In other words, CEPA has directly stimulated Hong Kong's increased investment in China.

One example is that in 2004 Hong Kong's TOM Group Ltd. decided to buy a 35 percent stake in the Beijing-based Huayi Brothers and Taihe Film Investment, which produced Huang Lei's TV drama *Song at Midnight.*[42] Founded in 1999 by Wang Zhongjun and Wang Zhonglei, Huayi Brothers and Taihe Film Investment (HTF) invests diversely in film and TV production and distribution, talent management, music recording, and advertising. It plays an important role in facilitating Chinese coproductions with foreign enterprises, including Sony's Columbia Pictures Film Production Asia (set up in Hong Kong in September 1998). The media conglomerate that results from HTF's partnership with Hong Kong's TOM Group Ltd. further stimulates coproductions and integrated marketing across the border in East Asia. As such, it actively promotes a Chinese-language media culture that is characterized by coproduction and coconsumption between mainland China, Hong Kong, and Taiwan. Huang Lei's TV drama rendition of *The Phantom Lover* emerged precisely from this context. Unsurprisingly, the subaltern politics that is explicit in the 1937 *Song at Midnight* and implicit in the 1995 *Phantom Lover* now gives way to euphoric participation in contemporary Chinese commercial culture that increasingly aspires to the global market.

Over the past century of film history, the phantom genealogy has experienced numerous transformations. This chapter had delineated two modes of subaltern and peripheral remaking (the domesticating mode that calls for collective resistance of dark forces in semicolonized China and the interventional mode that strategically positions postcolonial Hong Kong vis-à-vis its would-be motherland—China). These are followed by the twenty-first-century drive to project a pan-Chinese media culture predicated upon polylocal resources and markets. Clearly, the "student's" tribute to the "teacher" and the reconfiguration of the teacher-student dynamic will continue to inspire future reworking of the phantom genealogy. To that extent, the haunting of the phantom allegorizes the continuous film remaking in response to shifting local/global politics. As it recurs at different historical conjunctures, the phantom challenges the audience to decipher the past, repressed "prehistory" in order to regenerate his "afterlife" for the present and the future. The projective vision of the future, therefore, resides embryonically in the historical past, as it does in the spatially removed "Other" film(s).

Ultimately, we cannot think of the predecessor(s) without the remakes or understand Chinese-language cinema without considering its multiple internal and external "Others," just as we cannot think of ideological constraints without the utopic drive or vice versa. To maintain the dual, even multiple foci, we find ourselves constantly returning and resorting to Benedict Anderson's "spectre of comparison"—a spectre that is unleashed in the cross-Pacific and transregional film remaking that I have studied in this book. My hope in tracing, reconstructing, and scrutinizing the remaking trajectories has been to illuminate the ways in which the "spectre of comparison" produces diverse remaking strategies across some of the major twentieth-century political formations such as (semi)colonialism, the Cold War, postcolonialism, and globalization. In my concluding chapter, I will turn to the other half of the cross-Pacific film remaking loop, namely, Hollywood's recent remaking and appropriation of East Asian (especially Hong Kong) cinemas. My goal is to ponder the significance of the increasingly permeable contours of Chinese cinema and the active role that contemporary border-crossing Chinese media workers play in restructuring the global cinemascape.

Conclusion

Mr. Undercover Goes Global

> Recently, a number of American businessmen came to Hong Kong, armed with ample capital, poised to launch film production companies. They seek to recruit famous actors, writers, playwrights, and historians in southern and northern China . . . with the goal of producing big-budget spectacular medieval epics. If this goal did materialize, how could China's current film companies compete? How would we know Chinese people would not sell out? This is the most severe crisis our Chinese cinema has experienced.
>
> —Ma Shizeng, "Zhongguo dianying de weiji"

Writing in 1935, four years after his San Francisco trip and two years before the outbreak of the Second Sino-Japanese War, Cantonese opera master Ma Shizeng identified a crucial trend in Hollywood's endeavor to harness China's resources and market. For Ma, Hollywood's plan of setting up production arms in Hong Kong to make quasi-Chinese epics for Chinese audiences would only jeopardize Chinese cinema. It would pose unfair competition to China-made films and coerce Chinese filmmakers into "selling out," or losing their Chinese identity. Ma's anxiety with identity erosion or deidentification in Chinese cinema is at once striking (given his endeavor to modernize and "foreignize" Cantonese opera and film, as discussed in Chapter 3) and unsurprising (given the increasingly prominent nationalist discourse in the 1930s).

Ma's anxiety is not only symptomatic of the interstitial condition in the "contact zone"—places such as colonial Hong Kong and semicolonial China—in the early twentieth century. It also anticipates the present-day debate over what Chinese cinema is and how it can sustain itself in the face of, or even with the aid of, globalization (which has sometimes been dubbed "Hollywoodization"). Like Ma's bifurcated responses (apprehensive of the Western incursion in his writing, yet actively engaging with Western influences in his practice), the present-day debate on the crisis and future of Chinese cinema similarly displays anxiety and tenacious hope all at once. This ambivalent stance responds to none other than Hollywood's new round of incursions into China since the 1990s, a crusade that oftentimes feels like déjà vu, albeit on a more immersive and intensive level.[1]

The Other Side of the Loop

If pre-1949 semicolonial China was fully exposed to Western forces and Hollywood influx, then newly independent China after1949 sought to reverse the subjugated position by stymieing the public exhibition of Hollywood productions, which were successfully barred in the 1950s.[2] When China reopened its market to Hollywood in the 1980s, a strict quota system was implemented. Toward the end of the twentieth century, especially after China officially joined the World Trade Organization in November 2001, however, China once again actively engaged with Hollywood. China's increasingly important role in the global economic game combined with the persistent quota and censorship systems compels Hollywood to more systematically and strategically interact with China's postsocialist (nationalist) politics in its contemporary crusade. Their ostensibly more cooperative, although no less tension-ridden, relationship has developed in accordance with waning Cold War–style border politics and spreading global capitalism.

One of the most recent articulations of the coimplicating Sino-US relationship is Tim Burton's version of *Alice in Wonderland* (2010). In this digital 3D readaptation, Alice, the nineteenth-century Victorian girl–turned–armor-clad woman warrior, concludes her story by sailing to China, the country of long history and rich culture, now repositioned as her new destination of adventure and as an outpost in new trading routes. Here the childhood fantasy dovetails with maritime trade economy, which in turn prefigures neoliberal global capitalism in the new millennium. The apparently tangential reference to China in the Euro-American-centered female bildungsroman tellingly testifies to the increased attention directed to Sino-US interactions in the economic, cultural, and political domains.

In the field of filmic interactions, Hollywood's post-1990s crusade into Chinese (and other East Asian) markets has adopted two main strategies: (1) aggressive negotiation with the Chinese government for increased imports, screening time, revenue share, and investment in China's multiplex construction and (2) buying the remake rights to Hong Kong (as well as Japanese and Korean) box office hits. The second strategy is linked with the increasing use of "Chinese elements" (*Zhongguo yuansu* 中国元素) in a wide spectrum of Hollywood (co)productions. Examples include the Disney version of *Mulan* (dir. Tony Bancroft, Barry Cook, 1998); Yuan Woo Ping's action choreography in *The Matrix* (dir. Andy Wachowski, Lana Wachowski, 1999); DreamWorks' computer animation *Kung Fu Panda* (dir. Mark Osborne, John Stevenson, 2008) and *Kung Fu Panda 2* (dir. Jennifer Yuh Nelson, 2011), which mix and match a variety of posited Chinese elements (including puppetry, landscape, as well as the iconic Chinese kung fu and panda); and the latest installment of *The Mummy* series, *The Mummy: Tomb of the Dragon Emperor* (dir. Rob Cohen, 2008), which features a Chinese emperor played by Jet Li. Additionally, recent American remakes of earlier American films also insert China and Chinese elements in order to cash in on the enhanced marketability of "Chineseness" (however that is defined). This trend is exemplified by *The Karate Kid* (dir. Harald Zwart, 2010) and *Red Dawn* (dir. Dan Bradley, 2012).

The Karate Kid, coproduced by Sony and China Film Group, is reset from California (in the 1984 version) to Beijing, with Japanese karate replaced by Jackie Chan's Chinese kung fu. This transformation coincides with three recent developments: (1) the transnational (re)emergence of kung fu and martial arts following the landslide success of *Crouching Tiger Hidden Dragon* (dir. Ang Lee, 2000); (2) Hollywood's outsourcing from southern California to China (and other low-cost areas); and, finally, (3) the increasing number of Americans losing jobs during the current economic depression and finding themselves landed in countries like China for work opportunities.

Interestingly, not only was the Beijing portion in *The Karate Kid* shot in Beijing, but the American kid's hometown in Detroit, shown briefly before his relocation to Beijing with his mother, who gets a job transfer to China from an unidentified car factory, was also shot in Beijing— more specifically, the faculty dorm building at Beijing Forestry University.[3] The American mother's transfer to China within the film parallels the extradiegetic Hollywood outsourcing to China not only for location shooting, but also for settings that may be dressed up and passed as American locations. Furthermore, the contrast between the ersatz Detroit (as lifeless ruins resulting from the declining car industry) and the seemingly authentic China (as the "new land" of challenge and opportunities) suggests an all-out effort to sell the post-Olympics kung fu China to Western as well as Chinese audiences.[4] In contrast to the American karate kid's relocation to China and apprenticeship with a Chinese kung fu master, the unreleased 2010 version of *Red Dawn* delivers a paranoid narrative of an alien invasion of an American town, this time by the People's Liberation Army—the violent face of the Chinese government that replaces the invading Russian force from the film's 1984 Cold War version. (See Final Thoughts on p. 164 for further comments.)

Both of these remakes revolve around key Chinese symbols yet bespeak two conflicting American perceptions of contemporary China. For some observers, Hollywood's courtship with China prognosticates the birth of "Chollywood," with China promising to become Hollywood's largest single market, from which films like *The Karate Kid* tries to profit.[5] Meanwhile, the continued Sino-US conflict means that China's perceived market value in the world system is cause for anxiety—even paranoia—as well as celebration. Consequently, the various forms of Sino-US filmic interactions are both stimulated and plagued by Hollywood's simultaneously enamored and embattled relationship with East Asian (especially

Chinese) film industries and markets. In this light, Hollywood's incorporation and manufacturing of "Chinese elements," which leads to the "Asianization of Hollywood" (as Christina Klein terms it), necessarily produce multivalent economic and geopolitical ramifications.

From the Chinese perspective, Hollywood's current crusade into China is a double-edged sword. It may open up a new vista for Chinese cinema. Yet, like Hollywood's incursion into China in the early twentieth century, the current crusade also threatens to erase the identity of Chinese cinema and compromise Chinese self-esteem, thus once again (as Ma Shizeng worried in 1935) instigating a crisis of self-recognition and self-positioning on the part of a peripheral cinema.

In tackling the present-day Sino-American filmic interactions that can be characterized as "Hongkongification of American cinema"[6] and Hollywoodization of Chinese cinema, our main challenge is to stay sensitive to border politics that are assuming different forms and to develop empowering local positions that partake in and reshape global flows while striving toward the fairest possible play for all participants. More specifically, we need to ask how we can reevaluate and deploy the specificity and subject positioning of "Chinese cinema" on the local, regional, subnational, supranational, as well as national levels when global capitalism is rapidly redrawing and permeating borders, resulting in what Appadurai calls "an altogether new condition of neighborliness" comprising "communities with 'no sense of place.'"[7] In other words, when "global designs" and "local histories" (à la Walter Mignolo)[8] become increasingly intertwined and coimplicating, in what ways does the "local" persist as a flexible and dynamic structure that is not only self-generative and transformative, but also instrumental in reconfiguring the global?

My goal in asking these questions is to envision a fair and equitable power structure, which necessarily remains unattainable owing to its utopic nature. Yet this ideal power structure guides us to dissect the complex ramifications of cross-Pacific film remaking in the new millennium and to design strategies that can potentially undermine Hollywood's hegemony and reconfigure the center-periphery politics. These moments of intervention and microlevel strategization cumulatively enable gradual morphing (instead of an instant change) that approximates (even if not reaching) the ultimate goal of an equitable power structure.

In this concluding chapter, I explore these possibilities by examining two instances of contemporary Hollywood's absorption of "Chinese elements" in comparison with the innovative film/stage work by Shi-zheng Chen, a diasporic Chinese media artist. The Hollywood instances are (1) Martin Scorsese's remaking of *Infernal Affairs I* (dir. Andrew Lau, Alan Mak, 2002) into *The Departed* (2006), which won Scorsese his first Academy Award, and (2) DreamWorks' 3D animation *Kung Fu Panda 2* (2011), which was applauded by some Chinese reviewers as "a Chinese animation film made by the United States" (*Meiguo zhizao de Zhongguo donghuapian* 美国制造的中国动画片). In comparison and contrast with these mainstream big productions, Shi-zheng Chen's films, *Dark Matter* (2007) and *Disney High School Musical: China* (2010), and the stage performance *Monkey: Journey to the West* (launched in 2007) are more marked by the unsettling "spectre of comparison" and a correlated bifocal perspective.

Yet all these examples dramatize issues of identity confusion, collision, erasure, and transformation, which allegorically echo the risk of dedifferentiation, deidentification, and the related opportunity of self-repositioning that all emerge from the processes of remaking and appropriation in the global economy. *The Departed* and *Kung Fu Panda 2* foreground provincialization of Hollywood from the peripheral (in this case Chinese) perspective and redefinition of "Chinese cinema" as a cinema with a wide spectrum of fluctuating "Chinese elements." These developments lead us to ponder the new role of (diasporic) Chinese film-media workers (as exemplified by Shi-zheng Chen) in the arena of global media production and exchange.[9]

The Promises and Perils of Being Remade

The complex ramifications of American incorporation of Chinese cinema and elements must be assessed in the context of critical discourses instigated by this phenomenon. Hollywood remaking of East Asian cinemas is not merely a contemporary phenomenon. Akira Kurosawa's postwar films *Rashomon* (1950) and *Seven Samurai* (1954) were both remade in America. However, these remakes were sporadic, instance-oriented, and short-lived, contrary to the more sustained and systematic remaking of East Asian popular films since the late twentieth century. In the contemporary cycle of remaking, Roy Lee and his Vertigo Entertainment have played a key role. A Korean-American trained in law, Lee has made a career of brokering the remake rights of successful East Asian genre films to American studios. He has also served as executive producer or producer for most of America's post-2001 remakes, including the remakes of Japan's *Ringu* (1998), *Ju-on: The Grudge* (2002), and *Dark Water* (2002); Korea's *Il Mare* (2000) and *My Sassy Girl* (2001); Hong Kong–Singapore–Thailand's *The Eye* (2002); and Hong Kong's *Infernal Affairs I* (2002).

Lee's brokerage, according to Tad Friend, facilitates a win-win situation: "Asian studios get a windfall; American studios get a buffet of market-tested ideas; and Lee gets a producer's fee in the range of three hundred thousand dollars whenever one of his remakes goes into production."[10] Along this line yet with a more interesting spin, Christina Klein suggests that being remade by Hollywood generates extra revenues for Korean and Japanese filmmakers, which may in turn help rejuvenate local film industries.[11] Indeed, the prospects of being adapted and adopted by Hollywood are so appealing that some East Asian filmmakers choose to solicit Hollywood's attention (possibly selling the remake rights) before completing the film.[12] In view of the convergence, even coalition, between Hollywood and the East Asian mainstream film industries, mediated by industry-savvy brokers, it seems that the power asymmetry endemic to the early-twentieth-century colonial era is yielding to a more mutually beneficial relationship.

One should certainly question the extent to which a film industry can really break away from its peripheral position if it relies on Hollywood's uptake (even if partially). Relatedly, the apparently free-flowing coalition is compromised by profit-minded brokers' exclusive focus on heavily commercial and genre-driven films,[13] which makes them gatekeepers as well as mediators. Such gatekeeping means that only a narrow repertoire of East Asian films is funneled into the border-crossing circulation, which further skews Western perceptions of East Asian cinemas.

Similar criticism can be leveled at Quentin Tarantino, another important figure in popularizing and cultifying specific East Asian filmic elements among Western audiences. Through his carnivalesque reenactment of violent scenes culled from various Hong Kong and Japanese action films, Tarantino's postmodern pastiche pays homage to the 1960s and 1970s East Asian action genres (especially Hong Kong's Shaw Brothers action flicks), while cultivating the Western audience's retro interest in them.[14] Additionally, his style of rampant simulacra and pastiche foregrounds the cultural-political issue of the West's self-reinvention through selective incorporation of peripheral film cultures. This process of borrowing, mimicry, and self-reinvention resembles the foreignizing translation exemplified by the Western-costume Cantonese opera films made in the 1930s and 1950s (Chapter 3) or the reverse ventriloquism in Hong Kong's postcolonial rewriting of Hollywood's *The Phantom of the Opera* and Shanghai's *Song at Midnight* (Chapter 4).[15] The important difference, however, is that this time it is a filmmaker occupying the dominant position that is mimicking and expropriating the peripheral film culture.

If Hong Kong's partaking in global capitalism enables a remake such as *The Phantom Lover* that challenges mainland China's filmic and cultural authority, thus rendering Hong Kong's postcolonial position both subaltern and empowered (as I have argued in the previous chapter), then Tarantino's reverse mimicry from the center further complicates the forms and ramifications of border-crossing film interactions. As Kenneth Chan argues, "The line between intertextuality and neocolonial pilfering is a fine one indeed, especially when Tarantino sutures disparate elements from the various cinemas by stripping them out of their original context"[16] and transforming them into "commodities of Chinese cinematic culture in bite-size form for easy transcultural and transnational consumption."[17] In view of the underlying power inequity, which allows Tarantino to commercialize and decontextualize Chinese and other peripheral cinemas, Chan suggests that "contact zones" resulting from such filmic interactions are "zones of anxiety, slippage, and fragmentation, unveiling the uneasy suturing of the local to the global."[18]

Chan's incisive critique echoes the concerns expressed by many critics wary of Hollywood's hegemony. The reasoning is that Hollywood's remaking deprives the original films of their cultural specificity, replacing it with American mainstream ideology, which is then transmitted to the broadest possible markets (including the original films' countries) thanks to Hollywood's powerful publicity machinery. Such unfair competition marginalizes and represses peripheral cinemas, even when the latter supply the sustenance for Hollywood's new-millennium expansion.

The unequal competition is easily detected through a comparison of the budget and box office revenues of East Asian predecessor films and their American remakes. *Ringu* in Japan cost $1.2 million to make and made $6.6 million. Its American remake, *The Ring,* cost $48 million (with $1 million spent on purchasing the remake rights) and generated nearly $250 million, of which $8.3 million was from Japan during the film's first two weeks running.[19] Although *Ringu*'s remake rights sale alone almost offset its production costs, therefore easily convincing East Asian filmmakers of the benefits of developing and investing in potentially remakable films, the fact that its remake's budget and worldwide revenue were both multiplied forty times underscores the drastic discrepancy between the Hollywood and Japanese (and other East Asian) film industries, especially in their production conditions, marketing strategies, and profit margins. Such discrepancies are ultimately linked with the persistent power hierarchy that privileges the capital-intensive party (Hollywood) over the labor-intensive party (East Asian industries).

To understand both the optimistic and the critical assessments of Hollywood's remaking and incorporation of East Asian popular films outlined above, we must maintain dual perspective. On the one hand, we must not lose sight of the exploitative power relationship inherent in the new-millennium cross-Pacific filmic transactions. On the other hand, we must respect East Asian filmmakers' enthusiastic response to Hollywood's attention. We should seriously discern and account for the benefits (both collective and individual, both long-term and short-term) yielded by their production of market-proven templates as remakable films. One possible benefit is that remake rights revenues may help cultivate filmmaking practices that deviate from the homogenizing commercial appeal, thereby contributing to a full spectrum film culture.

To maintain the dual perspective, we must first address the deep-rooted anxiety with East Asian cinemas' imitative history (especially of Hollywood but also of European productions) starting from the early twentieth century. Whereas such anxiety posits imitation as the antinomy of an independent local or national cinema, my contention throughout the book has been that such remaking and the resulting apparent derivative status constitute the very basis for envisioning and producing location-based collective subjective positioning in the Chinese context. More recent imitation, that is, the manufacturing of remakable films that oftentimes echo Hollywood conventions and expectations, involves multiple layers of duplication, which in turn derive from the closer-range negotiation between the local position and Hollywood's commercial logic. This form of imitation self-consciously produces a tight feedback loop that sutures American and East Asian commercial cinemas into a mise-en-abìme, or mutually reflexive, relationship, which facilitates their increasing convergence coupled with persistent inequity and division. The coexistence of the Self-Other division, on the one hand, and dedifferentiation, on the other, reinforces a fundamental conundrum that foregrounds the role of the foreign in self-construction. This conundrum necessitates the dual perspective that characterizes the "spectre of comparison," and it already underpins Chinese diasporic filmmakers' encounter with Hollywood even before it permeates the East Asian production of remakable films.

John Woo, who switched his career from Hong Kong to Hollywood in the early 1990s, for instance, accurately captured the ironic feedback loop by describing Hollywood as imitating late 1980s and 1990s Hong Kong commercial movies, which have been more or less imitating Hollywood films. He concludes, "[S]o Hollywood is imitating Hollywood."[20] Or, more exactly, Hollywood does not simply imitate itself, but rather it imitates the Other that uncannily evokes the Self. Thus, it reinvents itself via foreign mediation. A decade later, Ang Lee similarly highlighted the irony of becoming the (Chinese) Self through becoming the (Western) Other. Commenting on the landslide success of his *Crouching Tiger, Hidden Dragon* (2000),[21] Lee observes, "The subtext is very purely Chinese. . . . But *to be more Chinese you have to be Westernized.*"[22]

In both Woo's and Lee's border-crossing films, to become foreign means to become derecognized, even disowned (by certain audience groups), which reveals the complex mechanisms (including incommensurability and failure as well as assimilation) in border-crossing self-translation. *Hard Target* (1993), Woo's first US film, for instance, was dismissed as "a pale imitation" of *Hard Boiled* (1992), Woo's last Hong Kong film. "Like a photograph that is not quite as sharp as the original, *Hard Target* was more like an eager fan paying homage to Woo than a true John Woo original. . . . In other words, it's very American."[23] Woo's perceived retrogressive self-imitation was attributed to Hollywood constraints that blunted

Woo's violent edge, when this could have helped to regenerate the American gangster genre. This view is a salutary critique of Hollywood's conservative homogenization. Yet it fails to acknowledge Woo's influence by the Hollywood gangster genre even prior to his immigration. As a result, it risks essentializing Woo's Hong Kong style as a pristine alternative to Hollywood. Thus, for devotees who uphold Woo's integrity and purity in his Hong Kong oeuvre, to become the American Other means to undermine his Hong Kong Self.

By the same logic, Lee's *Crouching Tiger, Hidden Dragon* encountered indifference in some East Asian markets, despite its attempt to appeal to a wide range of audiences. Responding to the Chinese critique that this film "twist[s] the genre" and fails to be "Chinese," Lee observes that "to be more Chinese you have to be Westernized" and that "you have to use Freudian or western techniques to dissect what I think is hidden in a repressed [Chinese] society."[24] Thus, Lee simultaneously maintains an essentialist view of repressive "Chineseness" and champions a Westernized representational form that can more effectively depict "Chineseness," thus making the film more fundamentally "Chinese."

The imperative or requirement to remain "Chinese" or "Hong Kong" stems from the fear of being perceived as imitative of Hollywood and thus losing national/regional specificities through mainstreaming and globalization. In other words, the investment in the notion of specificity and locality suggests an effort to maintain an alternative site outside of homogenizing globalization.[25] For critics like Zygmunt Bauman, local specificity in such defensive and essentialist terms is increasingly impossible and undesirable. As Bauman puts it, "travelling light, rather than holding tightly to things deemed attractive for their reliability and solidity . . . is now the asset of power." Light travel is possible only when we relinquish the "heavy weight, substantiality and unyielding power of resistance" usually associated with local, national, and regional subject positions."[26]

Nevertheless, we must be cognizant that such light travel can be unbearable and impossible for those who do not occupy positions of power in the world system and whose power, if any, can only come from heavy weight and the solidity of local, national, or regional specificity, even if the latter is under constant erasure and reconstruction. To revitalize their persistent political and affective appeals, we must deessentialize notions of local, regional, and national specificities. The move to deessentialize starts with our recognition of the local-foreign coimplication, or the role of the foreign Other in the construction of the local Self, as already amply demonstrated in John Woo and Ang Lee's diasporic filmmaking experiences. Furthermore, not only is the East Asian local constituted by the Hollywood foreign, but Hollywood should also be seen as a local reconstituted by the East Asian foreign. Martin Scorsese's remake of *Infernal Affairs* into *The Departed* (2006) illustrates precisely the production of a location-specific subject position on the American side.

Provincializing Hollywood: Hong Kong's Mr. Undercover Goes to Boston

One indication of a film's "identity" is its authorship and the related copyright. Unsurprisingly, authorship becomes a point of contention in the American remaking of an East Asian film. As many antihegemonic critics worry, the Hollywood remake will usurp the original authorship and monopolize market profits as well as artistic value. Consequently, the East Asian film will become decontextualized or even disfigured, thus losing its identity. This fear of deidentification, dedifferentiation, and unfair competition is hardly alleviated even though Scorsese duly honored the copyright law by purchasing the remake rights of *Infernal Affairs I* and acknowledging the original inspiration at the end of his remake. The acknowledgment was repeated in Scorsese's acceptance speech for Best Director at the seventy-ninth Academy Awards ceremony. Yet the public concern with American hegemony resurfaced with a scandalous slip of tongue at the same ceremony, when the MC described *The Departed* as a remake of a Japanese film. This slip combined with Scorsese's incorporation of elements from *Infernal Affairs II* and *III* while purchasing only the first episode's remake rights suggest an implicit discount (if not total denial) of Hong Kong authorship, which, unsurprisingly, led to dissatisfaction on Hong Kong's part.

My focus here is that the confusion and contention over the authorship of *Infernal Affairs* not only reconfirm Hollywood's hegemony, but also draw attention to the trilogy's complex interactions with other film industries/cultures in both mainland China and America, which in turn reinforce the role of the foreign other in the construction of the location-based cinema and self-identity. The trilogy demonstrates Hong Kong cinema's increasing outreach to the mainland Chinese film industry. The first episode offers a different ending for the mainland Chinese release. The second episode was coproduced with China's Eastern Dragon Film Company Ltd. and Singapore's Mediacorp Raintree Pictures. The last episode involved two more Chinese companies: Tianjin Film Studio and China Film Coproduction Corporation. Additionally, *Infernal Affairs II* and *III* both cast mainland Chinese actors in positions of authority and mix Mandarin Chinese language into the overall Cantonese films. All of these factors suggest increasing mutual dependence and coimplication between mainland Chinese and Hong Kong cinemas.

Compared to pre-1997 coproduction as illustrated by *The Phantom Lover*, post-1997 Sino–Hong Kong interactions have accelerated for three reasons. First, Hong Kong cinema suffered severe talent drain during the collective anxiety in anticipation of the 1997 handover. Some of these emigrant filmmakers later decided to come back to Hong Kong and/or engage with mainland Chinese cinema.[27] Second, Hong Kong's film industry was severely affected by the 1997

Asian Financial Crisis,[28] putting Hong Kong in the position of being rescued from the crisis by the mainland Chinese government. Finally, the new-millennium Chinese government has proactively engaged with global capitalism by strategically opening up its resources and market. Realigned with mainland China with the common ethos of global capitalism, Hong Kong's late-twentieth-century collective identity anxiety is gradually being rechanneled, leading to reauthorship and transfiguration of Hong Kong cinema and Chinese-language cinema as a whole.

In addition to collaborating with China, the *Infernal Affairs* trilogy also draws from the American gangster genre, which further complicates the film's Hong Kong identity. Andrew Lau, one of the trilogy's directors, calls attention to this intertextuality by naming Scorsese his idol and claiming to have seen all Scorsese's films. Such intertextuality is manifested in Lau and Scorsese's filmic resonances. As if echoing Scorsese's "mean street" gangster milieu, Lau's directorial debut, *Against All* (1990), along with his cinematographic work for Ringo Lam's *City on Fire* (1987) and Wong Kar Wai's *As Tears Go By* (1988) already demonstrate a strong interest in lawless street fighting. By identifying Scorsese as his inspiration, Lau not only reenacts the ironic intertextual circle of American film imitating Hong Kong film imitating American film (as John Woo puts it), he also ostensibly relinquishes his authorship (if only as diplomatic rhetoric) to the American auteur and submits to the structural power inequity. Indeed, Lau explicitly admitted the ironic ways in which *The Departed* helped to promote *Infernal Affairs*. He thanked Scorsese: "The success of *The Departed* demonstrates that we in Hong Kong can make films on a par with an Oscar award winner. It also exposes the international audience to the excellence of Hong Kong's filmmakers."[29]

This stoic optimism could also potentially implicate a strategic reversal: if his Hong Kong film can be recognized only through its American remake, then one can pervert the logic by arguing that the value of the remake is simply to promote the Hong Kong film to the international audience—at least from the Hong Kong perspective. Thus, we encounter a scenario reminiscent of the master-disciple hierarchy and its reversal as dramatized in the remaking of *The Phantom of the Opera* discussed in Chapter 4. The positions of the master and the disciple constantly shift and mutate into each other with the allegorical implications that the predecessor film may become the successor while the afterlife (remake) fulfills the prehistory (the predecessor film). The positional shifting means that the site of authority is subjected to renegotiation, which can potentially puncture the overall power asymmetry. In this sense, to prematurely characterize American remakes as mere exploitation and marginalization of Hong Kong cinema would foreclose the possibility of center-periphery renegotiation. It would also fail to address the complex ramifications of the Asianization of Hollywood as well as the Hollywoodization of Asian cinema.

One way to assess the impact of East Asian cinemas on Hollywood is to examine the ways in which Hollywood's remaking of East Asian cinemas entails its own localization and provincialization rather than simple global domination. To provincialize Hollywood means to reconnect its supposedly universal appeal with underlying historical and cultural specificities. *The Departed* offers a good illustration in three ways. First, Scorsese's auteurist approach to the gangster genre already distinguishes his films from mainstream entertainment (as perhaps testified by his frequent nominations for Academy Awards, though he did not win until *The Departed*). Second, the film is specifically set in Boston, within its Irish community, which has historically been associated with gangster activities. Additionally, William Monahan, the screenwriter, and Matt Damon, who plays the undercover gangster, are both originally from the Boston area (Monahan is from an Irish-American background), thus bringing a strong local flavor to the film. Furthermore, Jack Nicholson's mobster role is based on James Bulger, a real-life Irish-American mobster in Boston. And the film's technical advisor, Thomas Duffy, is a former major in the Massachusetts State Police who handled Bulger's case. All these Boston connections and indexes within and outside the diegesis are further reinforced by the film's location shooting. Despite partial shooting (both exterior and interior) in New York (which stands in for Boston), the film liberally displays the Boston cityscape, including local streets, Chinatown, the golden dome of the Massachusetts State House, Boston's Back Bay skyline, and the South Boston Seaport District (in the rooftop scenes).

The last dimension that plants *The Departed* firmly in post-9/11 America is its emotional resonance with post-9/11 collective paranoia. The double undercover narrative, inherited from *Infernal Affairs,* now refracts a loss of trust owing to the prevailing fear of betrayal and terrorism in a "nation of rats."[30] In this light, the cold, relentless cruelty, as opposed to the graceful romanticism in *Infernal Affairs,*[31] does not simply manifest Scorsese's signature style, but also acquires special relevance as a symptom of America's post-9/11 geopolitics and collective sentiment. In short, three factors—an idiosyncratic style, a specific immigrant community in the Boston area, and post-9/11 American society—combine to make Scorsese's remake a case of localization that registers and addresses location-specific politics and subject position. This strategy of localization is akin to the ways in which so many Shanghai and Hong Kong remakes domesticate Hollywood productions, although the political circumstances and available resources in the two remaking situations are very different.

The historical and geopolitical specificity of the American remake makes it a "walker's" product. A walker, according to Walter Benjamin, is a different traveler from the pilot. If the pilot resembles a common reader, who weaves his or her way dreamily through the text, the walker is more akin to a copyist, who is subjected to the discipline of the text and discovers whole inner worlds of detail. Benjamin's prime example of a copyist is a Chinese transcriber who copies books and transmits China's literary culture.[32] On the surface, the production crew of *The Departed* can hardly be seen as the "walker" or the "copyist" type. Monahan, the screenwriter, made it a point not to view *Infernal Affairs* before writing the script. The nonengagement with the predecessor film suggests a typical anxiety of influence. Yet, for Monahan, it also guaranteed his untainted creativity. Scorsese and the two male leads admitted to having seen the Hong Kong film but stressed that their film had only borrowed the latter's structure and had become very different and specific to Boston—a unique city even in America.

Yet, despite their emphasis on the difference, the remake does reproduce several key scenes from *Infernal Affairs*. Such scenes include the head gangster's secret meeting with his mole in a movie theater, a fatherly senior police officer's death from falling off the rooftop (rendering the undercover cop's true identity irretrievable), the two moles' rooftop encounter (Figures 5.1, 5.2), and the violent shootout

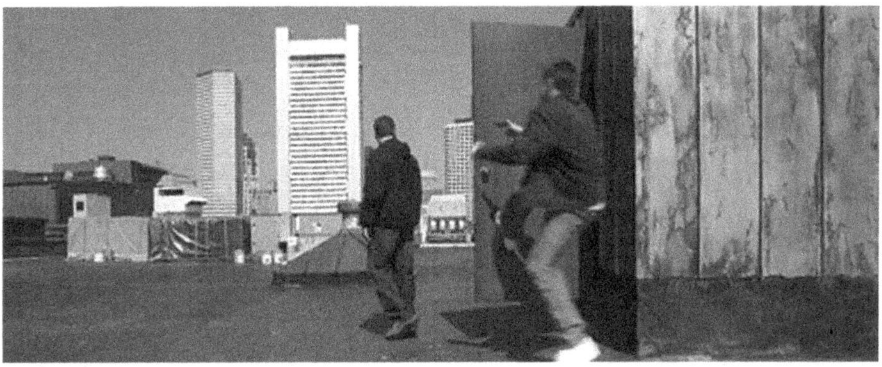

Figure 5.1 Rooftop encounter between the undercover cop and the undercover gangster in *The Departed*

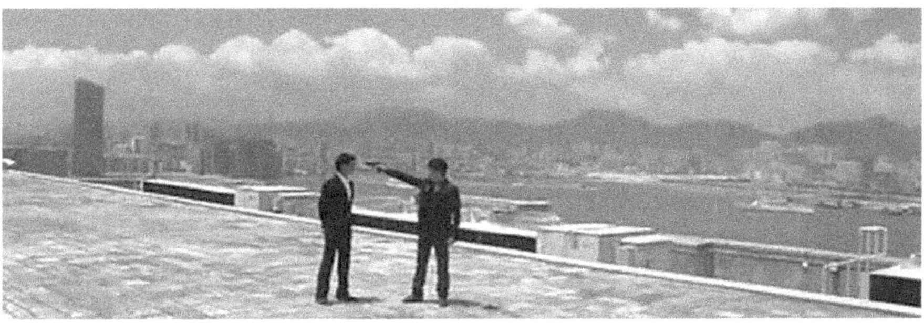

Figure 5.2 Rooftop encounter against Hong Kong's trademark landscape in *Infernal Affairs*

in the elevator. In both films, these scenes constitute major turning points or minor climaxes. The remake's rehearsal of these specific scenes suggests its engagement with selected details from the Hong Kong predecessor (even if its filmmakers may not admit to the full extent). The different rendering emphasized by the remake crew and cast also resembles the book copying process, for the copyist inevitably introduces changes and cumulatively reshapes the book, even when he or she studiously traces the details of the text.

By gleaning dramatic twists from *Infernal Affairs* and stitching them into *The Departed,* Scorsese and his crew evoke the Benjaminian "walker" who produces a specific, grounded, material territory with layers of textual interactions. This connection with the "walker" or "copyist" type (rather than the "pilot" type) allows us to refocus on the American remake's time- and place-specific (rather than the presumed universal) appeal. Thus we can bracket the habitual sweeping dismissal of the remake as just another example of Hollywood's hegemonic pillaging of a peripheral cinema. Instead, we can start to provincialize Hollywood by unpacking its intricate strategies of border-crossing transposition, designed in accordance with border politics underlying the multi-directional, cross-Pacific film remaking during and beyond the twentieth century.

Re-/Decentralizing Hollywood: Panda Po returns to China and Monkey King Goes to the West

Needless to say, global power geometry still matters. In fact, this larger structure continues to circumscribe cross-Pacific film remaking, including the types of East Asian films selected by Hollywood, the competition (as well as complementation) between the peripheral predecessor film and its Hollywood remake, and, finally, the ways in which the box office performance of the US remakes boomerang to reconfigure East Asian film industries. Meanwhile, we must also be sensitive to the pressures that American cinema is going through. Two main pressures at this point come from post-9/11 politics and the multiplied vectors of globalization, which necessitate recalibration of American cinema. In this light, Daniel Herbert argues that Hollywood's increasing involvement (rather than just leadership) in world cinema and politics not simply reconfirms Hollywood's continued dominance among the global film-cultural industries, but also "reveal[s] Hollywood's increased need for financial and geographic flexibility." Furthermore, Hollywood remakes of East Asian hit films "reveal the shifting and mobile conditions—the dislocations—of the contemporary global cultural industries."[33]

If, as I have demonstrated in this book, Shanghai and Hong Kong's remaking of Hollywood and of each other (consciously or not) figure forth (in a utopian, anticipatory, and provisionary manner) location-specific, subaltern, and peripheral subject positions, then, logically, we may expect Hollywood's remaking of East Asian cinemas to similarly refashion Hollywood and reposition American subjectivity (hegemonic as it may remain). If *The Departed* localizes and domesticates the Hong Kong gangster genre, suggesting provincialization of American cinema, we need also to attend to the other side, namely, its decentralization under new vectors of globalization. Hollywood's remake of the Japanese *Ju-on* (2002) is a case in point. Not only was the remake, *The Grudge* (2004), helmed by the predecessor film's director, Takashi Shimizu, but it was also shot in Japan and reprised a few Japanese actors from the predecessor film for secondary roles. Given the heavy dose of not-quite-American components in this remake, Daniel Herbert describes this remake as an "internationally financed, Hollywood-owned and distributed film," which represents "an industrial hybrid that mapped out a vast transnational space of cultural production."[34] Such border-crossing hybridity, however, does not harbinger the dissolving of Americanness. Rather, it suggests that the American remake is no longer "American" in the traditional sense, nor can American cinema as a whole stay the same. Both are undergoing complex transformation and decentralization.

Transnational authorship and flexible production as noted by Herbert are further illustrated in Hollywood's increasing mobilization of Chinese (and other East Asian) resources, demonstrated by recent DreamWorks productions—*The Kite Runner* (dir. Marc Forster, 2007) and *Kung Fu Panda 2* (dir. Jennifer Yuh Nelson, 2011). *The Kite Runner* is set in Afghanistan, but all of the Afghan scenes were actually shot in western China (including Kashgar, the Pamir Mountains, Tashgarkan, and Xinjiang), where the streets were described as "dripping with production value. All you have to do is change the signs."[35] Additionally, the production was green-lighted by the Chinese government, which temporarily went from barring Westerners from Xinjiang—the proseparatist region—to welcoming Western film crews. The film thus resulted from an assembly line that brought together American money; Chinese locations, extras, and government support; an Iranian, Afghan, and British cast; and an American-Afghan bestselling novel written in English.

In *The Kite Runner,* the Chinese location and extras that are used to stand in for an Afghan town and Afghan Muslims remain unnamed and unarticulated as mere picturesque background. DreamWorks' 3D animation *Kung Fu Panda 2,* in contrast, flaunts its "Chinese elements." Riding the tide of the global success of *Kung Fu Panda* (2008), the sequel goes to great lengths to integrate a range of regional ingredients from the city of Chengdu in Sichuan Province. In August 2008, following the first episode's successful screening in China, Jeffrey Katzenberg, CEO of DreamWorks, and Jennifer Yuh Nelson, the sequel's Korean-American director, took the production crew to Chengdu. During their ten-day trip, they visited Chengdu Research Base of Giant Panda Breeding, Mt. Qingcheng, and Jinsha Site, while sampling local cuisine.[36] The regional scenery and lifestyle were distilled into the lush green backdrop, the narrow street lined with folk food stalls, the traditional Chinese architecture, and the puppet play, which are all paraded in the sequel. The crew even found a panda cub on which they modeled the childhood Kung Fu Panda, as well as a peacock that was cast as the panda's archenemy. Indeed, this film is so saturated with China's regional elements that a Chinese film commentator, Zhang Xiaobei, dubbed it "a Chinese animation film made by the United States" (*Meiguo zhizao de Zhongguo donghuapian*).[37]

Zhang's affirmation of the "Chinese identity" of a DreamWorks product was echoed in the raving reviews in China and the Chinese audience's enthusiastic embrace of the film's Chinese icons. Contrary to the first episode, which was described as a "China-born, US-raised" (*tusheng yangzhang*) hybrid that troubled the Chinese identification and therefore aroused anxiety as well as excitement among Chinese film workers,[38] the sequel three years later seems to have been accepted as a true-blooded "native" Chinese film that happens to have been delivered by its US surrogate parent. As the Chinese public media have it, the sequel demonstrated the DreamWorks production crew's new in-depth understanding of Chinese culture (as opposed to their superficial display of several Chinese symbols in the first episode).

To the extent that the DreamWorks production can pass for a "Chinese" film, American cinema and Chinese cinema seem to have become unified on the basis of shared "Chinese elements." As an American film takes on a "Chinese" face and becomes decentralized, the palatable audio-visual "Chinese elements" also become decoupled from the geographical or geopolitical China, transforming into a reproducible brand with flexible authorship. In celebrating the sequel as a "Chinese film," the Chinese media did not so much state a fact as express a wish to brand China or a Chinese city (Chengdu in this case) as a global commodity, thereby facilitating China's participation in the global commercial media culture. The production of films with "Chinese elements" signals the formation of a cost-effective "assembly line" that converges global resources to coproduce films that parade multicultural interests (if not exoticism) for the widest possible market. To sustain the "assembly line," the global space is systemically binarized into labor-intensive areas and capital-intensive areas with the result of global redivision of labor, often supported by local industry and government.

One of the feared results of the transnational and transregional assembly line production is homogenization or dedifferentiation of different national or regional cinemas. If the paradox of national cinema is that "to be nationally popular it must also be international in scope,"[39] as Andrew Higson argues in 1989 (a time that significantly coincided with the collapse of the socialist bloc and the apparent triumph of capitalism), then this paradox takes on a more disturbing twist in more recent years. That is, national and regional specificity is flattened and hollowed into generic global commercial icons in the name of going international or transregional. Such dedifferentiation takes place not only across the Pacific, but also within the Asian and Sinophone contexts. Yang Yuanying, a Beijing-based Chinese-film historian, argues that Hong Kong cinema has become de–Hong Kong–ized (*gangpian bugang* 港片不港) through increasing Sino–Hong Kong coproductions since the signing of the Closer Economic Partnership Arrangement in 2003.[40] Analogously, Bliss Cua Lim points out that "Asian horror film" is a despecified category. It is a regionalist-globalist appellation that "play[s] with cultural/regional identity that, in the same breath, discounts cultural specificity, claiming a universal, culture-neutral appeal."[41]

Both Higson and Lim attribute standardization and dedifferentiation to the juggernaut of Hollywood. Higson reasons that to achieve the "international scope," peripheral national cinemas must strive to reproduce the Hollywood standard, with the result of "colluding with Hollywood's systems of funding, production control, distribution and marketing."[42] Along the same logic, Lim sees Hollywood's remaking as deracinating because "what is being mimicked is not just genre, but globalised film culture writ large, the internationalisation of film standards, and the imbrication of this internationalisation/standardisation with the national-popular."[43] Such criticism rightfully alerts us to Hollywood's global hegemony. Yet it also over hastily equates globalization with Hollywoodization and Americanization. Whereas I do not deny their structural connections or significant overlapping, I think it is also important for us to consider ramifications of provincializing and decentralizing American cinema undertaken from the American side, as argued above.

Furthermore, I seek to open up a space of fault lines in the global power structure in order to think beyond the binary of Hollywood versus peripheral cinemas. I do so by considering globalization from a different angle, namely, East Asian (especially Chinese in this context) media workers' engagement with the West in contemporary global flows. Such engagement takes different forms, including producing films that may attract Hollywood attention (as described earlier), directly participating in filmmaking in America (as in the cases of John Woo and Ang Lee), and offering technical assistance and other resources to American productions (as in *The Kite Runner* and *Kung Fu Panda 2*). In addition to these forms of commercial interactions, some Chinese diasporic media artists have also critically engaged with independent as well as mainstream media, and more consciously worked against the seemingly irresistible tide of being either submerged in or flowing with the global commercial culture.

Commanding "situated agency" like their early-twentieth-century predecessors,[44] these contemporary Chinese media workers have not only generated commercial gains, but also subtly transformed the Western "mecca" of cinema. Their journey to the West does not simply produce "flexible citizens" that readily fit into the commercial logic. It also gives rise to what I call "inflexible noncitizenship," whose obstinate misfit fractures and foreignizes the environment they encounter, with the result of resetting the stage, much as the internal outsiders, Alfred and Ali, have done in *The Love Parade* and *My Kingdom for a Husband* (discussed in Chapter 3).[45]

This approach of troubling and foreignizing the Western (as well as Chinese) media status quo is represented by Shi-zheng Chen. Having studied regional opera and experienced the Cultural Revolution in China, Chen moved to America in the late 1980s and has since established himself as a New York–based experimental dramatist-filmmaker. His award-winning film debut, *Dark Matter* (2007), based on the real incident of a 1991 campus shootout perpetrated by a frustrated Chinese student, "explore[s] the mysterious and powerful forces unleashed when a young Chinese immigrant strives to make his mark in a culture that is at once seductive and impenetrable."[46] The difficulty of accessing a new culture accurately captures the lure and frustration of border-crossing. The destructive power arising from frustration forces us to deglamorize the journey to Hollywood and the West, and to ponder the complex ramifications of crossing.

If *Dark Matter* ends with an "inflexible noncitizen's" failure to adapt, Chen's experimental circus-opera, *Monkey: Journey to the West* (initially staged in 2007), suggests a more successful border-crossing intervention. This show adapts a classic Chinese mythic fiction into a mind-boggling hybrid stage experience that interweaves animation, opera, hip-pop, and acrobatics. The original novel *Journey to the West* follows a Tang dynasty monk's perilous journey to India (the "West" in the minds of ancient Chinese) with the mission of obtaining Buddhist sutras. He was able to reach his destination only with the help of the shape-shifting trickster, Monkey King, along with three other mythical characters/disciples. Each chapter in the novel describes one obstacle en route that only the resourceful Monkey King can overcome. In Chen's circus-opera adaptation, the classic narrative of journeying through tribulations toward success is replaced by visual and vocal spectacles with little dialog. Furthermore, the Western operatic convention is completely fractured by the insertion of extended acrobatic performance. The vocal performance by ten vocalists singing in Mandarin Chinese with operatic inflections is also deliberately foreign and foreignizing to the Western audience. The "journey to the West" thus symbolizes the Chinese "monkey's" encounter with and innovative transformation of Western culture. It is a performance that simultaneously entertains the Euro-American audience and reshapes their understanding of Western opera.

Contrary to the Chinese "monkey" who journeys to the West to transform the Western operatic convention, Chen's second film, *Disney High School Musical: China* (*Gewu qingchun*) (2010), traverses in the opposite direction with potentially more problematic ramifications. As the title indicates, this musical is a Disney-China coproduction that cashes in on the company's internationally successful film series *High School Musical* (2006–2008). Illustrating Disney's strategy of developing local content to harness non-American audiences, the Chinese version of *High School Musical* seems to be no more than a passive copycat of the American "original" with a Chinese face. To that extent, it seems to have materialized Ma Shizeng's nightmare of 1935, namely, American businessmen coming to China, recruiting local talent, and producing big-budget China-themed movies that would monopolize the Chinese market, forcing Chinese filmmakers to sell out and thereby bankrupting Chinese cinema. In the contemporary case, Disney's strategy of developing local content in China (as well as India and Russia) goes hand in hand with its exporting the Disney theme park to Hong Kong and Shanghai, making Ma's prescient anxiety even more alarming.

On closer analysis, however, the Chinese version exceeds Ma's 1930s nightmare in its conception and diegesis. Shi-zheng Chen, the director, once again interweaves Chinese and Western performance styles so as to highlight their productive clash and negotiation. His interest is not to reinscribe or rehearse sanctified iconic "local" content, but rather to subject it to external pressures so as to stage its inevitable reconfiguration as a result of multilevel crossings. Given this overarching concern, it is not surprising that he rejected the original Disney script that describes a Chinese rural boy who initially wants to study kung fu and then switches to dancing. Chen deemed this story too cliché and opted to project a metropolitan China teeming with hip-hopping first-year college students committed to pursuing their own dreams.

Consequently, the film features spectacular hip-hop and other styles of performance set in the classroom, the gym, the dorm, the street, the home, and the stage—all stripped of locational specificity. When the "Chinese locality" does crop up at one point, it appears as urban ruins, the rubble left behind by bulldozers that demolish old residential areas to make way for bigger roads and gentrified skyscrapers. The ruins are set against and surrounded by gray high-rises on the distant horizon, creating a sharp visual contrast between the old and postmodern China. Yet, in the midst of the ruins stands a gray-stone residential building where the older generation clings to Peking opera and denigrates the younger generation's hip-hop performance. The proplike old building inserted into the panoramic ruins produces a surreal effect.

Indeed, the nonrealistic style is a dominant feature of this film, allowing Chen to construe a China that does not exist in reality and to present a style of life that is unavailable to the audience. He sees the surreal musical style as a major departure from and a contribution to realism-oriented Chinese cinema.[47] In this light, the promised "local content" in the Chinese version of *High School Musical* is deessentialized. It is both iconized and opened up for resignification. Moreover, Chen's surreal hip hop does not mean that "China" in this film simply becomes Westernized. Rather, the stalwart presence of the old house and the Peking opera amid urban ruins surrounded by postmodern high-rises underscores an awkward copresence of different temporalities. This awkward anomaly is symptomatic of a rapidly changing China stripped of teleological developmentalism. The coexistence of hip-hop spectacles and Peking opera in the urban ruins enhances their mutual out-of-place-ness.

Here we can detect a parallel between Chen's hip-hop musical and the Cantonese Western-costume opera/films discussed in Chapter 3. In both cases, what is assumed local and regional becomes foreignized through taking on Western audio-visuality. The result is not complete Westernization but rather a prolonged "trans" state of contact and clash, which destabilizes the local Self and the foreign Other simultaneously. Thus, Shi-zheng Chen's Chinese version of *High School Musical* hardly masquerades as a "local content" production. Instead, it displays the impossibility of pinning down the local and the necessity of reconfiguring the local from the foreign perspective. In this same process, the foreign is recontextualized and resignified rather than simply adopted as the dominant force.

Reconfiguring the Global Power Structure: The Undercover Goes Global

Despite their different production apparatuses, Chen's three projects—*Dark Matter, Monkey: Journey to the West,* and *Disney High School Musical: China*—share the figure of the misfit "internal foreigner" (i.e., the Chinese student who fails to adapt to the American academic environment, the acrobatic Monkey King singing Western opera in Mandarin Chinese, and Chinese college students hip-hopping in urban ruins). The position of "internal foreigner" defamiliarizes Western operatic conventions and troubles Chineseness by presenting fantastic acrobatics and hip-hop performance as much as it results in the Chinese student's explosive violence against the Western Other in *Dark Matter.*

The foreignizing perspective addresses the cross-Pacific power asymmetry in two ways. First, it engages with and confronts it by rejecting foreclosed discourses of essentialism, be it Westward assimilation or Eastward domestication. Second, it exposes and ruptures the power structure by demystifing the ideal of "flexible citizenship" and insisting on differences and discrepancy as significant values that persist in various migrating and shuttling processes (fantastic and real, diegetic and extradiegetic).

Driven by the "spectre of comparison," the "internal foreigner" juxtaposes the "Chinese" and the "Western" with the result of transforming both. This figure enables Shi-zheng Chen, who himself shuttles in the zone of "trans," to simultaneously work with and work against the "seductive and impenetrable" mainstream system. Herein lies the new "situated agency" of East Asian media workers who actively participate in today's intensified global flows and potential counterflows. While the end results of their globalization (or global shuttling) are hard to predict, they strive to envision and perform strategic interventions that may improve the rules of the game (even if the improvement is conceivable only in the "negative utopian" mode as theorized by Fredric Jameson).

One such strategic intervention is akin to one of the Monkey King's ploys, which is to conquer the "Ox Demon" by sneaking into his belly; that is, becoming an "internal foreigner" and wreaking havoc from within.[48] Or, one can become an undercover agent (as in *Infernal Affairs* and *The Departed*) with the hope of deconstructing the system from below. Such internal subversion, unsurprisingly, is also the strategy adopted by Shanghai's leftist film workers when they made a foray into Shanghai's commercial film industry in the early 1930s.[49] Their participation culminated in 1933, dubbed the year of leftist films, which contributed to what has become known as the golden era of Chinese silent cinema.

Despite the drastic difference between the 1930s and the new millennium (if not only because of China's radically changed status in the Pacific Rim and the world), what have remained consistent in border-crossing film/media encounters and more general border/identity politics are the imbrications between the mainstream and the visionary, the local and the foreign, the participatory and the subversive. From China's national crisis in early-twentieth-century colonialism to its present-day confluence with globalized media culture, the strategy of wreaking havoc from within the "Ox Demon's belly" always assumes an intimate symbiosis and osmosis between the Demon and the Monkey King. This entails identity erasure and/or exchange (as thematized in the double undercover cop-gangster films discussed in this chapter). To remake Hollywood films and to allow one's own films to be remade by Hollywood fosters precisely such a form of cross-Pacific symbiosis and undercover exchange, which makes internal subversion and transformation possible. The same potential exists in Sino-American mutual appropriation in broader film and media practices.

Chinese cinema started with "internal foreigners" imitating, adopting, mobilizing, and transforming the so-called Western technology of cinema in the early twentieth century. Now, new generations of "internal foreigners" as globalized undercover agents/game players are poised to envision ways of remaking Chinese cinema, reconfiguring American cinema, and reshuffling the global order while redefining location-specific collective positioning. With their vision, globalization gains a different vector from Hollywoodization. On this basis, we can anticipate the global reinvention of a sustainable political and affective structure that in turn facilitates a new situated yet shuttling collective subjectivity. A crucial link in this process is none other than Chinese cinema. Resulting from and instigating border-crossing remaking and appropriation, Chinese cinema has served and will continue to serve as a "trans" port or a revolving prism through which the global and the local, the Self and the Other, the past and the future are doubly exposed, mutually reinflected, and thereby reciprocally constitutive.

Final Thoughts

As this book was going to press, *Red Dawn* went through yet another "remake." Its original release in 2010 was cancelled owing to the production company MGM's declaration of bankruptcy. In 2011 potential distributors of the film voiced concerns about the likelihood of the film's alienating the Chinese government, which would have led to the loss of China's lucrative box office. As a result, the invading Chinese army and Chinese symbols were digitally replaced with a North Korean army and North Korean symbols in the 2012 theatrical release.

Red Dawn's last-minute makeover highlights the overpowering concern with box office. Yet it does not address the US media's deep-seated anxiety and mistrust when faced with the "Oriental" Other. Indeed, such paranoia foregrounds American cinema's dependence on the global market, which leads to self-censorship while undermining its hegemony. This "two sides (paranoia/self-censorship and hegemony) of the same coin" situation is clearly evident in the remaking of *Red Dawn*, with its imaginary enemies cycling from Russian to Chinese to North Korean. The "face-off" further encapsulates the tension-ridden yet neighborly feedback loop that I have been tracing throughout this book. What I hope emerges from this loop, however, is a "foreign perspective" that is not demonized or assimilated but rather prompts a fundamental remaking of the Self—be it a national cinema or a collective identity.

Notes

Introduction

1. Ruiz, *Poetics of Cinema*, 111.

2. Grossing nearly 110,000,000 Chinese yuan (RMB) (roughly US$20 million) by July 2, 2008, this film broke the animated films box-office record in China. See "*Kung Fu Panda* Breaks Chinese Box Office Records."

3. Zhu Jidong, "*Gongfu xiongmao* weihe mofang Zhongguo gongfu ye rang Zhongguo yingren wangchen moji?"

4. "Meiguo zhizao de Zhongguo donghuapian Haolaiwu zhong de Zhongguo yuansu."

5. For an important comprehensive study of contemporary Hollywood's global success, see Miller et al., *Global Hollywood 2*.

6. Recent examples include Hollywood remakes of *Il Mare* (2000, South Korea), *My Sassy Girl* (2001, North Korea), *Infernal Affairs* (2002, Hong Kong), and *The Eye* (2002, Hong Kong/Singapore).

7. Carolyn L. Cartier, *Globalizing South China* (Oxford, UK: Blackwell, 2001), 26, quoted in Yingjin Zhang, "Transnationalism and Translocality in Chinese Cinema," 138. Zhang develops the paradigm of translocal and polylocal study of contemporary independent Chinese filmmaking in *Cinema, Space, and Polylocality in a Globalizing China*.

8. Sheldon Lu's pioneering work on transnational Chinese cinemas has played a key role in reshaping Chinese film studies. My reconsideration of the "national" in relation to other forms of the "collective" is inspired Lu's edited volumes such as *Transnational Chinese Cinemas: Identity, Nationhood, Gender* and *Chinese-Language Film: Historiography, Poetics*.

9. Bloch, *The Principle of Hope*.

10. Jameson, "Reification and Utopia in Mass Culture."

11. Brooks, *The Melodramatic Imagination*.

12. Bloch, *The Utopian Function of Art and Literature*, 11.

13. Cheng Jihua et al., *Zhongguo dianying fanzhanshi*.

14. See Berry, "Poisonous Weeds or National Treasures?" (1989); Ning Ma, "The Textual and Critical Difference of Being Radical" (1989); Pickowicz, "The Theme of Spiritual Pollution in Chinese Films of the 1930s" (1991).

15. Major works include Li Suyuan, "Sanshi niandai Zhongguo dianying yundong mingcheng chuyi" (2004); Xiao Zhiwei, "Sanshi niandai 'zuoyi dianying' de shenhua" (2007); Hu Jubin and Li Suyuan, *Zhongguo wusheng dianying shi* (1996); Harris, "Silent Speech" (1997); Yingjin Zhang, ed., *Cinema and Urban Culture in Shanghai, 1922–1943* (1999); Leo Ou-fan Lee, *Shanghai Modern* (1999); Dong Xinyu, *Kan yu beikan zhijian: dui Zhongguo wusheng dianying de wenhua yuanjiu* (2000); Stephenson, "The Occupied Screen" (2000); Lai Kwan Pang, *Building a New China in Cinema* (2002); Hu Jubin, *Projecting a Nation* (2003); Vivian Shen, *The Origins of Left-Wing Cinema in China* (2005); and Zhang Zhen, *An Amorous History of the Silver Screen* (2006).

16. "Cosmopolitanism" is elaborated in Leo Ou-fan Lee, *Shanghai Modern;* "vernacular modernism" is extended to Chinese cinema in Hansen, "Fallen Women, Rising Stars, New Horizons," and Zhang Zhen, *An Amorous History*.

17. Tani Barlow similarly stresses the importance of colonialism and semicolonialism as analytical categories. According to her, the occlusion of these terms has to do with Cold War politics, and it serves to justify a Western presence in China. See Barlow, "Colonialism's Career in Postwar China Studies."

18. See Sun Yat-sen's *Sanmin zhuyi* for his explication of the Three Principles of the People. Sun's discussion of "subcolony" appears in the section on the second principle—nationalism (*minzu zhuyi* 民族主义). Shu-mei Shih also discusses Sun's subcolony in her book *The Lure of the Modern;* see pp. 31–32.

19. See Lu Mengshu, "Xin yingxiong zhuyi." A year later, in his essay "Geming yu dianying," Lu further elaborated on the necessity of "neoheroism" in Chinese cinema owing to China's subcolonial status. In this essay, he quotes Sun Yat-sen's discussion of subcolonialism at length. See Lu Mengshu, "Geming yu dianying," 37.

20. Massey, "Power-Geometry and a Progressive Sense of Place," 61–62.

21. de Kock, "Interview with Gayatri Chakravorty Spivak," 45; Spivak, "Can the Subaltern Speak?"

22. I derive this term from F. Jameson's discussion of "situated consciousness" in Third World cultural production. See Jameson, "Third World Literature in the Era of Multinational Capitalism." Elizabeth Grosz further elaborates the idea of situated agency by attributing it to the dilemma of Third World intellectuals. Grosz describes these intellectuals' task as figuring out "how to speak a language of the colonizer which nevertheless represents the interests and positions of the colonized. If the subaltern can speak, what language is able to articulate, to speak or adequately represent the subaltern's position?" See "Judaism and Exile," 78. Whereas Grosz is mainly concerned with Third World intellectuals, I argue that the same dilemma applies to those filmmakers who have historically occupied the subaltern position, which does not necessarily overlap with the Third World position, but rather takes on different meanings at

variant historical conjunctures. Because of the commercial imperative of filmmaking and the shifting meanings of the subaltern position, the filmmakers' agency is even more overdetermined and situation-specific.

23. See Wong Wang-chi, *Fouxiang Xianggang*, 25–26. Such Shanghai-centrism finds expression in Yang Yanqi's essay "Half a Year in Hong Kong," written nearly a century ago. Yang writes, "In the past three years, whatever Shanghai has, Hong Kong also desires. Even something as inconsequential as Shanghai's Paramount dancing hall has been duplicated in Hong Kong, although the Hong Kong version can hardly compare with its Shanghai counterpart." Quoted in ibid., 68.

24. Examples of coproductions included Shaw Brothers musicals with Japanese directors and a Hong Kong cast, such as *Xiangjiang huayue ye* (Hong Kong Nocturne) (dir. Inoue Umetsugu, 1967), and vampire films coproduced with Britain's Hammer Studios, such as *The Legend of the 7 Golden Vampires* (dir. Roy Ward Baker, Chang Cheh, 1974). For more detailed industrial and textual analysis, see Wong Ain-ling, ed., *Guotai gushi* and *The Shaw Screen*.

25. Rey Chow's polemic is representative of this stance, as illustrated in her 1992 article "Between Colonizers."

26. Beijin Xiangxiang Caucus, "Beijin xiangxiang: Xianggang hou zhimin lunshu zai dingwei."

27. Examples include Stanley Kwan's *Centre Stage* (1992), *Lan Yu* (2001), and *Everlasting Regret* (2005). Ronny Yu's *The Phantom Lover* (1995) is a relatively early example that I examine in depth in this book.

28. The Wachowski Brothers' *The Matrix* trilogy (1999–2003) and Quentin Tarantino's *Kill Bill* I and II (2003–2004) demonstrate the extent to which Hong Kong martial arts genres have inspired visual effects in American filmmaking.

29. See Horton and McDougal, eds., *Play It Again, Sam*; Forrest and Koos, eds., *Dead Ringers;* Durham, *Double Takes;* Mazdon, *Encore Hollywood;* Verevis, *Film Remakes;* Schliesser, "Toward a Cinema of Exhaustion."

30. Patricia Aufderheide's "Made in Hong Kong" offers a rare intervention by studying Hong Kong cinema's imitative tendency. Nevertheless, she fails to examine the historical and ideological circumstances that contribute to this practice. Consequently, she highlights the intertextuality and the hybridity of a film like *Eastern Condors* (dir. Sammo Hung, 1986) without offering a specific and systematic methodology for studying remakes as a theoretical as well as practical category.

31. Mazdon, *Encore Hollywood*, 27.

32. De Certeau, *The Practice of Everyday Life*, 37–38.

33. Benjamin, "The Work of Art in the Age of Mechanical Reproduction," 220.

34. Benjamin, "A Small History of Photography," 242, 243.

35. Willemen, "Bangalore."

36. Jameson, "Third World Literature in the Era of Multinational Capitalism," 71.

37. Xavier, "Historical Allegory," 354.

38. Ibid., 360–361.

39. See Berry, "If China Can Say No, Can China Make Movies?"

40. Jameson, *The Political Unconscious,* 99.

41. Ibid., 99, emphases mine.

42. The terms *Urgeschichte* and *Nachleben* are used by Benjamin in "Re The Theory of Knowledge, Theory of Progress"—Konvolut N in his *Arcades Project.* Rolf Tiedemann translates them into "prehistory" and "afterlife" respectively. See Smith, ed., *Benjamin: Philosophy, Aesthetics, History,* 51, N 3a.2, and 47, N 2.3.

43. Ruiz, *Poetics of Cinema.*

44. Benjamin, "Theses on the Philosophy of History," 255, emphasis mine.

45. In this book, I stick to familiar terms such as "Chinese cinema" and "Chinese-language cinema" as a way of engaging in a dialog with the notion of "Sinophone cinema" posited by Shu-mei Shih in her *Visuality and Identity.* Shih excludes mainland Chinese cinema from Sinophone cinema in order to (1) debunk China/Mandarin Chinese–centered nationalism and (2) critique the notion of "diaspora" for implicitly privileging the ancestral home over the adopted land. In my study, I put mainland China and Mandarin Chinese back onto the "Sinophone" map in order to unpack the interactions and tensions between different regions where a spectrum of Chinese languages and dialects are used. My goal is not to reinstate the central position of mainland China or Mandarin Chinese, but rather to highlight the mutual constitution (even if in the form of contention) between the various regions. Such a constellation necessarily entails each region shifting position relative to the entire field, which in turn experiences constant decentering and recentering. To comprehend the unfolding of this interactive terrain, we must start with a broad and heterogeneous conception rather than preclude any of its components.

46. Venuti, *The Translator's Invisibility*, 25.

Chapter 1: *The Goddess*

1. For a foundational study of genre films and motherhood, see Lucy Fischer, *Cinematernity.*

2. See *Yin xing* (The Movie Guide), no. 10 (July 1927): n.p.

3. See http://www.archive.org/details/thegoddess.

4. For a useful and innovative study of Chinese cinema in relation to Euro-American cinema in the 1920s Shanghai, see Qin Xiqing, *Oumei dianying yu Zhongguo zaoqi dianying.*

5. See Macherey, *A Theory of Literary Production,* 92.

6. Importantly, the Cantonese-based southern Chinese subject position is not confined to southern China, but is rather fostered through the network of southern China and the Chinese diaspora in Southeast Asia and beyond. This is evidenced in the fact that the Cantonese version of *Rouge Tears* was elected number four, just above *The Critical Moment* (*Zuihou guantou*) (1938)—the high-profile "national defense film" (*guofang dianying* 国防电影) collaborated on by six Hong Kong film studios—among the ten most popular Cantonese films shown in Singapore in the year from early 1938

to early 1939. The top-ranking film was *Blood-Bathed Baoshan City* (*Xuejian Baoshan cheng*) (dir. Sutu Huimin. 1938), another national defense film made in Hong Kong. See "Shida mingpian xuanju yeyi gongbu," n.p. For more on "national defense cinema," see Chapter 2, note 41.

7. See note 2.

8. See Kaplan,"The Case of the Missing Mother," 83.

9. See Linda Williams, "'Something Else besides a Mother,'" 320.

10. See de Lauretis, *Technologies of Gender,* 10.

11. See Cavell, "Stella's Taste," 220, emphasis mine.

12. Ibid., 219, emphasis mine.

13. Ibid., 219–220.

14. See Hansen, "Fallen Women, Rising Stars, New Horizons," 10.

15. See Gleber, "Women on the Screens and Streets of Modernity," 57. Gleber argues that scenes depicting women's presence in *Berlin, Symphony of a Great City* (dir. Walter Ruttmann, 1927) "are not (at) all sites of prostitution but are instead comprised of at least four distinct instances of female figures, fashions, and habits in the street." See page 69.

16. See Barlow, ed., *Formations of Colonial Modernity in East Asia.*

17. See Bordwell, "Camera Movement and Cinematic Space," 229–246.

18. Tianyi, Mingxing (Star Motion Pictures Co.), and Lianhua 联华 (United China Photoplay and Publishing Service) constituted the tripod of the 1930s Shanghai film industry. Tianyi was the first company to establish a distribution network in Southeast Asia, which became the predecessor of Shaw Brothers Ltd., which dominated the Hong Kong film industry from the late 1950s to the early 1980s.

19. See Wu Yonggang, "*Shennü* he wo," 130.

20. The transition to sound was a prolonged process in China and was not completed until 1938. The use of sound facilitated four developments: more elaborated depiction of the urban setting, more explicit inscription of political messages, more attention to the construction of Chinese cinema (or *guopian* 国片), and, finally, the flourishing of Cantonese cinema. According to Zheng Junli (1911–1969), a prominent Shanghai actor, translator, and critic, sound played a crucial role in promoting modern Chinese nationalism in the struggle against Hollywood incursion. See Zheng Junli, *Xiandai Zhongguo dianying shi lue.*

21. Arguably, the sound transition undermined Shanghai's position as the center of Chinese cinema owing to the rapid development of Cantonese cinema, buttressed by strong followings in both China and Southeast Asia, especially among diasporic Cantonese populations. A 1936 article titled "Guochan yingpian Nanyang lizu nan: Dianying shichang wei Meiguo bazhan, guoyu yingpian wei Yueyu pian suo yadao" (China-Made Films Experiencing Setback in Southeast Asia: Film Market Monopolized by Hollywood, Mandarin Films Overwhelmed by Cantonese Films) spelled out the declining market share of Mandarin Chinese films vis-à-vis that of Hollywood and Cantonese productions. See *Diansheng zhoukan* 5.21 (1936): 509. Commenting on such developments, Stephen Teo writes, "Hong Kong gained a film industry as sound

came in circa 1933–34 . . . whereas in the silent years, a film industry based in the colony always seemed a precarious idea. It could only develop as a center of Cantonese film production." See Teo, *Hong Kong Cinema,* 19.

22. See Wu Yonggang, "*Shennü* wancheng zhilou" (1934), reprinted in Wu, *Wo de tansuo he zhuiqiu,* 134, emphases mine.

23. See the film's English transcript by Yomi Braester.

24. Zhiwei Xiao identifies this relief as the work of Norwegian sculptor Stephan Abel Sinding titled *The Captive Mother.* See Xiao, "Wu Yonggang and the Ambivalence in the Chinese Experience of Modernity."

25. Petro, *Joyless Street.* Petro's book title echoes *The Joyless Street* (*Die Freudlose Gasse*) (dir. G. W. Pabst, 1925), a silent German expressionist film dealing with forced prostitution during the post–World War I depression. Based on the textual and artistic inscription of woman in Weimar, Petro seeks to discern "a way to reread early discussions of modernity in the Weimar period so as to *situate woman as an inhabitant of the city* she so frequently serves to represent." See page 43, emphasis mine.

26. The Bund originated as a muddy road stretching about a mile along the Huangpu River, which flows northward at this bend and eventually empties into the Pacific Ocean. Ceded to Britain in the mid-nineteenth century, the Bund had developed into a financial hub by the 1930s, lined on the west with fifty or so Western buildings of various architectural styles. The International Settlement (1854–1943) was the combination of British and American concessions, lying to the west of the Bund and north of the old walled Shanghai city where most Chinese resided.

27. For neon lights as a Shanghai trademark, see a tip offered to tourists by Rev. C. E. Darwent, the late minister of Union Church, Shanghai. Writing in 1920, shortly after Sincere and Wing On's Shanghai branches were opened, Rev. Darwent encouraged foreign visitors to "see the Road at night for its illuminations," which also meant to share "the Chinese delight in brilliant light." See Darwent, *Shanghai,* 15.

28. Such deterioration had to do with Western and Japanese companies' predatory dumping in the Chinese market. By dumping merchandise at prices lower than market value, these foreign companies sought to monopolize the Chinese market, resulting in severe damage to the local rural economy.

29. Aside from *The Goddess,* another prominent example is *Street Angel* (*Malu tianshi*) (dir. Yuan Muzhi, 1937).

30. See Pratt, *Imperial Eyes,* 6–7.

31. Hao, "Chinese Visual Representation," 47–49.

32. Wu Yonggang, "Lun dianying bujing," 173.

33. Ibid., 173.

34. The close-up tracking shot of the walking feet bears striking resemblance to the opening sequence of *Dirnentragödie* (Tragedy of the Street) (dir. Bruno Rahn, 1927), which illustrates the elliptical editing characteristics of Weimar street film. As Petro describes it, the opening sequence is composed of "a series of abstract and elliptical images: the camera tracks a woman's legs as they move cautiously across a cobblestone pavement until they meet a man's legs, at which point both pairs enter

a doorway and disappear out of sight." See *Joyless Street,* 165. Unsurprisingly, the low angle framing of the meeting of the legs in this Weimar street film also implies urban prostitution.

35. This overhead shot could be referencing a similar shot of prostitution in *Street Angel* (1928), directed by Frank Borzage, who inspired many Shanghai-based filmmakers in the 1930s. A significant difference, however, is that the overhead shot in *The Goddess* is from an anonymous perspective, while the shot in *Street Angel* is authored by Janet Gaynor's character, who, overseeing the scene of prostitution, winces at the idea that she could also be forced to prostitute herself in order to help her sick mother.

36. See Lotte Eisner's discussion of *Dirnentragödie* in her *The Haunted Screen,* 264.

37. Paul Willemen describes cinephilia as "what is seen is in excess of what is being shown." See Willemen, *Looks and Frictions,* 237. For Siegfried Kracauer, Walter Benjamin, and Thomas Elsaesser, the cinephiliac ability to unsuture the audience enables spectatorial agency, reactivates stymied sensorial, sensuous experiences, and thereby undermines mainstream ideology. For a critical summary of Benjamin's, Kracauer's, and Elsaesser's cinephiliac theories, see Keathley, "The Cinephiliac Moment."

38. Žižek, "I Hear You with My Eyes; or, The Invisible Master," 90.

39. Lacan, *The Four Fundamental Concepts of Psychoanalysis,* 67.

40. Žižek, "I Hear You with My Eyes," 90.

41. Yingjin Zhang similarly discusses the film's concealment of female sexuality and momentary expression of the "narrative desire" embodied by the male intellectual trying "to penetrate the unknown world of urban prostitution." He concludes that the film ultimately reinscribes the conservative "paternal law." See Zhang, "Prostitution and Urban Imagination," 170. If this is indeed the end result, we should not attribute this to Wu Yonggang's presumed fixed ideological stance but should rather take into account his laborious negotiation with the multiple and multivalent sociopolitical and filmic determinants in carrying out his debut work and its remake.

42. See Chen Wu, "*Shennü* ping yi," 551–552. Along these lines, Wei Yu argued that Wu's personification of social evil in the figure of the urban thug might lead the audience to attribute the tragedy to "a bad individual, rather than the entire social system." See Wei Yu, "Kuyan chao," 554.

43. Wang Yunman, "Supu yunhan de *Shennü*" (1986), 192. Chen Huiyang, "Wushi nianlai, zongcheng yimeng," 76. One exception came from Yu Muyun, a veteran Hong Kong film historian, who reclaimed *Rouge Tears* as one of the best among the eight Hong Kong–made Mandarin Chinese films released in 1938 and 1939. See Yu Muyun, *Xianggang dianying bashinian,* 19.

44. See *Nanyue* 6 (May 1938): n.p. The film was also treated as a major Hong Kong production as reflected in the extraordinarily high remuneration for the leading actress, Hu Die. See Huang Sumin and Zhang Zuokang, eds., *Yijiusanba zhi Zhongguo dianying.*

45. See Xuan Ren, "Yinian lai de Zhongguo dianying jie," 7–8.

46. See "Xu Hao laigang zhengchi yueyupian teji," 22–25. Xu Hao was the wartime director of the Guomingtang-controlled Film Censorship Board.

47. New China Film Company was founded in 1934 and developed into a major film company after the outbreak of the war in 1937, replacing Shanghai's three major film studios (Star, Tianyi, and United China Photoplay and Publishing Service), which either folded or relocated following Japan's bombing in August of 1938.

48. Before *Rouge Tears,* Chang had already successfully finished a period drama titled *Diao Chan* (The Sable Cicada) in Hong Kong. The film was started in Shanghai but was interrupted by the war, then resumed in Hong Kong. Its release in 1938 helped to establish the reputation of Mandarin Chinese cinema in a colony characterized predominantly by Cantonese culture. See Zhou Chengren and Li Yizhuang, *Zaoqi Xianggang dianyingshi (1897–1945)*, 251–252.

49. Because of the mass migration of Shanghai film workers to Hong Kong during the war, re-presenting and remaking the Shanghai urban landscape became a common practice in a number of Hong Kong–made films that depict resistance activities in Shanghai. *Orphan Island Paradise* (*Gudao tiantang*) (dir. Cai Chusheng, 1939), produced by the Hong Kong–based Earth (Dadi 大地) Film Studio, for instance, offers an allegorical narrative of the struggle between the evil Gang of Skulls and the revolutionaries in a place called "Orphan Island"—a clear reference to Shanghai between 1937 and 1941, before Japan's occupation of Western settlements in Shanghai following the outbreak of the Pacific War. To visualize "Orphan Island" in a Hong Kong studio, the film opens with a still photograph of one of Shanghai's most recognizable landmarks—the panorama of the Bund. With this image as the background, the male and female protagonists pose in the foreground, singing a duet about people's miseries as a result of various exploitations. As the song goes on, the protagonists are repositioned in the lower right corner of the frame, looking toward the upper left side of the frame, where a cut-out space shows footage of the Shanghai landscape—the suffering masses, the debauched party-goers, and the evil schemers. These moving images are simultaneously indexical and fictional. They are supposed to objectively reflect the landscape and social problems of "Orphan Island." Yet, they also quote the staple filmic imagery drawn from 1930s films set and made in Shanghai. The framed presentation in the cut-out space conjures the movie-viewing experience, with the protagonists standing in for the actual audience. The re-presentation of Shanghai in this Hong Kong–made film is therefore both immediate and mediated, which aptly corresponds with the shooting circumstances, that is, the simultaneous absence and presence of Shanghai's urbanscape.

50. My analysis below is based on the Mandarin Chinese version held in the China Film Archive. I also use the 1930s publicity materials on the Cantonese version. These materials are drawn from Hong Kong newspapers and magazines, especially Nanyue Studio's 1938 special issue on *Rouge Tears. Hong Kong Filmography,* vol. 1, uses the identical synopsis, film still, and release date (December 16, 1938) for both versions, which suggests their close proximity.

51. For Peirce's semiotic theory that divides the sign into three levels: firstness-the icon, secondness-the index, and thirdness-the symbol, see his "Division of Signs."

52. Friedberg, *Window Shopping.*

53. Barthes, "The Reality Effect," 11, 15.

54. This review was partially quoted in "Xianggang chuanshuo" n.p.

55. Armes, "The Stars," 138, emphases mine.

56. Wu Yonggang's metaphor of Ruan being the most sensitive film stock that instantly registered the most appropriate emotions effectively reinforced the myth of her natural fit. See *Wo de tansuo he zhuiqiu,* 132, 133.

57. Carlson, *The Haunted Stage.*

58. Armes, "The Stars," 139.

59. Barthes, "The Face of Garbo," 57.

60. The term "metaphysical prostitute" is borrowed from Hong Kong critic Chen Huiyang's discussion of *The Goddess.* See "Wushi nianlai, zongcheng yimeng," 19–20. Chen further argues that Ruan's character is more transcendental than lifelike.

61. Baudrillard, "The Ecstasy of Communication," 130.

62. See Introduction, note 42.

63. Benjamin, "The Task of the Translator."

64. Derrida, *Of Grammatology,* 145.

65. Thompson, "Screen Acting and the Commutation Test," 58.

66. Ibid., 59.

67. Comolli, "Historical Fiction: A Body Too Much," 49.

68. One of the movie posters included in the background is *The New Peach Blossom Fan* (*Xin taohua shan*) (dir. Ouyang Yuqian, 1935). Produced by New China Film Company, which also funded *Rouge Tears,* the film adapts a classic drama by resetting it in the 1920s warlord period, thereby delivering an allegory of war and resistance.

69. This was related to the "national goods campaigns" (*guohuo yundong*) that escalated in the mid- to late 1930s in response to the Japanese invasion of the Chinese market.

70. See Jameson, "Class and Allegory in Contemporary Mass Culture," 44.

71. Rothman, "*The Goddess,*" 69, emphasis in original.

72. Bloch, *The Principle of Hope,* vol. 1, 157.

73. Brooks, *The Melodramatic Imagination,* ch. 3.

74. See Raymond Williams, *Marxism and Literature,* 132–135.

75. Gramsci, *Selections from Cultural Writings,* 238, emphases mine.

76. Jameson, "Reification and Utopia in Mass Culture," 33.

77. According to Tony Bennett, the positioning of a work is not an abstract theory, but a praxis, a "political advance." The position is neither fixed nor natural to texts, but "a product of a historically particular organization of the field of cultural relations and of the particular ways in which the texts concerned are produced for consumption within that field." See Bennett, *Formalism and Marxism,* 166, 167.

78. The Hong Kong director, Chen Pi, only played a complementary role by directing the Cantonese cast to reenact a Shanghai-based narrative.

79. These publicity materials are gathered from 1938 Hong Kong newspaper advertisements and the *Rouge Tears* special issue of *Nanyue* (South China Film Magazine), no. 6.

80. Yanli Han emphasizes the absence of "Hong Kong" in the labeling and argues that Hong Kong cinema was not an a priori concept automatically derived from Hong Kong's geographical existence. Rather, to understand the formation of Hong Kong cinema requires that we examine its eclecticism, instability, and border-crossing processes. See Yanli Han, "Cong guofang pian de zhizuo kan zaoqi yueyu dianying he Zhongguo dalu de guanxi," 56–67. Yingjin Zhang makes a similar argument in "Beyond Binary Imagination," 83–84.

Chapter 2: Family Resemblance, Class Conflicts

1. I translate the Chinese title literally into "Sister Flowers" (instead of adopting the conventional translation, "Twin Sisters") in order to emphasize two things: (1) the audience appeal held by a narrative centering on a pair of beautiful young women compared to flowers, which led to (2) the increasing use of the term *zimei hua* in popular discourses that went beyond literal twinship to indicate the doubling of female youth and beauty as a new social trend. The replacement of literal twinship with metaphorical sisterhood also lent itself to politicization and expansion of the sisterhood community, as I shall argue in relation to the 1964 Shanghai film *Stage Sisters.*

2. The film instantly triggered three literary-media texts in the same year. They were a radio drama by Li Changjian, a ten-chapter screen fiction by Chen Mutao, and a sequel by He Ke'ren.

3. Between the 1940s and 1950s, four films titled *Zimei hua* appeared in Hong Kong, in addition to a dozen other films with *zimei hua* as part of the title. The closest remake was the 1940 *Sister Flowers* (dir. Yang Hongguan), which has an identical plot, reenacted by an all-Cantonese cast, with the twin sisters played by a top Hong Kong star, Bai Yan 白燕 (1920–1987). It simultaneously revived and competed with its Shanghai predecessor by inviting the audience to compare Hu and Bai, and by confirming the Hong Kong remake's enhanced appeal through the use of Cantonese. This is evidenced by a Hong Kong poster dated September 11, 1940, in the Hong Kong Film Archive. Another close remake was shot in the Amoy dialect by Chen Huanwen in 1958. These proliferating Hong Kong "sister flowers" films, shot in various dialects during a relatively short time span, speak to the vitality and malleability of the image and the subject.

4. According to Leitch's taxonomy, a remake may adopt four stances toward the "original" film: readaptation, update, homage, and true remake. See "Twice-Told Tales," 47.

5. Hollander, "Versions, Interpretations, Performances," 220.

6. Such linkage between the sisterhood scenario and the musical genre is also prevalent in Hollywood backstage musicals that parade singing and dancing sisters. *White Christmas* (dir. Irving Berlin, 1954) is a case in point. Between the 1950s and 1960s, Hong Kong's two major film companies, Shaw Brothers and Motion Pictures and General Investment (later renamed Cathay), also produced a spate of films centered on

singing-dancing sisters. These song-and-dance films tended to result from Hong Kong's importation of Japanese filmmakers, composers, and choreographers, who in turn drew heavily on Hollywood musicals. Two prominent examples are Motion Pictures and General Investment's *Our Sister Hedy* (*Si qianjin*) (dir. Tao Qin, 1957) and Shaw Brothers' *Hong Kong Nocturne* (*Xiangjiang huayue ye*) (dir. Inoue Umetsugu, 1967).

7. Dyer, "Entertainment and Utopia," 184.

8. Zheng Zhengqiu, "*Zimei hua* de ziwo pipan," 40.

9. The "civilized play" was a hybrid dramatic form that emerged at the turn of the twentieth century in Shanghai, partially inspired by modern Western drama. Zheng Zhengqiu started out as a playwright of "civilized plays" with a humanist bent, specifically concerned with women's subordinate position in feudal and patriarchal China. Early Chinese cinema was heavily influenced by the "civilized play" in terms of acting and narrative. For a historical account of the transition from the civilized play to early silent film, see Zhong Dafeng, Zhang Zhen, and Yingjin Zhang, "From Wenmingxi (Civilized Play) to Yingxi (Shadowplay)."

10. In Zheng Zhengqiu's original plan, the father is driven to weapon trafficking by Chinese comprador capitalists—a special social sector that emerged to mediate China's encounter and negotiation with Western economic, cultural, and political penetration. Zheng also intended to tackle the dire effect of weapon trafficking on Chinese society in general. He ultimately abandoned these ideas because of difficulties of production. However, he stressed the importance of understanding each film and filmmaker in relation to their sociopolitical circumstances. See Zheng, "*Zimei hua* de ziwo pipan," 40.

11. In her analysis of the gender relationship in this film, Vivian Shen similarly discusses how the four characters are reconfigured spatially through framing. However, she pays closer attention to how the characters' *dialogs* register their shifting stances. See Vivian Shen, *The Origins of Left-Wing Cinema in China,* 97–99.

12. Ibid., 99.

13. See Zheng Zhengqiu, "Ruhe zoushang qianjin zhi lu."

14. The film contest was conducted by a Chinese Film Selection Committee formed by the Guomindang's Central Executive Committee, Ministry of the Interior, Ministry of Education, and China Educational Film Association.

15. See Ya Fu's and Han Cun's reviews of the film, originally published in the newspaper column titled "Everyday Cinema" (Meiri dianying), in *Chen bao* (Morning Newspaper), Feb. 24, 1934. Reprinted in Chen Bo, ed., *Sanshi niandai Zhongguo dianying pinglun wenxuan,* 34–36.

16. See Tang Na's "Muqian Zhongguo dianying de jige qingxiang," reprinted in Cheng Jihua et al., *Zhongguo dianying fazhan shi.* 239.

17. Lu Xun, "Yunming," 29–31.

18. Luo Yunwen, "Youlun *Zimeihua* ji jinhou dianying wenhua zhi lu," 476–478. Also see "A Glimpse of Film": "The success of *Sister Flowers* has to do with the fact that it allows lower-middle-class urban viewers to release their pent-up frustration under a progressive cover that seemingly presents a social critique. Its techniques are

far from superb. The director and actors also erroneously slip back to the model of the civilized play."

19. See Marchetti, "Two Stage Sisters," 72–75.

20. Barthes, "Diderot, Brecht, Eisenstein," 73.

21. Poshek Fu, "Between Nationalism and Colonialism," 218–219.

22. Ibid., 219.

23. Ibid., 218–219. For a critique of Fu's reading of the film, see Yingjin Zhang, "Fandui xiuzheng," 104–114.

24. When the war broke out in 1937, severely damaging the film industry (among other things), both Star (which produced *Sister Flowers*) and United China Photoplay and Publishing Service (which produced *The Goddess*) were closed, while Tianyi moved to Hong Kong completely and was renamed Nanyang Film Company (Nanyang Yingpian Gongsi).

25. An advertisement for the film appeared in Shaw Brothers' house magazine in Singapore, *Dianying quan* 电影圈 (Screen Voice Semimonthly), 48 (July 1, 1939): n.p. This advertisement bills the film as a "funny and romantic singsong Cantonese masterpiece."

26. Lanfen's fiancé seems more like a placeholder, and his relationship with Lanfen is far less important than the sisters'.

27. The use of a latex mask recurs in *Romance of a Teenage Girl* (*Shaonü xin*) (dir. Chen Yun, 1966), starring the 1960s youth idol Josephine Siao. This youth film features Siao playing three roles and performing eighteen songs and dances—an extreme development of what He Lan, the leading actress in *The Happy Reunion,* pioneered in the early 1960s.

28. See chart 3 of Ye Fuqiang, "The Cantonese Cinema in the 1960s Hong Kong and Social Change," 19.

29. See "*Xin zimei hua,* huahua xuxu." The publicity photo shows He Lan posing in a male suit next to the director Hu Peng and the producer Huang Tao.

30. It was reported that the film attracted intense overseas interest and that overseas Chinese, especially those from Southeast Asia, frequently visited the shooting set. See ibid.

31. Hu's other mother roles in postwar Hong Kong films include *Back Door* (*Hou men*) (dir. Li Hanxiang, 1960), shot in Mandarin Chinese, and *Maternal Love* (*Mu ai*) (dir. Zhu Ji, 1961), shot in Cantonese.

32. A similar use of singing could be found at the formative stage of the Hollywood musical. According to Rick Altman, the late 1920s inclusion of singsong sequences prefigured the Hollywood musical, which solidified as a genre in the late 1930s. *Broadway Melody* (1929), for instance, was billed by MGM as an "all talking, all singing, all dancing dramatic sensation." Its music was treated simply as a way to present the narrative, with the purpose of cashing in on the audience's curiosity about the novelty of talkies. See Altman, *Film/Genre,* 31–34.

33. The film was sold to the Philippines for 18,000 yuan and to Indonesia for 16,000 yuan, which was eight or nine times more than the highest price of a silent film.

See Cheng Jihua et al., *Zhongguo dianying fazhan shi,* 163, note 1. Documents suggest that Southeast Asian film distributors would sometimes specify the rate they would pay for each song number. This economic incentive unsurprisingly encouraged film producers to emphasize singing sequences and sound recording quality.

34. Gong Jianong, *Gong Jiannong congying huiyi lu,* vol. 2, 296.

35. The film's box-office record was considered by a contemporary reviewer to be a big victory for Chinese cinema. This reviewer attributed the success to director Zheng Zhengqiu's successful tapping into the Chinese audience's psychology and viewing habits. He further warned against the self-indulgent pursuit of "artsy" and "trendy" film styles that "leave the audience behind." See Xu Xu, "Dui *Zimei hua* maizuo dapo jilu de ganxiang," 12.

36. See Hu Die, *Hu Die huiyilu,* 163.

37. *Diansheng zhoukan* 4, no. 22 (May 24, 1935): 436. The reason for the protest was not specified. In the previous issue, however, it was reported that *Sister Flowers, Spring Silkworms,* and another Mingxing (Star) Motion Pictures Co. production were all sold to Chinese in Germany for the price of 10,000 yuan. See *Diansheng zhoukan* 4, no. 21 (May 24, 1935): 418.

38. *Mingxing yuekan* 2, no. 4 (Nov. 1934): 20.

39. In recognition of her performance in Honululu for overseas Chinese, Hu was conferred a golden medal with the engraving "A beautiful lady from the south" (*nanguo jiaren*)—an apt anticipation of her 1939 film discussed here. See Huang Sumin and Zhang Zuokang, eds., *Yijiusanba zhi Zhongguo dianying,* 40. Hu's first talkie, *Romance of the Songsters,* was billed as "a huge production completely made in America, with Cantonese dialogue and songs, titillating, romantic and didactic" (*quanbu zai Meiguo shezhi zhi yueyu duibai gechang xiangyan langman aiqing jingshi jupian* 全部在美国摄制之粤语对白歌唱香艳浪漫爱情警世巨片).

40. Cantonese opera was integrated into Cantonese cinema from the very beginning. Stephen Teo pinpoints 1939, the year this film was made, as the peak of Cantonese opera film production. See Teo, *Hong Kong Cinema,* 40.

41. Unlike the Shanghai-centered leftist cinema from the early to mid-1930s, "national defense cinema" spread to Hong Kong with the wartime migration of leftist filmmakers. Owing to the spread of war and nationalist discourses, both diasporic mainland Chinese filmmakers and Hong Kong film workers participated and sometimes collaborated in producing national defense films. In Hong Kong, national defense cinema was only one "genre" that coexisted and vied with films that carried no apparent political message. For the wartime collaboration between mainland Chinese and Hong Kong filmmakers, see Law and Bren, *Hong Kong Cinema,* 129–141. A major film project that indicated Hong Kong film workers' investment in national defense cinema was six local studios' collective work on *The Critical Moment* (*Zuihou guantou*) (1938). The profits of the film were donated for war relief.

42. For coverage of Hong Kong film workers' fund-raising activities, see *Xianggang zaoqi dianying guiji,* 42–43.

43. Gunning, "An Aesthetic of Astonishment."

44. Television was introduced into Hong Kong on May 29, 1957, but was confined to only a tiny number of families owing to its exorbitant rental fees. By 1966, the only TV station, Rediffusion cable TV, had only 67,000 subscribers. See Law Kar, "Xinxing yu jingguan," 48–50. Also see note 55 in Chapter 3 for a brief history of Rediffusion.

45. See "Guan Meiguo Yingxi ji." I have made slight modifications to Jay Leyda's translation in his *Dianying: An Account of Films and the Film Audience in China,* 2.

46. According to Paul S. N. Lee, the TV shows provided by the RTV cable system were mostly imported from United Kingdom and America. See Lee, "The Absorption and Indigenization of Foreign Media Cultures," 81.

47. Poshek Fu, "The 1960s," 82.

48. The 1961 official census showed that half of the total Hong Kong population was under the age of twenty-one. See *Hong Kong Annual Report,* in ibid.

49. Cheuk, "The Characteristics of Sixties Youth Movies," 73–79.

50. Poshek Fu, "The 1960s," 72.

51. For a detailed account of how the music of the film was composed, see Huang Zhun, "Tantan *Wutai jiemei* de yinyue chuangzuo," 285–291.

52. In her performance of the revolutionary version of *The White-Haired Girl,* for instance, Chunhua plays the lead without singing a single line. The performance ends with the chorus singing: "The old society turned me from a human into a ghost; the new society brings me back into the human world." This line then instigates the diegetic audience's collective shouting, "Avenge the white-haired girl!"

53. Dyer, "Entertainment and Utopia," 184.

54. For a detailed acount of the One Hundred Flowers Campaign, see MacFarquhar, *The Hundred Flowers Campaign and the Chinese Intellectuals.*

55. See Xie Jin et al., "*Wutai jiemei,*" 147.

56. The "Gang of Four" (Siren Bang), headed by Madame Mao (aka Jiang Qing), was an ultraleftist political clique with highly concentrated power. After the Cultural Revolution, it has been conventionally and conveniently held responsible for perpetrating violence during the Cultural Revolution (1966–1976). Its dissolution in October of 1976 brought the Cultural Revolution to an end.

57. For Western critics' comments on the film, see McCarthy, "Two Stage Sisters," 23, 24; and Tony Rayns and Scott Meek, "Two Stage Sisters," n.p. To help Western audiences understand the Chinese film (and, implicitly, to overcome the Cold War divide that made post-1949 Chinese films barely accessible in the West), Rayns and Meek specifically note the film's Ophulsian precision and sensuousness as well as the noir lighting and composition in the backstage confrontation sequences in the film's Shanghai part.

58. This building is featured in Josephine Siao's *Young Lovers* (*Qingchun zhi lian*) (dir. Chen Yun, 1967).

59. Law and Bren, *Hong Kong Cinema,* 178.

60. Eric Kit-wai Ma calls this "desinicization," which enabled "a distinctive local identity" and encouraged mass media depiction of mainlanders as "uncivilized"

outsiders as opposed to modern, cosmopolitan Hongkongers. See *Culture, Politics, and Television in Hong Kong,* 1.

61. Jameson, "The Politics of Utopia," 46, emphasis mine.

Chapter 3: *The Love Parade* Goes On

1. Quoted in Braudy, "The Double Detachment of Ernst Lubitsch,"1084, note 11.
2. Mai Xiaoxia "Guangdong xiju shilue,"
3. Venuti, *The Translator's Invisibility,* 25.
4. "Xizhuang ju" refers to a set of Cantonese operas and films that derived from the encounter between Western cinema and Cantonese opera in the early twentieth century, which triggered the reform of Cantonese opera. One major trait of the reformed Cantonese opera was the adoption of Western costumes (*xizhuang*), hence the term, "xizhuang ju".
5. See film advertisement in *Shen bao,* Oct. 29, 1930. Three months later, Star Theater previewed China's first Vitaphone film, *Singsong Girl Red Peony* (*Genü Hong Mudan*) (dir. Zhang Shichuang, 1931), produced by Star Motion Pictures Co. and starring Hu Die.
6. See *Guangzhou nianjian* (Guangzhou Almanac), vol. 8, 88, quoted in Zhang Fangwei, "Sanshi niandai Guangzhou yueju shengshuai ji."
7. Liyuan Huangsou, "Xue Juexian dashiji." Although Liyuan Huangsou does not explicitly describe Xue's cross-dressing performance in *Xuangong yanshi,* he does mention that Xue's opera troupe experienced a period when the leading actor who specialized in female roles left the troupe, and Xue ended up filling the female roles with great success. This period coincided with the time when Xue's *Xuangong yanshi,* along with other programs, was staged.
8. The title *Baijin long* was originally a cigarette brand manufactured by Nanyang Xiongdi Yancao Gongsi (Nanyang Brothers Tobacco Company). The company asked Xue to name his opera's male protagonist after the brand name in order to boost the cigarette's competitive ability vis-à-vis Western brands in the Chinese market. Packs of Baijin Long cigarettes were offered to the audience, while newspaper advertisements encouraged viewers to "watch the famous opera *Baijin long* and enjoy Baijin Long cigarettes." The tie-in strategy successfully boosted the popularity of both the opera and the cigarettes in China and Southeast Asia. See Lee Pui-tak, "Jin yu fanjin," 29.
9. When asked about the message of the film, Xue cryptically responded, "My goal in making the film is to encourage the Chinese to expand overseas business in order to achieve victory in the war of business at a time of global depression." See Liu Feng, "Fangwen," 13.
10. Mai Xiaoxia, "Guangdong xiju shilue" 792. *Xieyi* also characterizes *The Goddess,* directed by Wu Yonggang, as discussed in Chapter 1.
11. Ouyang's critique originally appeared in *Xiju* 戏剧 (Theater), 1 (1929), quoted in Xie Binchou谢彬筹, "Dui Yueju yanjiu de cuqian ganzhi" 对粤剧研究的粗浅感知

(A Preliminary Study of Cantonese Opera), unpublished manuscript, cited in Luo Li, "Yueju yanjiu yu Yueju yanjiu shi chuyi (shang)," 28.

12. Ma Shizeng, "Wo de xinju tan," n.p.

13. Ma Shizeng, "Wo daile yiqiang biange Yueju de recheng huilai," 171–173.

14. Ma Shizeng, "Wo you mei yanju zhi zongzhi," n.p.

15. Xue Juexian, "Nanyou zhiqu."

16. Xue Juexian, *Yilin* 艺林 (Artland) (1938), quoted in Luo Li, "Yiling yixing yu yingju hudong," 44.

17. Mai Xiaoxia, "Guangdong xiju shilue."

18. Mai Xiaoxia, "Wanjiu Zhongguo xiju zhi weiwang," 183–198.

19. Ibid.

20. Anderson, *The Spectre of Comparison*, 229.

21. Ibid.

22. In a 1925 publicity essay, Lubitsch's style was described as "detached and nuanced" (*lengjun youwei* 冷峻幽微) as opposed to D. W. Griffith's stimulating entertainment (*ciji* 刺激) style. Lubitsch's *The Marriage Circle* (1924) and *Three Women* (1924), shown in Shanghai and praised for expressive visuality, inspired Chinese urban marriage films. See Star Motion Pictures Co.'s house magazine, *Mingxing tekan* (1925).

23. Braudy, "The Double Detachment of Ernst Lubitsch," 1073.

24. Ibid., 1073–1074.

25. Xiang Lin, "Dianying de chulu: yifeng gongkai xin," n.p.

26. Ibid.

27. Zhao Zhongyu, "Zhongguo dianying shiye de mianmian guan," 11.

28. Ibid.

29. Wei Nan, "Dianying de wenyi hua," 10–11.

30. Sang Hu, "Hanxu."

31. Braudy, "The Double Detachment of Ernst Lubitsch," 1075.

32. Ibid., 1078.

33. Weinberg, *The Lubitsch Touch: A Critical Study.*

34. Braudy, "The Double Detachment of Ernst Lubitsch," 1078, 1080, emphasis mine.

35. Ibid., 1080.

36. Harvey, *Romantic Comedy in Hollywood, from Lubitsch to Sturges*, 17. Harvey argues that MacDonald's self-mocking, laconic comedian persona was very much invented by Lubitsch, who instantly signed her up as the queen in *The Love Parade* after seeing her in a screen test and a stage performance.

37. Braudy, "The Double Detachment of Ernst Lubitsch," 1083.

38. Willemen, "The National Revisited," 36, 40, my emphasis.

39. Farquhar and Berry, *China on Screen*, 15.

40. Venuti, *The Translator's Invisibility*, 25.

41. This company was founded in 1956 in Hong Kong by Lu Yuntao 陆运涛 (Lok Wan Tho in Cantonese), a Britain-educated business tycoon from a Malaysian/Singaporean Chinese family. It was a major rival of Shaw Brothers (which was derived

from Tianyi) in Hong Kong in the 1950s and 1960s. For a comprehensive study of the two companies' histories, see Ain-ling Wong, ed., *Guotai gushi* and *The Shaw Screen* (2003).

42. For a historical account of the Shanghai and Hong Kong genealogy initiated by *The Love Parade*, see Yung Sai-shing, "Cong *Xuangong yanshi* dao *Xuangong yanshi*," 190–289.

43. The term *yanshi* 艳史 (passionate romance) also appears in the Chinese translation of the titles of many later musicals starring Maurice Chevalier and Jeanette MacDonald, either together or separately. *The Vagabond King* (dir. Ludwig Berger, 1930), starring MacDonald, was translated into *Fagong yanshi* 法宫艳史 (The Passionate Romance in the French Palace). *One Hour with You* (dir. Ernest Lubitsch, 1932), starring MacDonald and Chevalier, was translated into *Honglou yanshi* 红楼艳史 (The Passionate Romance in the Red Chamber).

44. According to Mai Xiaoxia, opera critic and publicity director for Xue Juexian's theater troupe, the southern Chinese *kunqu* opera in the early twentieth century used twelve instruments, the northern Peking opera used fifteen instruments, whereas the Cantonese opera used forty instruments, and Western instruments were used only in Cantonese opera. See Mai Xiaoxia, "Guangdong xiju shilue," 813–814.

45. Wu Tingzhang, *Yueju dashi Xue Juexian*, 55–56.

46. Excerpts of the script appear in Ma Shizeng, *Qianli zhuangyou ji*.

47. Yung Sai-shing, "Cong *Xuangong yanshi* dao *Xuangong yanshi*," 192. *Xuangong yanshi* was not the first Western-costume Cantonese opera to depend heavily on Western props. *Baijin long* had already paraded eye-catching props including cigars, chocolate, a telephone, Western-style costuming, furnishings, and an exotic-looking barbarian tent. See Gong Bohong, "Lingnan feng,"

48. The advertisement is included in the Loke Wan Tho Collection held at the National Archives of Singapore.

49. For a chronological account of the competition between Motion Pictures and General Investment and Shaw Brothers, see Zhao Weifang, "Wuliushi niandai jingzheng geju zhong de Xianggang guoyu dianying gongye." For Loke Wan Tho's film enterprise, see Chung, "A Chinese Movie Mogul and the Transformation of His Movie Empire."

50. The Snow Country is translated as "Non-Such" in the English synopsis included in the film's publicity materials for its screening at the World Theatre in San Francisco.

51. Lee Cheuk-to, "Zuo Ji liushi niandai zuopin de chubu yanjiu," 59–60.

52. See "Xuangong yanshi yu liangfei."

53. Ibid.

54. Miao Jieke, "Zhang Ying Luo Yanqing de tianmi jingtou."

55. Rediffusion is a radio and TV broadcasting company originally formed in Britain. Branches were set up after World War II in British colonies. In Hong Kong, Rediffusion was founded in 1949 as Li de Husheng (丽的呼声, transliterated from Rediffusion; literally, "Beautiful Sounds"). In 1957, Rediffusion launched a subscription

cable television service known as Li de Yingsheng (丽的映声, literally, "Beautiful Images"), which was renamed Rediffusion Television Limited, or RTV, in 1973. For the publicity stunts for this film, see "Tou Hou-fun," 285. The film made over HK$400,000 and became one of the highest grossing films at the time. It ran for two weeks at two major Hong Kong theaters (*Da shijie* 大世界 and New York), breaking the box office record. Less than ten days later, it was brought back into the theater, with Zhang Ying, Luo Yanqing, and Liang Xingbo in attendance and performing their song numbers. See "Yingju xinwen," n.p.

56. Chen Shibai, "Huisu qishi nianqian Xianggang."

57. Chen Guanzhong, "Zazhong xiucheng zhengguo."

58. Farquhar and Berry, *China on Screen,* 15.

59. Prominent examples include *Manbo nülang* (Mambo Girl) (dir. Yi Wen, 1957) and *Longxiang fengwu* (Calendar Girl) (dir. Tao Qin, 1959).

60. See Shu-mei Shih, *Visuality and Identity,* 16.

61. I draw the notion of "espacement" from Aiten and Zonn, eds., *Place, Power, Situation, and Spectacle,* 211.

62. Kwai-cheung Lo, *Chinese Face/off,* 123. Whereas Lo's analysis focuses on post-1990s Hong Kong cinema, which undoubtedly demonstrates more conspicuous transnational transactions, I argue that the simultaneously contradictory yet complementary relationship between the local and the foreign also played an important role in earlier Hong Kong filmmaking.

63. Mignolo, *Local Histories/Global Designs,* 253.

64. Venuti, *The Translator's Invisibility,* 25.

65. Jameson, "Globalization and Hybridization," 316.

66. Ibid., 316.

Chapter 4: Mr. Phantom Goes to the East

1. In the first version directed by Rupert Julian, previewed on January 1925 in Los Angeles, Christine kisses the phantom, which makes him shudder like "an injured animal," but also "redeems his soul." He releases Christine's fiancé, plays the wedding march for them at his piano, then dies as the vengeful mob approaches him. After a poor reception, the film was transferred to Edward Sedgewick, who reedited it and inserted new footage of the chase sequence that replaced the original death in the catacomb. This chase sequence was retained in the third cut, done by Lois Weber, which had a successful premiere in New York. This last cut defines the silent version we see today. See Birchard, *Early Universal City,* 111.

2. This ending resembles not only that of *The Phantom of the Opera,* but also that of *Frankenstein* (1931) and *Bride of Frankenstein* (1935), directed by James Whales. In the sequel, *Song at Midnight II* (dir. Maxu Weibang, 1941), the phantom is saved by a mad doctor, who then performs surgery on him. He emerges from the surgery more hideous than ever. This perpetuates his haunting presence as alienation incarnate.

3. See Birchard, *Early Universal City,* 111. This publicity stunt was required by Lon Chaney in his contract with Universal, which stipulated that Chaney's phantom makeup should not be revealed until well after the film's release.

4. Chion, *The Voice in Cinema,* 28.

5. Ibid., 23, 24.

6. Rutsky, "The Mediation of Technology and Gender," 16.

7. Chion, *The Voice in Cinema,* 24.

8. Lon Chaney's effective portrayal of the inaudible phantom with his nimble fingers owes a lot to his real-life experiences living with his deaf-mute parents.

9. Doane, "The Voice in the Cinema," 363. When the film was reedited and reissued with dialogue and sound effects in 1929, using the Western Electric sound-on-disk technology, all of the main cast members dubbed their roles except Lon Chaney, whose voice was not available for use owing to his contract with MGM, which was producing his upcoming first and only talkie, *The Unholy Three* (dir. Jack Conway). Consequently, the shadow of Chaney's phantom was "ventriloquized" by an uncredited voice actor. In other words, despite the publicity emphasis that the new sound version allows the audience to "hear as well as see" (according to the 1929 reissue trailer), Chaney's phantom remains inordinately silent. To add another twist, shortly after the release of *The Unholy Three,* Chaney died of throat cancer, which wiped out his voice physically and symbolically. All of these factors seem to reinforce the phantom of the opera as a categorically silent shadow, whose voice is as forbidden to his film audience as it is "angelic" to Christine. See also Robert Spadoni's in-depth study of the gap between the sound and the image, and the ways in which this gap is foregrounded and thematized in early horror talkies. Spadoni, *Uncanny Bodies.*

10. Giles, "Conditions of Pleasure in Horror Cinema," 47.

11. See Mordaunt Hall's movie review in *New York Times,* Sept. 7, 1925: 15.

12. Linda Williams, "When the Woman Looks," 86–87.

13. Chion, *The Voice in Cinema,* 28, 29.

14. Maxu originally intended to play this role himself, but it eventually went to Jin Shan, a popular film and spoken drama actor, owing to the intervention of S. K. Chang, producer of the film.

15. See Guiqu Shanzhuang's blog, "Wo de yeye MaXu Weibang (4)."

16. Yomi Braester summarizes the film's multiple appeals in terms of revolution and revulsion, which are at odds with each other. He argues that the phantom's scar entails a revolutionary message that tends to be overshadowed or undermined by the film's emphasis on "a repugnant monstrosity" as "a fascinating object of consumption." See Braester, *Witness against History,* 90. In my analysis below, I take a different perspective and examine the ways in which entertainment (derived from the romantic twists) and politicization (necessitated by the national crisis) are dialectically and allegorically intertwined (the former being the proxy figure of the latter) and that they both revolve around the sentiment of emergency and liminal presence.

17. The transition to talkie was a prolonged process in China, lasting from 1930 to 1938, according to the consensus of Chinese film historians. The fact that silent

films were produced as late as 1938 can be partially attributed to the impact of the Second Sino-Japanese War, which not only drastically reduced the resources for film-making, but also decentralized filmmaking to areas including the hinterlands, where basic filmmaking infrastructure was not available.

18. Tang Yu, *Erliutang jishi,* 125–127.

19. See Zhang Zhen, *An Amorous History of the Silver Screen,* 318. Departing from Zhang's technology-oriented interpretation, I focus on teasing out the layers of acoustic doubling, splitting, and relaying within and without the diegesis. On this basis, I analyze the intersubjective and intergenerational power structure and the ways it shapes the relationship between the past and the present, between the Other and the Self, and also between the predecessor film and the remake.

20. For a useful discussion of the aesthetic of disgust in horror film, see Roth, "Twice Two."

21. Similar criticism was also targeted at the sequel, *Song at Midnight II* (1941). See Xin Xie, "Ping *Yeban gesheng xuji.*" Cheng Jihua et al. also criticize this film for slavishly imitating the Hollywood horror genre as represented by *The Phantom of the Opera.* See Cheng Jihua, Li Shaobai, Xing Zuwen, *Zhongguo dianying fazhan shi* (1998), vol. 1, 490–491.

22. Any reference to Japan (Riben) in films had to be replaced by the vague term *diren* (enemy) or written as "xx" (a placeholding sign indicating censorship) in silent film intertitles. Such coded and oblique references can be found in Sun Yu's left-leaning films such as *Small Toys* (*Xiao wanyi*) (1933, starring Ruan Lingyu) and *The Big Road* (*Da lu*) (1934). Whereas readily understood by the contemporaneous audience, this coded presentation makes the films inevitably allegorical.

23. Braester, *Witness against History,* 90.

24. In addition to revising Maxu's script for *Song at Midnight* and writing song lyrics for the film, Tian Han also wrote the script and theme-song lyrics for *Children of Troubled Times* (*Fengyun ernü*) (dir. Xu Xingzhi, 1935) as well as song lyrics for *Street Angel* (*Malu tianshi*) (dir. Yuan Muzhi, 1937). Tian Han's "March of the Volunteers" (Yiyongjun jinxing qu 义勇军进行曲), the theme song of *Children of Troubled Times,* was selected in 1949 as the national anthem for the newly founded People's Republic of China. This song calls on the Chinese people to rise above slavery and to brave "the enemy's battle fire." The call for collective resistance of the allegorical "enemy" who enslaves China is repeated in "Love on the Yellow River" in *Song at Midnight.* Xian Xinghai, the composer of the three songs in this film, was born into a poor family in Macao and then converted to Christianity and was educated in France. Upon graduation in 1930, he joined the Pathé Record Company in Shanghai. He later became the head of the music department of Xinhua Film Company. See Kraus, *Pianos and Politics in China,* 40–69. Two years after composing for *Song at Midnight,* Xian Xinghai wrote the "Yellow River Cantata" (Huanghe da hechang 黄河大合唱), which develops the Yellow River theme originated in "Love on the Yellow River."

25. For an important study of modernism in 1980s China, see Xudong Zhang, *Chinese Modernism in the Era of Reforms.* For a study of the femininity and monstrosity

in Maxu's and Yang's phantom remakes, see Yiman Wang, "Here, Again, Comes the Bride-to-Be."

26. See Stokes and Hoover, *City on Fire*, 346, note 19.

27. The director, Ronny Yu, was to make the American comedy/horror film *Bride of Chucky* (1998). The cinematographer, Peter Pau, later shot Ang Lee's *Crouching Tiger Hidden Dragon* (2000), which won him the Academy Award for Best Cinematographer. The film's score was composed by Hong Kong–Filipino musician Chris Babida, the "Godfather of Pop and Cross-Over Music," who shuttles between Hong Kong, Taiwan, and mainland China, and has produced major projects for the Chinese government. For example, he served as the music director of the 1997 Hong Kong handover ceremony and wrote the theme song for the 2008 Beijing Olympics. Finally, costuming was done by Hong Kong production designer and film editor William Chang, who has collaborated with various Hong Kong New Wave directors including Stanley Kwan and Wong Kar-wai.

28. See Abbas, *Hong Kong;* Chow, "A Souvenir of Love"; and Lim, "Spectral Times."

29. Bloom, *The Anxiety of Influence*, 15–16.

30. See Bhabha's discussion of "sly" tactics in *The Location of Culture*, 93–101.

31. In an interview, director Ronny Yu indicated his original plan to make Cheung's face more gruesome but was unable to do so owing to the tight schedule and inadequate digital technology at the time. Meanwhile, he also admitted that even the modest disfiguration in the film already provoked some female viewers to protest against Cheung's "uglification." Yu's interview appears in the bonus materials included in the film DVD released by Tai Seng Video.

32. The disfiguration of the male actor as a punishment is a recurring theme in films and literature set in pre-1949 China. Cheung's fear of disfiguration places him squarely in the discursive tradition of male actors' suffering and mutilation. Cheung's interview appears in the bonus materials included in the film DVD released by Tai Seng Video.

33. Roth, "Twice Two," 106.

34. Before filming *The Phantom Lover*, Leslie Cheung had already undergone intensive Mandarin Chinese drilling for his role in *Farewell My Concubine* (dir. Chen Kaige, 1993), a China–Hong Kong coproduction adapted from a novel by a Hong Kong writer, Lillian Lee (Li Bihua). Cheung plays the character of a famous Peking Opera actor who specializes in playing female roles. Until recently, it had been commonly believed that this was Cheung's first film in which he spoke Mandarin Chinese in his own voice. However, in actuality, his voice was mostly dubbed by Yang Lixin, a Chinese spoken drama actor who agreed to relinquish credit in order to avoid jeopardizing the film's eligibility for competition at international film festivals. Chen Kaige did retain Cheung's original voice in two scenes where Cheung's character's voice is supposed to be "distorted" (*shi zhen*) by physical and mental distress. The dubbing went unnoticed because Yang "pretended so well" (as Cheung's phantom accuses Huang's student). By bending his neck backward, Yang was able to preserve Cheung's slightly husky voice quality. See Ju Jianfu, "Bawang bieji de miwen." Yang's dubbing of Cheung interestingly

parallels the multiple layers of dubbing and ventriloquism in *The Phantom Lover.* In all these cases, the location of credit, authorship, and authority becomes ambiguous and subjected to intricate power play.

35. Statistics show that over 90 percent of films screened in 1930s China were imported from America.

36. Lianhua's campaign may sound overly essentialist to contemporary scholars. Nevertheless, understood within its context, the efforts to wrest the indigenous market from Hollywood's hegemony registered a decolonizing impulse in urban cultural production. Furthermore, the emphasis on *guopian* (Chinese national cinema or China-made films) indicates precisely an attempt to construct and define a category that is not yet materialized and, therefore, not given.

37. Chow, "Between Colonizers," 151. Chow's observation was already anticipated in the 1965 memoir of Sir Alexander Grantham, the twenty-second British governor of Hong Kong. Grantham describes Hong Kong's fundamental political problem as its relationship with China rather than self-governance or independence. See Grantham, *Via Ports*. The theme of "decolonization without independence" becomes a major argument regarding Hong Kong's political development. See Lau Siu-kai, *Decolonization without Independence.*

38. For an important study of cultural production in postsocialist China, see McGrath, *Postsocialist Modernity.*

39. See Beijin Xiangxiang Caucus, "Beijin xiangxiang."

40. Appadurai, "Disjuncture and Difference in the Global Cultural Economy"; see 325.

41. See Ying Hong and He Mei, "Gongzao hou hepai shidai de Huayu dianying," 31–32.

42. Ada Shen, "Tom Buys 35% of Huayi Brothers."

Conclusion

1. For a detailed account of Hollywood's efforts to increase its market share in mainland China in the 1990s, see Ting Wang, "Hollywood's Pre-WTO Crusade in China." For a nuanced discussion of the impact of globalization on the Hollywood and East Asian film industries, see Klein, "Martial Arts and the Globalization of US and Asian Film Industries." One specific instance of Hollywoodization of Asian cinema industries, according to Klein, is achieved through Hollywood's production of local-content films via companies such as Sony's Columbia Pictures Film Production Asia. The similarity with Hollywood's early-twentieth-century attempt to make quasi-Chinese films (decried by Ma Shizeng) is hard to miss. The difference, however, is also obvious. Hollywood since the late twentieth century is no longer geographically confined but rather seeps into other conglomerates, thus becoming apparently de-Hollywoodized, as exemplified by Japan-based Sony's acquisition of Columbia Pictures Entertainment, Inc. from the Coca-Cola Company in 1989.

2. For a study of the socialist government's campaign to cleanse the Chinese market of Hollywood films, see Rao Shuguang and Shao Qi, "Xin Zhongguo dianying de diyige yundong."

3. See "*Gongfu meng*." This film, released in the United States and mainland China on June 11 and June 22, 2010, respectively, topped box office revenues in the opening week in both markets. Although criticized in China for its negative portrayal of Chinese kung fu kids, who viciously beat up the African American "stranger in a new world" (a line from the trailer that eerily evokes *Alice in Wonderland*) and also for its conclusion that shows the African American kung fu kid defeating his Chinese enemies in the latter's game, the film is generally viewed as an entertaining China-US coproduction that spotlights China's cultural traditions—kung fu, Mt. Wudang (the origin of Shaolin kung fu), old Beijing *hutong* residential areas, the Great Wall—while also showcasing Beijing's new architectural marvels including the Bird's Nest (Beijing National Stadium) and the new CCTV (Central China TV) headquarters.

4. Hollywood's olive branch to China becomes even more pronounced in the film's DVD and Blu-ray versions released in October 2010, which include interactive Chinese language lessons and a map of China. *Washington Post* commentator Howard Schneider sensationalizes the Sino-US courtship and power play in his film review titled "Lessons from 'The Karate Kid'—Japan Out, America Down, China on the Rise." For Schneider, the film amounts to "a two-hour-plus advertisement for the country [China], featuring stunning landscapes, smog-free skies and a Forbidden City void of police," to which China contributed US$5 million and granted permission to shoot on the Great Wall and in the Forbidden City.

5. See Sisci, "From Hollywood to Chollywood."

6. Bordwell, *Planet Hong Kong*, 19.

7. Appadurai, "Disjuncture and Difference in the Global Cultural Economy," 325.

8. Mignolo, *Local Histories/Global Designs*.

9. I follow Rob Wilson and Wimal Dissanayake, who usefully maintain the dual perspective of globalization and localization. Thus, they describe a "new world-space of cultural production and national representation which is simultaneously becoming more *globalized* (unified around dynamics of capitalogic moving across borders) and more *localized* (fragmented into contestatory enclaves of difference, coalition, and resistance) in everyday texture and composition" (original emphasis). Consequently, the nation-state is undone by the "imploding heteroglossic interface of the global with the local," or the "*global/local* nexus" (original emphasis). See Wilson and Dissanayake, "Introduction," 1, 3. Building on this argument, I further stress the shuttling position in the global/local nexus, in between the globalization of the local and the localization of the global. This shuttling position is characterized by tension, suspension, indeterminable possibilities, and openness. It therefore defies the telos of both globalization and localization, and instead dwells in the tension-ridden uncertainty of the zone of "trans," as theorized in Chapter 3.

10. Friend, "The Remake Man."

11. Klein, "Martial Arts and the Globalization of US and Asian Film Industries," 367.

12. For East Asian filmmakers being lured to produce remakable films, see Gary G. Xu, "Remaking East Asia, Outsourcing Hollywood." In this essay, Xu also discusses Scorsese's remake of *Infernal Affairs*. He concludes that the remake deracinates the Hong Kong gangster triology, while sneaking Cold War politics back into the film by privileging Western technological and moral superiority over China's dark power. See pages 198–200. Xu's critique of Hollywood's (and, by extension, Western) hegemony in global media and of Hollywood's remaking of East Asian genre films as a form of outsourcing is well taken. However, as I argue below, Scorsese's remake also invites us to explore ways of provincializing Hollywood. This move does not negate Hollywood's continued hegemony, but seeks to reposition it in the dynamic and shifting power geometry of contemporary global flow of film and media.

13. Roy Lee, for instance, privileges horror and high-concept films (over films with more local and national specificity) as the basis of American remaking. See Herbert, "Remaking Transnational Hollywood."

14. For further development of Tarantino as a gatekeeper and Asiaphiliac, see Hunt, "Asiaphilia, Asianization and the Gatekeeper Auteur."

15. Speaking of his preparation for shooting *Kill Bill* (2003/2004), Tarantino stresses his act of mimicry: "[T]he reason I was [watching up to three Shaw Brothers movies every day] is that I wanted to immerse myself so much in that style of filmmaking so that the things that they did would be second nature to me." See "Interview with Quentin Tarantino," in *Screenwriter's Monthly.* Tarantino's comments closely resemble the voice of the phantom's student, who reverse ventriloquizes the phantom's letter, as I have discussed with regard to Ronny Yu's *The Phantom Lover* in Chapter 4.

16. Chan, *Remade in Hollywood,* 146.

17. Ibid., 150.

18. Ibid., 159.

19. Friend, "The Remake Man."

20. See Woo's interview in Stokes and Hoover, *City on Fire,* 309.

21. This martial arts film is based on a script adapted from a Chinese novel that was first rewritten in English by James Shamus, then translated into Chinese by Wong Hui-ling—Lee's longtime collaborator—and eventually retranslated into English dialog. The convoluted back-and-forth translation connotes the cautious management and strategizing of cultural and aesthetic discrepancies in order to best address Western as well as Chinese audiences. In other words, Lee's reinvention of the Chinese martial arts genre is enabled by his negotiation and collaboration with global film cultures.

22. See Hajari, "Erasing the Boundaries," emphasis mine.

23. Donovan, *Asian Influence on Hollywood Action Films,* 4–5. Wen Yiduo (1899–1946), a Chinese poet who studied Western fine arts in the United States in the 1920s, deployed a similar trope of the original versus the copy in comparing Caucasian and Chinese facial features: "A Caucasian (white) face [is] an original print, with clearly defined sense organs, contrary to a Mongolian (yellow) face that has become blurred

due to frequent photocopying." See Liang Shiqiu, *Tan Wen Yiduo,* 30. The difference is that Donovan sees John Woo's Hong Kong work as the authentic action film that is compromised by formulaic Hollywood, whereas Wen Yiduo, in his self-racialization, saw the Caucasian face as the standard that makes the Mongolian face derivative. Nevertheless, both Donovan and Wen reference technologies of mechanical reproduction (i.e., photography and photocopy) that actually minimize the difference between the original and the copy, rendering them veritable simulacra of each other. The hierarchical differences they set up are therefore more ideological than factual.

24. Hajari, "Erasing the Boundaries," 79.

25. Michael Cronin describes "globalization-as-homogenization" as "a McWorld bereft of difference because under colonialism everything turns out to be a replica, a simulacrum, a copy of a limited set of economically and culturally powerful originals." See *Translation and Globalization,* 129.

26. Bauman, *Light Modernity,* 13.

27. Among the Westward flow were John Woo and Chow Yun-fat, who went on to become key contributors to Hong Kong/Chinese diasporic cinema and who have respectively directed and starred in major Chinese productions.

28. The two Hong Kong box office hits between 1997 and 2003 were *Shaolin Soccer* (dir. Stephen Chow, 2001) and *Infernal Affairs I.* Whereas *Shaolin Soccer* led box office records until 2004, when they were broken by Chow's *Kungfu Hustle,* coproduced by Hong Kong, China, and the United States, the success of *Infernal Affairs I* triggered a string of remakes and parodies, and revived the gangster genre in Hong Kong.

29. "Yuanban *Wujian dao* daoyan Liu Weiqiang."

30. In a press conference, Scorsese observed that the film evinced "a sense of paranoia and betrayal—one person never knowing who the other person is or what the other person is doing, or if you can believe anybody. It reflects the world now, the America that we know now, post September 11th." He further explains that the tragic deaths at the end reflect the "moral Ground Zero," "a sadness and a sense of despair" since 9/11. See Balfour, "Meeting with Martin and *The Departed.*" Also see Sarris, "Scorsese Takes Boston, and Electrifies with *Departed.*" The metaphoric "rat" or mole becomes literalized at the end of the film: after Damon's gangster mole is shot in his apartment, a rat appears, gnawing on croissants, just below the golden dome of the State House in the background. Scorsese sees this image as a metacinematic moment that comments on the film from a detached distance, which evokes similar endings of classic gangster movies such as *Scarface* (dir. Brian De Palma, 1983) and *White Heat* (dir. Raoul Walsh, 1949). See Balfour, "Meeting with Martin and *The Departed.*"

31. This stylistic distinction is made by a Chinese blogger, whose commentaries are representative of the Chinese netizens' overall sentiments. See Mei Jianchi, "Dang langman bei canku dianfu." For more Chinese internet reviews, see http://www.mtime.com/movie/22657/.

32. Benjamin, *One-Way Street and Other Writings,* 50.

33. Herbert, "Trading Spaces," 160.

34. Ibid., 158.

35. French, "Where to Shoot an Epic about Afghanistan?"

36. "Chengdu Elements Stand Out in *Kung Fu Panda 2*"; Jonathan Landreth, "*Kung Fu Panda 2* Returns to Its Chinese Home."

37. See "Meiguo zhizao de Zhongguo donghuapian."

38. Zhu Jidong summarized the Chinese filmmakers' discomfort by asking, "How does *Kung Fu Panda*'s imitation of Chinese kung fu outperform Chinese productions?" Zheng Hu, the deputy manager of the Shanghai Animation Studio, reasoned that Hollywood had outstanding merchants, whereas China only had outstanding artists. Thus, the Chinese film industry must undergo full-scale marketization, follow Hollywood's commercial strategy, and produce animations such as *Kung Fu Monkey King* and *The Happy Pig Monk*. See Zhu Jidong "*Gongfu xiongmao* weihe mofang Zhangguo gongfu ye rang Zhongguo yingren wangchen moji?"

39. Higson, "The Concept of National Cinema," 41.

40. Yang Yuanying and Ding Ning, "Xianggang dianying de beijin xiangxiang."

41. Lim, "Generic Ghosts," 118.

42. Higson, "The Concept of National Cinema," 41.

43. Lim, "Generic Ghosts," 124.

44. See Jameson, "Third World Literature in the Era of Multinational Capitalism"; see also note 22 in the Introduction.

45. For elaboration of the notion of "inflexible noncitizenship" in Chinese diasporic cinema (counterpoised with Aihwa Ong's "flexible citizen"), see Yiman Wang, "Alter-centering Chinese Cinema."

46. Shi-zheng Chen, "Director's Statement."

47. Liu Xiaozhuo, "Zhuanfang Chen Shi-zheng."

48. The Ox Demon (*niu mowang*) is an obstacle that blocks the Tang dynasty monk's journey to the West in the classic novel. It can be metaphorically reread as any obstacle en route to a more equitable interactive global structure or other desired goals.

49. See the autobiography of Xia Yan, a leftist scriptwriter and critic, *Lanxun jiumeng lu*, 245.

Bibliography

Abbas, Ackbar. *Hong Kong: Culture and the Politics of Disappearance*. Minneapolis: University of Minnesota Press, 1997.

Aiten, Stuart C., and Leo E. Zonn. *Place, Power, Situation, and Spectacle: A Geography of Film*. Lanham, MD: Rowman and Littlefield, 1994.

Altman, Rick. *Film/Genre*. London: BFI, 1999.

Anderson, Benedict. *The Spectre of Comparison: Nationalism, Southeast Asia and the World*. New York: Verso, 1998.

Andrew, Dudley. "Adaptation." In James Narremore, ed., *Film Adaptation*, 28–37. New Brunswick, NJ: Rutgers University Press, 2000.

Appadurai, Arjun. "Disjuncture and Difference in the Global Cultural Economy" (1990). In Patrick Williams and Laura Chrisman, eds., *Colonial Discourse and Postcolonial Theory*, 324–339. New York: Columbia University Press, 1994.

Armes, Roy. "The Stars." In Armes, *Film and Reality: An Historical Survey*, 132–140. Middlesex: Penguin Books, 1974.

Aufderheide, Patricia. "Made in Hong Kong: Translation and Transmutation." In Andrew Horton and Stuart Y. McDougal, eds., *Play It Again, Sam: Retakes on Remakes*, 191–199. Berkeley, CA: University of California Press, 1998.

Balfour, Brad. "Meeting with Martin and *The Departed*." *PopEntertainment*, Feb. 25, 2007. http://www.popentertainment.com/scorsese.htm (accessed May 16, 2010).

Barlow, Tani. "Colonialism's Career in Postwar China Studies." *Positions* 1, no. 1 (Spring 1993): 224–267.

———, ed. *Formations of Colonial Modernity in East Asia*. Durham, NC: Duke University Press, 1997.

Barthes, Roland. "Diderot, Brecht, Eisenstein." In Barthes, *Image-Music-Text*, edited by Stephen Heath, 69–78. New York: Hill and Wang, 1977.

———. "The Face of Garbo." In Barthes, *Mythologies*, translated by Annette Lavers, 56–57. New York: The Noonday Press, 1972.

———. "The Reality Effect." In Tzvetan Todorov, ed., *French Literary Theory Today*, 11–17. Cambridge: Cambridge University Press, 1982.

Baudrillard, Jean. "The Ecstasy of Communication." In Hal Foster, ed., *Anti-Aesthetic: Essays on Postmodern Culture*, 126–134. Port Townsend, WA: Bay Press, 1983.

Bauman, Zygmunt. *Light Modernity*. Cambridge: Polity Press, 2000.

Beijin Xiangxiang Caucus 北进想象专题小组. "Beijin xiangxiang: Xianggang hou zhiming lunshu zai dingwei" 北进想象：香港后殖民论述再定位 (Northward

Advancing Imaginary: Reassessing Postcolonial Theory in Hong Kong). In Stephen C. K. Chan 陈清侨, ed., *Wenhua xiangxiang yu yishi xingtai: dangdai Xianggang wenhua zhengzhi lunping* 文化香港与意识形态：当代香港文化政治论评 (Cultural Imaginary and Ideology: Contemporary Hong Kong Culture and Politics Review), 3–10. Hong Kong: Oxford University Press, 1997.

Benjamin, Walter. *Illuminations.* Edited by Hannah Arendt; translated by Harry Zohn. New York: Schoken Books, 1968.

———. *One-Way Street and Other Writings.* Translated by Edmund Jephcott and Kinglsey Shorter. London: New Left Books, 1979

———. "A Small History of Photography" (1931). In Benjamin, *One-Way Street and Other Writings,* 240–257.

———. "The Task of the Translator" (1923). In Benjamin, *Illuminations,* 69–82.

———. "Theses on the Philosophy of History" (1940). In Benjamin, *Illuminations,* 253–267.

———. "The Work of Art in the Age of Mechanical Reproduction" (1936). In Benjamin, *Illuminations,* 27–251.

Bennett, Tony. *Formalism and Marxism.* New York: Routledge, 1989.

Berry, Chris. "If China Can Say No, Can China Make Movies? Or, Do Movies Make China? Rethinking National Cinema and National Agency." *Boundary 2* 25, no. 3 (1998): 129–150.

———. "Poisonous Weeds or National Treasures? Chinese Left Cinema in the 1930s." *Jump Cut,* no. 34 (March 1989): 67–94.

Bhabha, Homi. *The Location of Culture.* New York: Routledge, 1994.

Birchard, Robert S. *Early Universal City.* Charleston, SC: Arcadia Publishing, 2009.

Bloch, Ernst. *The Principle of Hope.* 3 vols. Translated by Neville Plaice et al. Cambridge, MA: MIT, 1986.

———. *The Utopian Function of Art and Literature: Selected Essays by Ernst Bloch.* Translated by J. Zipes and F. Mecklenburg. Cambridge, MA: MIT Press, 1988.

Bloom, Harold. *The Anxiety of Influence: A Theory of Poetry.* New York: Oxford University Press, 1973.

Bordwell, David. "Camera Movement and Cinematic Space." In Ron Burnett, ed., *Explorations in Film Theory: Selected Essays from Ciné-tracts,* 229–246. Bloomington: Indiana University Press, 1991.

———. *Planet Hong Kong: Popular Cinema and the Art of Entertainment.* Cambridge, MA: Harvard University Press, 2000.

Braester, Yomi. *English Transcript of "The Goddess."* N.d. http://faculty.washington.edu/yomi/goddess.html (accessed Jan. 5, 2005).

———. *Witness against History: Literature, Film, and Public Discourse in Twentieth-Century China.* Stanford, CA: Stanford University Press, 2003.

Braudy, Leo. "The Double Detachment of Ernst Lubitsch." *Comparative Literature* 98, no. 5 (Dec. 1983): 1071–1084.

Brooks, Peter. *The Melodramatic Imagination: Balzac, Henry James, Melodrama, and the Mode of Excess.* Princeton, NJ: Princeton University Press, 1985.

Brower, Reuben Arthur, ed. *On Translation.* Cambridge, MA: Harvard University Press, 1959.

Carlson, Marvin. *The Haunted Stage: The Theatre as Memory Machine.* Ann Arbor: University of Michigan Press, 2001.

Cavell, Stanley. "Stella's Taste: Reading Stella Dallas." In Cavell, *Contesting Tears: The Hollywood Melodrama of the Unknown Woman*, 197–222. Chicago: University of Chicago, 1996.

Chan, Kenneth. *Remade in Hollywood: The Global Chinese Presence in Transnational Cinemas*. Hong Kong: Hong Kong University Press, 2009.

Chen Bo 陈播, ed. *Sanshi niandai Zhongguo dianying pinglun wenxuan* 三十年代中国电影评论文选 (A Selected Collection of 1930s Film Criticism). Beijing: China Film Press, 1993.

———, ed. *Zhongguo zuoyi dianying yundong* 中国左翼电影 (The Chinese Leftist Cinema Movement). Beijing: China Film Press, 1993.

Chen Guanzhong 陈冠中. "Zazhong xiucheng zhengguo" 杂种修成正果 (The Bastard Canonized). *Zhongguo shibao* 中国时报 (China Times), Jan. 2007.

Chen Huiyang 陈辉扬. "Wushi nianlai, zongcheng yimeng: Sun Yu Wu Yonggang chuangzuo licheng chutan" 五十年来，总成一梦：孙瑜吴永刚创作历程初探 (A Dream That Lasted Fifty Years: A Preliminary Exploration of Works by Sun Yu and Wu Yonggang). In Chen, *Mengying ji: Zhongguo dianying yinxiang* 梦影集：中国电影印象 (A Collection of Dreams and Shadows: Impressions on Chinese Cinema), 41–100. Taipei: Yunchen wenhua shiye gufen youxian gongsi, 1990.

Chen Mutao 陈慕陶. "*Zimei hua*": *Shihui* 姊妹花：10回 (*Sister Flowers:* Ten Chapters). Hankou: Dianying xiaoshuo she, 1934.

Chen Shibai 陈世柏. "Huisu qishi nianqian Xianggang" 回溯七十年前香港 (Remembering Hong Kong Seven Decades Ago). *Lingnan jianbao* 岭南简报 (Southern China Newsletter), 2000. http://www.puichingsf.org/SFPCAA_Essays/Esy210101HongKong.htm.

Chen, Shi-zheng. "Director's Statement." *Dark Matter Press Kit*. N.d. http://www.darkmatterthefilm.com/ (accessed Dec. 19, 2009).

Chen Wu 尘无. "*Shennü* ping yi" 神女评一 (*The Goddess*—Review One). In Chen Bo, ed., *Zhongguo zuoyi dianying yundong*, 551–552. Originally published in the "Meiri dianying" (Everyday Film) column of *Chen Bao* 晨报 (Morning Paper) (Dec. 1934).

Cheng Jihua 程季华, Li Shaobai 李少白, and Xing Zuwen 邢祖文. *Zhongguo dianying fazhan shi* 中国电影发展史 (The History of Chinese Cinema). Vol. 1. Beijing: China Film Press, 1998. Originally published in 1963.

"Chengdu Elements Stand Out in *Kung Fu Panda 2*." *China Daily*, June 1, 2011. http://www.chinadaily.com.cn/china/2011-06/01/content_12623100.htm (accessed June 2, 2011).

Cheuk, Pak-tang 卓伯棠. "The Characteristics of Sixties Youth Movies." In *Zaodong de yidai*, 73–79.

Chion, Michel. *The Voice in Cinema*. Translated by Claudia Gorbman. New York: Columbia University Press, 1999.

Chow, Rey. "Between Colonizers: Hong Kong's Postcolonial Self-Writing in the 1990s." In Chow, *Ethics after Idealism: Theory, Culture, Ethnicity, Reading*, 140–167. Bloomington: Indiana University Press, 1998.

———. "A Souvenir of Love." *Modern Chinese Literature* 7, no. 2 (Fall 1993): 59–78.

Chung, Stephanie Bo-ying. "A Chinese Movie Mogul and the Transformation of His Movie Empire—the Loke Wan Tho Family and the Cathay Organisation in

Southern China and Southeast Asia (1915–2000)." *Asia-Europe Journal* 7, nos. 3–4 (Dec. 2009): 463–478.

Comolli, Jean-Louis. "Historical Fiction: A Body Too Much." *Screen* 19, no. 2 (Summer 1978): 41–53.

Cronin, Michael. *Translation and Globalization.* New York: Routledge, 2003.

Darwent, Rev. C. E. *Shanghai: A Handbook for Travellers and Residents to the Chief Objects of Interest in and around the Foreign Settlements and Native City.* 2nd ed. Shanghai: Kelly and Walsh, 1920.

de Certeau, Michel. *The Practice of Everyday Life.* Berkeley: Univerity of California Press, 1984.

de Kock, Leon. "Interview with Gayatri Chakravorty Spivak: New Nation Writers Conference in South Africa." *Ariel: A Review of International English Literature* 23, no. 3 (July 1992): 29–48.

de Lauretis, Teresa. *Technologies of Gender: Essays on Theory, Film and Fiction.* Bloomington: Indiana University Press, 1987.

Derrida, Jacques. *Of Grammatology.* Translated by Gayatri Chakravorty Spivak. Baltimore: Johns Hopkins University Press, 1997.

Diansheng zhoukan 电声周刊 (Movie Tone Weekly). 4, no. 21 (May 24, 1935): 418; 4, no. 22 (May 24, 1935): 436.

Doane, Mary Ann. "The Voice in the Cinema: The Articulation of Body and Space" (1980). In Leo Braudy and Marshall Cohen, eds., *Film Theory and Criticism: Introductory Readings,* 363–375. New York: Oxford University Press, 1999.

Dong Xinyu 董新宇. *Kan yu beikan zhijian: Dui Zhongguo wusheng dianying de wenhua yuanjiu* 看与被看之间：对中国无声电影的文化研究 (Between Looking and Being Looked At: A Cultural Study of Chinese Silent Cinema). Beijing: Beijing Normal University Press, 2000.

Donovan, Barna William. *Asian Influence on Hollywood Action Films.* Jefferson, NC: McFarland and Company, 2008.

Durham, Carolyn A. *Double Takes: Culture and Gender in French Films and Their American Remakes.* Hanover, NH: University Press of New England, 1998.

Dyer, Richard. "Entertainment and Utopia." In Rick Altman, ed., *Genre: The Musical,* 175–189. London: Routledge and Kegan Paul, 1981.

Eisner, Lotte. *The Haunted Screen: Expressionism in the German Cinema and the Influence of Marx Reinhardt.* Berkeley: University of California Press, 1973.

Farquhar, Mary, and Chris Berry. *China on Screen: Cinema and Nation.* New York: Columbia University Press, 2006.

Fischer, Lucy. *Cinematernity: Film, Motherhood, Genre.* Princeton, NJ: Princeton University Press, 1996.

Forrest, Jennifer, and Leonard R. Koos, eds. *Dead Ringers: The Remake in Theory and Practice.* Albany, NY: State University of New York Press, 2002.

French, Howard W. "Where to Shoot an Epic about Afghanistan? China, Where Else?" *New York Times,* Dec. 31, 2006. http://www.nytimes.com/2006/12/31/movies/31fren.html?pagewanted=1&_r=1 (accessed Oct. 12, 2009).

Friedberg, Anne. *Window Shopping: Cinema and the Postmodern.* Berkeley, CA: University of California Press, 1994.

Friend, Tad. "The Remake Man: Roy Lee Brings Asia to Hollywood, and Finds Some

Enemies along the Way." *The New Yorker,* June 2, 2003. http://www.newyorker.com/archive/2003/06/02/030602fa_fact (accessed May 2, 2010).

Fu, Poshek. "Between Nationalism and Colonialism: Mainland Émigrés, Marginal Culture, and Hong Kong Cinema 1937–1941." In Fu and Desser, eds., *The Cinema of Hong Kong,* 199–226.

———. "The 1960s: Modernity, Youth Culture, and Hong Kong Cantonese Cinema." In Fu and Desser, eds., *The Cinema of Hong Kong,* 71–89.

Fu, Poshek, and David Desser, eds. *The Cinema of Hong Kong: History, Arts, Identity.* Cambridge, MA: Cambridge University Press, 2000.

Giles, Dennis. "Conditions of Pleasure in Horror Cinema." In Barry Keith Grant, ed., *Planks of Reason: Essays on the Horror Film,* 36–49. Metuchen, NJ: Scarecrow Press, 1984.

Gleber, Anke. "Women on the Screens and Streets of Modernity: In Search of the Female Flaneur." In Dudley Andrew, ed., *The Image in Dispute: Art and Cinema in the Age of Photography,* 55–86. Austin: University of Texas Press, 1997.

"A Glimpse of Film." *Diansheng zhoukan* 4. no. 2 (1935).

Gong Bohong 龚伯洪. "Lingnan feng: yang wei Zhong yong de yueju jumu" 岭南風: 洋为中用的粤剧剧目 (Southern Sinophone: The Cantonese Drama That Borrows from the West). *Jinyang wang* 金羊网, Jan. 30, 2007. http://www2.ycwb.com/big5/ycwb/2007-01/31/content_1369858.htm (accessed Oct. 20, 2010).

Gong Jianong 龚稼农. *Gong Jianong congying huiyi lu* 龚稼农从影回忆录 (Robert Kung's Memoirs of His Film Career). 3 vols. Taipei: Zhuanji wenxue chubanshe, 1980.

"*Gongfu meng:* muhou huaxu" 功夫梦：幕后花絮 (*The Karate Kid:* Behind the Scenes). June 10, 2010. http://www.mtime.com/movie/97723/behind_the_scene.html (accessed Mar. 15, 2011).

Gramsci, Antonio. *Selections from Cultural Writings.* Edited by David Forgacs Forgacs and Geoffrey Nowell-Smith; translated by William Boelhower. Cambridge, MA: MIT Press, 1985.

Grantham, Alexander. *Via Ports, from Hong Kong to Hong Kong.* Hong Kong: Hong Kong University Press, 1965.

Grosz, Elizabeth. "Judaism and Exile: The Ethics of Otherness." *New Formations,* no. 12 (Dec. 1990): 77–88.

Gu Kenfu 顾肯夫. "Fakan ci" 发刊词 (Mission Statement). *Dianying zazhi* 电影杂志 (Movies Magazine), 1 (May 1924): *jia* 甲4.

"Guan Meiguo yingxi ji" 观美国影戏记 (Watching American Shadow Plays). *Youxi bao* 游戏报 (The Amusement Paper), no. 74 (Sept. 1897).

Guiqu Shanzhuang 归去山庄. "Wo de yeye Maxu Weibang (4): Yeye yu *Yeban gesheng*" 我的爷爷马徐维邦（四）爷爷与《夜半歌声》(My Grandfather Maxu Weibang [4]: Maxu Weibang and *Song at Midnight*). *Guiqu Shanzhuang's Blog,* Dec. 23, 2009. http://blog.sina.com.cn/s/blog_61baad970100gyxn.html (accessed Feb. 10, 2011).

Gunning, Tom. "An Aesthetic of Astonishment: Early Film and the (In)Credulous Spectator." *Art and Text,* no. 34 (Spring 1989): 31–44.

"Guochan yingpian Nanyang lizu nan: Dianying shichang wei Meiguo bazhan, Guoyu yingpian wei Yueyu pian suo yadao" 国产影片南洋立足难：电影市场为美国霸占，国语影片为粤语片所压倒 (China-made Films Experiencing Setback in

Southeast Asia: Film Market Monopolized by Hollywood, Mandarin Films Overwhelmed by Cantonese Films). *Diansheng zhoukan* 电声周刊 5, no. 21 (1936): 509.

Hajari, Nisid. "Erasing the Boundaries." *Newsweek*, July–Sept. 2001: 79.

Hall, Mordaunt. "Review of *The Phantom of the Opera*." *New York Times*, Sept. 7, 1925: 15.

Han Cun 寒村. "*Zimeihua:* Ping er" 姊妹花：评二 (*Sister Flowers:* Review Two). In Chen Bo, ed., *Sanshi niandai Zhongguo dianying pinglun wenxuan*, 36. Originally published in *Chen bao* 晨报 (Morning Newspaper), Feb. 24, 1934.

Han Yanli 韩燕丽. "Cong guofang pian de zhizuo kan zaoqi Yueyu dianying he Zhongguo dalu de guanxi" 从国防片的制作看早期粤语电影和中国大陆的关系 (A Study of Early Cantonese Cinema's Relationship with Mainland China through the Lens of National Defense Cinema). In Wong Ainling 黄爱玲, ed., *Yuegang dianying yinyuan* 粤港电影因缘 (The Hong Kong–Guangdong Film Connection), 56–67. Hong Kong: Hong Kong Film Archive, 2005.

Hansen, Miriam. "Fallen Women, Rising Stars, New Horizons: Shanghai Silent Film and Vernacular Modernism." *Film Quarterly* 54, no. 1 (Fall 2000): 10–22.

Hao, Dazheng. "Chinese Visual Representation: Painting and Cinema." In Linda Ehrlich and David Desser, eds., *Cinematic Landscapes: Observations on the Visual Arts and Cinema of China and Japan*, 45–62. Austin: University of Texas Press, 1994.

Harris, Kristine. "Silent Speech: Envisioning the Nation in Early Shanghai Cinema." Ph.D. dissertation, Columbia University, 1997.

Harvey, James. *Romantic Comedy in Hollywood, from Lubitsch to Sturges*. New York: Da Capo Press, 1998.

He Ke'ren 何可人. *Xu zimeihua* 续姊妹花 (Sister Flowers: A Sequel). Shanghai: Datong tushu gongsi, 1934.

Herbert, Daniel. "Remaking Transnational Hollywood." *Spectator* 27, no. 1 (2007): 94–100.

———. "Trading Spaces: Transnational Dislocations in *Insomnia/Insomnia* and *Ju-on/The Grudge*." In Scott A. Lukas and John Marmysz, eds., *Fear, Cultural Anxiety, and Transformation: Horror, Science Fiction, and Fantasy Films Remade*, 143–164. Lanham, MD: Lexington Books, 2009.

Higson, Andrew. "The Concept of National Cinema." *Screen* 30, no. 4 (Autumn 1989): 36–47.

Hollander, John. "Versions, Interpretations, Performances." In Brower, ed., *On Translation*, 205–231.

Hong Kong Filmography, vol. 1, *1913–1941*. Hong Kong: Urban Council, 1997.

Horton, Andrew, and Stuart Y. McDougal, eds. *Play It Again, Sam: Retakes on Remakes*. Berkeley: University of California Press, 1998.

Hu Die 胡蝶. *Hu Die huiyilu* 胡蝶回忆录 (Memoirs of Hu Die). Edited by Liu Huiqin 刘慧琴. Beijing: Wenhua yishu chubanshe, 1988.

Hu, Jubin. *Projecting a Nation: Chinese National Cinema before 1949*. Hong Kong: Hong Kong University Press, 2003.

Hu Jubin 胡菊彬 and Li Suyuan 郦苏元. *Zhongguo wusheng dianying shi* 中国无声电影史 (The History of Chinese Silent Cinema) . Beijing: China Film Press, 1996.

Huang Sumin 黄素民 and Zhang Zuokang 张作康, eds. *Yijiusanba zhi Zhongguo* *dianying: Minguo nianqi nian dianying nianjian 1938*之中国电影：民国廿七年电影年鉴 (Chinese Cinema in 1938). Hong Kong: Lingxing Magazine Press, 1939.

Huang Zhun黄准. "Tantan *Wutai jiemei* de yinyue chuangzuo" 谈谈舞台姐妹的音乐创作 (How I Created the Music for *Stage Sisters*). In *"Wutai jiemei": Cong tigang dao yingpian* 舞台姐妹：从提纲到影片 (*Stage Sisters:* From an Outline to a Film), 285–291. Shanghai: Shanghai wenyi chubanshe, 1982.

Hunt, Leon. "Asiaphilia, Asianization and the Gatekeeper Auteur: Quentin Tarantino and Luc Besson." In Hunt and Leung, eds., *East Asian Cinemas*, 220–236.

Hunt, Leon, and Leung Wing-Fai, eds. *East Asian Cinemas: Exploring Transnational Connections*. London: I. B. Tauris, 2008.

Iampolski, Mikhail. *The Memory of Tiresias: Intertextuality and Film.* Berkeley: University of California Press, 1998.

"Interview with Quentin Tarantino." *Screenwriter's Monthly* 2004. http://www.screenwritersutopia.com/SM/tarantino.html (accessed Feb. 15, 2008).

Jameson, Fredric. "Class and Allegory in Contemporary Mass Culture: *Dog Day Afternoon* as a Political Film" (1977). In Jameson, *Signatures of the Visible*, 35–54.

———. "Globalization and Hybridization." In Nataša Ďurovičová and Kathleen Newman, eds., *World Cinemas, Transnational Perspectives,* 315–325. New York: Routledge, 2010.

———. *The Political Unconscious: Narrative as a Socially Symbolic Act.* Ithaca, NY: Cornell University Press, 1981.

———. "The Politics of Utopia." *New Left Review* 25 (Jan.–Feb. 2004): 35–54.

———. "Reification and Utopia in Mass Culture" (1979). In Jameson, *Signatures of the Visible,* 9–34.

———. *Signatures of the Visible.* New York: Routledge, 1990.

———. "Third World Literature in the Era of Multinational Capitalism." *Social Text,* no. 15 (Fall 1986): 65–88.

Ju Jianfu 鞠健夫. "*Bawang bieji* de miwen" 霸王别姬的秘闻 (Secretes of *Farewell My Concubine*). In Ju, *Yule meiyou quan* 娱乐没有圈 (Another Eye on Entertainment), 171–173. Beijing: Dongfang chubanshe, 2008.

Kaplan, E. Ann. "The Case of the Missing Mother: Maternal Issues in Vidor's *Stella Dallas*." *Heresies* 4, no. 4 (1983): 81–85.

Keathley, Christian. "The Cinephiliac Moment." *Framework: The Journal of Cinema and Media* 42 (Summer 2000).

Klein, Christina. "Martial Arts and the Globalization of US and Asian Film Industries." *Comparative American Studies* 2, no. 3 (2004): 360–384.

Kraus, Richard Curt. *Pianos and Politics in China: Middle-Class Ambitions and the Struggle over Western Music.* New York: Oxford University Press, 1989.

"*Kung Fu Panda* Breaks Chinese Box Office Records." *Telegraph,* July 8, 2008. http://www.telegraph.co.uk/news/worldnews/asia/china/2268139/Kung-Fu-Panda-breaks-Chinese-box-office-records.html (accessed May 8, 2009).

Lacan, Jacques. *The Four Fundamental Concepts of Psychoanalysis.* Edited by J. A. Miller; translated by Alan Sheridan. New York: W. W. Norton, 1981.

Lai Bojiang 赖伯疆. *Xue Juexian yiyuan chunqiu* 薛觉先艺苑春秋 (The Art of Xue Juexian). Shanghai: Shanghai wenyi chubanshe, 1993.

Landreth, Jonathan. "*Kung Fu Panda 2* Returns to Its Chinese Home." *The*

Hollywood Reporter, May 25, 2011. http://www.hollywoodreporter.com/news/kung-fu-panda-2-returns-192452 (accessed June 1, 2011).

Lau, Siu-kai. *Decolonization without Independence: The Unfinished Political Reforms of the Hong Kong Government*. Hong Kong: Chinese University of Hong Kong, 1987.

Law Kar. "Xinxing yu jingguan—liushi niandai Yueyu pian yipie" 新星与景观—六十年代粤语片一瞥 (Stars in a Landscape: A Glance at Cantonese Movies of the Sixties). In *Zaodong de yidai,* 48–50.

Law, Kar, and Frank Bren. *Hong Kong Cinema: A Cross-Cultural View.* Lanham, MD: Scarecrow Press, 2004.

Lee Cheuk-to李焯桃. "Zuo Ji liushi niandai zuopin de chubu yanjiu" 左几六十年代作品的初步研究 (The Films of Zuo Ji in the 1960s—a Preliminary Study)." In *Yueyu dianying huigu 1960–69* 粤语电影回顾 (Cantonese Cinema Retrospective 1960–69), 56–71. Hong Kong: Hong Kong Urban Council, 1982.

Lee, Leo Ou-fan. *Shanghai Modern: The Flowering of a New Urban Culture in China, 1930–1945.* Cambridge, MA: Harvard University Press, 1999.

Lee, Paul S. N. "The Absorption and Indigenization of Foreign Media Cultures." In *Bashi niandai Xianggang dianying: Yu xifang dianying bijiao yanjiu* 八十年代香港电影：与西方电影比较研究 (Hong Kong Cinema in the Eighties: A Comparative Study with Western Cinema), 80–86. Hong Kong: The Urban Council, 1991.

Lee Pui-tak 李培德. "Jin yu fanjin—1930 niandai chuyu Hu Gang jiafeng de Yueyu dianying" 禁与反 禁：1930年代处于沪港夹缝的粤语电影 (To Ban or Counter Ban: Cantonese Cinema Caught between Shanghai and Hong Kong in the 1930s). In Ain-ling Wong, ed., *Yuegang dianying yinyuan* 粤港电影因缘 (The Hong Kong–Guangdong Film Connection), 24–41. Hong Kong: Hong Kong Film Archive, 2005.

Leitch, Thomas M. "Twice-Told Tales: Disavowal and the Rhetoric of the Remake." In Jennifer Forrest et al., eds., *Dead Ringers: The Remake in Theory and Practice,* 37–62. Albany: State University of New York, 2002.

Leyda, Jay. *Dianying: An Account of Films and the Film Audience in China.* Cambridge: MIT Press, 1972.

Li Changjian 李昌鑑. *Zimei hua: Boyin juben* 姊妹花：播音剧本 (Sister Flowers: A Radio Play). Shanghai: Yuanchang guangbo diantai, 1934.

Li Suyuan 郦苏元. "Sanshi niandai Zhongguo dianying yundong mingcheng chuyi" 30年代中国电影运动名称刍议 (A Preliminary Study of the Naming of the 1930s Chinese Film Movement). *Dangdai dianying* 当代电影 (Contemporary Cinema), 118, no. 10 (Jan. 2004): 39–43.

Liang Shiqiu. *Tan Wen Yiduo* 谈闻一多 (On Wen Yiduo). Taipei: Zhuanji wenxue chubanshe, 1967.

Lim, Bliss Cua. "Generic Ghosts: Remaking the New 'Asian Horror Film.'" In Gina Marchetti and Tam See Kam, eds., *Hong Kong Film, Hollywood and the New Global Cinema: No Film Is an Island,* 109–125. New York: Routledge, 2007.

———. "Spectral Times: The Ghost Film as Historical Allegory." *Positions* 9, no. 2 (Fall 2001): 287–329.

Lingxing er zhounian jinian zhuankan 伶星二周年纪念专刊 (Special Issue on the Two-Year Anniversary of Ling Sing—a Film Magazine). Guangzhou: Ling Sing zazhishe, 1933.

Liu Feng 流风. "Fangwen: Guangdong Mei Lanfang" 访问广东梅兰芳 (Interview with Mei Lanfang from Guangdong). In *Lingxing er zhounian jinian zhuankan*, 12–15.

Liu Xiaozhuo 刘小卓. "Zhuanfang Chen Shi-zheng: *Gewu qingchun* bushi shanzhai Meiguo ban 专访陈士争：歌舞青春不是山寨美国版 (Interview with Shi-zheng Chen: *Disney High School Musical: China* Is Not a Cheap Copycat of the American Version). *China Daily*, Aug. 5, 2010. http://www.chinadaily.com.cn/hqyl/2010-08/05/content_11105126.htm (accessed May 25, 2011).

Liyuan Huangsou 梨园黄叟. "Xue Juexian dashiji: *Baijin long* nan zhujiao xiaoshi" 薛觉先大事记:白金龙男主角小史 (Xue Juexian's Landmarks: A Short Biography of the Male Lead in *Golden Dragon*). In *Zhen "Baijin long" zhuanlan: Xinhua yousheng daxiyuan fukan* 真白金龙专栏：新华有声大戏院副刊 (Special Issue on the Real-Life *Golden Dragon:* Brochure Issued by Xinhua Sound Picture Theater), included in *Lingxing er zhounian jinian zhuankan*, 24.

Lo, Kwai-cheung. *Chinese Face/off: The Transnational Popular Culture of Hong Kong*. Urbana: University of Illinois Press, 2005.

"Loke Wan Tho Collection." National Archives of Singapore. N.d.

Lu Mengshu 卢梦殊. "Geming yu dianying" 革命与电影 (Revolution and Cinema). *Yin xing* 银星 (The Movie Guide), no. 9 (1927): 34–42.

———. "Xin yingxiong zhuyi" 新英雄主义 (Neoheroism). *Yin xing* 银星 (The Movie Guide), 1926.

Lu, Sheldon, ed. *Transnational Chinese Cinemas: Identity, Nationhood, Gender*. Honolulu: University of Hawai'i Press, 2007.

Lu, Sheldon, and Emilie Yueh-yu Yeh, eds. *Chinese-Language Film: Historiography, Poetics, Politics*. Honolulu: University of Hawai'i Press, 2005.

Lu Xun 鲁迅. "Yunming" 运命 (Fate). In Liu Siping 刘思平 and Xing Zuwen 邢祖文, eds., *Lu Xun yu diangying* 鲁迅与电影 (Lu Xun and Cinema), 29–31. Beijing: China Film Press, 1981. Originally published in "Ziyou tan" (Freedom Forum), supplement to *Shen bao* 申报, Feb. 27, 1934.

Luo Li 罗丽. "Yiling yixing yu yingju hudong—luetan Xue Juexian de dianying shijian huodong" 亦伶亦星与影剧互动—略谈薛觉先的电影实践活动 (Shuttling between Film and Opera: Notes on Xue Juexian's Film Activities). *Nanguo hongdou* 南国红豆 (Red Bean of Southern China), no. 4 (2009): 41–44.

———. "Yueju yanjiu yu Yueju yanjiu shi chuyi (shang)" 粤剧研究与粤剧研究史刍议(上) (Preliminary Thoughts on Cantonese Opera Study and History of Cantonese Opera Study). *Nanguo hongdou* 南国红豆 (Red Bean of Southern China), no. 1 (2009): 27–30.

Luo Yunwen 罗韵文. "Youlun *Zimeihua* ji jinhou dianying wenhua zhi lu" 又论姊妹花及今后电影文化之路 (Revisiting *Sister Flowers* and the Road of Film Culture in the Future). In Chen Bo, ed., *Zhongguo zuoyi dianying yundong*, 476–478. Originally printed in the "Torch" column in *Da wanbao* 大晚报 (China Evening News), Mar. 24, 1934.

Ma, Eric Kit-wai. *Culture, Politics, and Television in Hong Kong*. New York: Routledge, 1999.

Ma, Ning. "The Textual and Critical Difference of Being Radical: Reconstructing Chinese Leftist Films of the 1930s." *Wide Angle* 11, no. 2 (1989): 22–31.

Ma Shizeng马师曾. *Qianli zhuangyou ji* 千里壮游记 (Writings for My Long Journey to the United States). Hong Kong: Dongya yinwu youxian gongsi, 1931.

———. "Wo daile yiqiang biange Yueju de recheng huilai" 我带了一腔变革粤剧的热诚回来 (I Came Back with Great Expectations to Reform Cantonese Opera). In *Lingxing er zhounian jinian zhuankan,* 171–173.

———. "Wo de xinju tan" 我的新剧观 (My Views on New Opera). In Ma, *Qianli zhuangyou ji,* n.p.

———. "Wo you mei Yanju zhi zongzhi" 我游美演剧之宗旨 (The Goal of My Performance Tour in America). In Ma, *Qianli zhuangyou ji,* n.p.

———. "Zhongguo dianying de weiji" 中国电影的危机 (The Crisis of Chinese Cinema). *Ling xing* 伶星, May 20, 1935: n.p.

MacFarquhar, Roderick. *The Hundred Flowers Campaign and the Chinese Intellectuals.* New York: Praeger, 1960.

Macherey, Pierre. *A Theory of Literary Production.* Translated by Geoffrey Wall. London: Routledge and Keegan Paul, 1978.

Mai Xiaoxia 麦啸霞. "Guangdong xiju shilue" 广东戏剧史略 (A Concise History of Cantonese Opera)" (1940). *Guangdong wenwu* 广东文物 (Cantonese Cultural History), 2 (1941): 791–835.

———. "Wanjiu Zhongguo xiju zhi weiwang" 挽救中国戏剧之危亡 (How to Revive Chinese Opera). In *Lingxing er zhounian jinian zhuankan,* 183–198.

Marchetti, Gina. "Two Stage Sisters: The Blossoming of a Revolutionary Aesthetic." In Sheldon Lu, ed., *Transnational Chinese Cinemas: Identity, Nationhood, Gender,* 59–80.

Massey, Doreen. "Power-Geometry and a Progressive Sense of Place." In B. Curtis, T. Putnam, G. Robertson, L. Tickner, and J. Bird, eds., *Mapping the Futures: Local Cultures, Global Change,* 59–69. London: Routledge, 1993.

Mazdon, Lucy. *Encore Hollywood: Remaking French Cinema.* London: BFI, 2000.

McCarthy, Todd. "Two Stage Sisters." *Variety,* April 1981: 23, 24.

McGrath, Jason. *Postsocialist Modernity: Chinese Cinema, Literature, and Criticism in the Market Age.* Stanford, CA: Stanford University Press, 2008.

Mei Jianchi 眉间尺. "Dang langman bei canku dianfu" 当浪漫被残酷颠覆 (When Romanticism Is Subverted by Cruelty). *Mtime,* Dec. 25, 2006. http://i.mtime.com/101348/blog/297794/ (accessed May 16, 2010).

"Meiguo zhizao de Zhongguo donghuapian Haolaiwu zhong de Zhongguo yuansu" 美国制造的中国动画片 好莱坞中的中国元素 (A Chinese Animation Film Made by the United States: Chinese Elements in Hollywood). *Guoji caijing shibao* 国际财经时报, June 2, 2011. http://www.ibtimes.com.cn/articles/20110602/zhongguoyuansu-huamulan-xiongmao2.htm (accessed June 2, 2011).

Miao Jieke 缪捷克. "Zhang Ying Luo Yanqing de tianmi jingtou: Yinyue shi yanfu qitian" 张瑛罗艳卿的甜蜜镜头：音乐师艳福齐天 (The Sweet Double Shot of Zhang Ying and Luo Yanqing: Feast for the Musicians' Eyes). "*Xuangong yanshi*" *Programme* (held in Hong Kong Film Archive), n.d.: n.p.

Mignolo, Walter. *Local Histories/Global Designs: Coloniality, Subaltern Knowledges, and Border Thinking.* Princeton, NJ: Princeton University Press, 2000.

Miller, Toby, et al. *Global Hollywood 2.* London: BFI, 2005.

Mingxing tekan 明星特刊 (Star Special Issue), Oct. 1925.

Mingxing yuekan 明星月刊 (The Star Monthly), 2, no. 4 (Nov. 1934): 20.

Nanyue 南粤 (South China Film Magazine), 6 (May 1938): n.p.

Pang, Lai Kwan. *Building a New China in Cinema: The Chinese Left-Wing Cinema Movement, 1932–1937.* Lanham, MD: Rowman and Littlefield Publishers, 2002.

Peirce, Charles Sanders. *Division of Signs* (1897). Vol. 2 of Peirce, *The Collected Papers of Charles Sanders Peirce,* edited by C. Hartshorne and P. Weiss, 134–272. Bristol: Thoemmes Press, 1998.

Petro, Patrice. *Joyless Street: Women and Melodramatic Representation in Weimar Germany 1913–1933.* Princeton, NJ: Princeton University Press, 1989.

Pickowicz, Paul. "The Theme of Spiritual Pollution in Chinese Films of the 1930s." *Modern China* 17, no. 1 (1991): 38–75.

Pratt, Mary L. *Imperial Eyes: Travel Writing and Transculturation.* New York: Routledge, 1992.

Qin Xiqing 秦喜清. *Oumei dianying yu Zhongguo zaoqi dianying: 1920–1930* 欧美电影与中国早期电影: 1920–1930 (Euro-American Cinema and Early Chinese Cinema: 1920–1930). Beijing: China Film Press, 2008.

Rao Shuguang 饶曙光 and Shao Qi 邵奇. "Xin Zhongguo dianying de diyige yundong: Qingchu haolaiwu dianying" 新中国电影的第一个运动：清除好莱坞电影 (Cleansing Hollywood Cinema: The First Campaign in New China). *Dianying yishu* 电影艺术 (Contemporary Cinema), no. 5, 2006: 119–126.

Rayns, Tony, and Scott Meek. "Two Stage Sisters." *Los Angeles International Film Exposition,* April 6, 1981.

Roth, Marty. "Twice Two: *The Fly* and *Invasion of the Body Snatchers.*" *Discourse* 22, no. 1 (Winter 2000): 103–116.

Rothman, William. "*The Goddess:* Reflections on Melodrama East and West." In Wimal Dissanayake, ed., *Melodrama and Asian Cinema,* 59–72. Cambridge: Cambridge Univeristy Press, 1993.

Ruiz, Raúl. *Poetics of Cinema.* Translated by Brian Holmes. Paris: Editions Dis Voir, 1995.

Rutsky, R. L. "The Mediation of Technology and Gender: Metropolis, Nazism, and Modernism." *New German Critique,* no. 60 (Fall 1993): 3–32.

Sang Hu 桑弧. "Hanxu" 含蓄 (The Subtle Art). *Guanghua Daily* 光华日报 (May 1945): n.p.

Sarris, Andrew. "Scorsese Takes Boston, and Electrifies with Departed." *New York Observer,* Oct. 2, 2006. http://observer.com/2006/10/02/scorsese-takes-boston-and-electrifies-with-departed/ (accessed May 16, 2010).

Schliesser, John Templin. "Toward a Cinema of Exhaustion: Cross-Cultural Influence, Imitation, and Intertextuality in Film." Ph.D. dissertation, University of California, Berkeley, 1995.

Schneider, Howard. "Lessons from 'The Karate Kid'—Japan Out, America Down, China on the Rise." *Washington Post,* June 27, 2010. http://www.washingtonpost.com/wp-dyn/content/article/2010/06/25/AR2010062502159.html (accessed July 10, 2010).

Shen, Ada. "Tom Buys 35% of Huayi Brothers." *Danwei, Chinese Media, Advertising, and Urban Life,* Dec. 12, 2004. http://www.danwei.org/media_business/tom_buys_35_of_huayi_brothers.php (accessed Aug. 10, 2010).

Shen, Vivian. *The Origins of Left-Wing Cinema in China, 1932–1937.* New York: Routledge, 2005.

"Shida mingpian xuanju yeyi gongbu" 十大名片选举业已公布 (Announcing the

Selected Ten Top Films). *Dianying quan* 电影圈 (Screen Voice Semimonthly), no. 45 (May 1939): n.p.

Shih, Shu-mei. *The Lure of the Modern: Writing Modernism in Semicolonial China, 1917-1937*. Berkeley: University California Press, 2001.

———. *Visuality and Identity: Sinophone Articulations across the Pacific.* Berkeley: University of California Press, 2007.

Sisci, Francesco. "From Hollywood to Chollywood." *Asia Times,* April 1, 2010. http://www.atimes.com/atimes/China/LD01Ad01.html (accessed June 10, 2010).

Smith, Gary, ed. *Benjamin: Philosophy, Aesthetics, History.* Chicago: University of Chicago Press, 1989.

Spadoni, Robert. *Uncanny Bodies: The Coming of Sound Film and the Origins of the Horror Genre.* Berkeley: University of California Press, 2007.

Spivak, Gayatri. "Can the Subaltern Speak?" In Lawrence Grossberg and Cary Nelson, eds., *Marxism and the Interpretation of Culture,* 271–316. Urbana: University of Illinois Press, 1988.

Stephenson, Shelly. "The Occupied Screen: Star, Fan, and Nation in Shanghai Cinema, 1937–1945." Ph.D. dissertation, University of Chicago, 2000.

Stokes, Lisa Odham, and Michael Hoover. *City on Fire: Hong Kong Cinema.* London: Verso, 1999.

Sun, Yat-sen. *Sanmin zhuyi: The Three Principles of the People*. Trans. Frank W. Price. Shanghai: Commercial Press, 1928.

Tang Na 唐纳. "Muqian Zhongguo dianying de jige qingxiang" 目前中国电影的几个倾向 (Several Tendencies in Current Chinese Cinema). *Shidai dianying* 时代电影 (Contemporary Film), no. 6 (1934).

Tang Yu 唐瑜. *Erliutang jishi* 二流堂纪事 (Recollecting Life in the Vagabonds' Residence). Beijing: Sanlian shudian, 2005.

Teo, Stephen. *Hong Kong Cinema: The Extra Dimensions.* London: BFI, 1997.

Thompson, John O. "Screen Acting and the Commutation Test." *Screen* 19, no. 2 (Summer 1978): 55–69.

Topel, Fred. "Tarantino Talks *Kill Bill Vol. 2.*" In Paul A. Woods, ed., *Quentin Tarantino: The Film Geek Files.* London: Plexus, 2005.

"Tou Hou-fun: Dianmao de Yueyu zhizuo" 窦汉勋： 电懋的粤语制作 (Making Cantonese Films at Motion Pictures and General Investment: Tou Hon-fun Remembers). In Ain-ling Wong, ed., *Guotai gushi,* 280–289.

Venuti, Lawrence. *The Translator's Invisibility: A History of Translation.* New York: Routledge, 1995.

Verevis, Constantine. *Film Remakes.* New York: Palgrave Macmillan, 2005.

Wang, Ting. "Hollywood's Pre-WTO Crusade in China." *Jump Cut,* vol. 49 (Spring 2007).

Wang, Yiman. "Alter-centering Chinese Cinema: The Diasporic Formation." In Yingjin Zhang, ed., *A Companion to Chinese Cinema,* 535–551. Wiley-Blackwell, 2012,

———. "Here, Again, Comes the Bride to Be: Refiguring the Gender and Remaking the Horror." *Language and Literature* (special edition: *Studies of Asian and Asian American Literature*), 28 (2003): 43–65.

Wang Yunman 王云缦. "Supu yunhan de *Shennü*" 素朴蕴含的神女 (The Simple yet Subtle *Goddess*). In Wu Yonggang, *Wo de tansuo he zhuiqiu,* 188–192.

Wei Nan 尉南. "Dianying de wenyi hua" 电影的文艺化 (The Artistic Turn of Cinema). In Lu Mengshu 卢梦殊, ed., *Dianying yu wenyi* 电影与文艺 (Cinema and Literature-Art), 1–15. Shanghai: Young Companion Press.

Wei Yu 魏育. "Kuyan chao—guanyu *Shennü* yu *Taoli jie*" 苦言抄—关于神女与桃李劫 (A Few Critical Words—on *The Goddess* and *The Plunder of Peach and Plum*). In Chen Bo, ed., *Zhongguo zuoyi dianying yundong,* 554–555. Originally published in *Wenyi dianying* (Literature, Art, and Film), no. 1 (1934).

Weinberg, Herman G. *The Lubitsch Touch: A Critical Study.* New York: Dutton, 1968.

Willemen, Paul. "Bangalore." Feb. 2004. http://oldcscs.freecrow.com/html/BANGALORE1.htm (accessed Feb. 12, 2010).

———. *Looks and Frictions: Essays in Cultural Studies and Film Theory.* London: BFI, 1994.

———. "The National Revisited." In Valentina Vitali, Paul Willemen, and Paul Vitali, eds., *Theorising National Cinema,* 29–43. London: BFI, 2006.

Williams, Linda. "'Something Else besides a Mother': Stella Dallas and the Maternal Melodrama" (1984). In E. Ann Kaplan, ed., *Feminism and Film,* 479–504. Oxford: Oxford University Press, 2000.

———. "When the Woman Looks." In Mary Ann Doane, Patricia Mellencamp, and Linda Williams, eds., *Re-vision: Essays in Feminist Film Criticism,* 83–99. Los Angeles: University Publications of America, 1984.

Williams, Raymond. *Marxism and Literature.* Oxford: Oxford University Press, 1977.

Wilson, Rob, and Wimal Dissanayake, "Introduction." In Wilson and Dissanayake, eds., *Global/Local: Cultural Production and the Transnational Imaginary,* 1–18. Durham, NC: Duke University Press, 1996.

Wong, Ain-ling 黄爱玲, ed. *Guotai gushi* 国泰故事 (The Cathay Story). Hong Kong: Hong Kong Film Archive, 2002.

———, ed. *The Shaw Screen: A Preliminary Study.* Hong Kong: Hong Kong Film Archive, 2003.

Wong Wang-chi 王宏志. *Fouxiang Xianggang: lishi, wenhua, weilai* 否想香港: 历史, 文化, 未来 (Hong Kong Unimagined: History, Culture, and the Future). Taipei: Rye Field Publishing Group, 1997.

Wu Tingzhang 吴庭璋. *Yueju dashi Xue Juexian* 粤剧大师薛觉先 (Xue Juexian—the Cantonese Opera Master). Guangdong: Guangdong renmin chubanshe, 2006.

Wu Yonggang. "Lun dianying bujing" 论电影布景 (On Film Setting). In Wu Yonggang, *Wo de tansuo he zhuiqiu,* 173.

———. "*Shennü* he wo" 神女和我 (*The Goddess* and I). In Wu Yonggang, *Wo de tansuo he zhuiqiu,* 130. Originally published in *Dianying wenhua* 电影文化 (Film Culture), no. 1 (1980).

———. "*Shennü* wancheng zhihou" 神女完成之后 (After Finishing *The Goddess*) (1934). In Wu Yonggang, *Wo de tansuo he zhuiqiu,* 134.

———. *Wo de tansuo he zhuiqiu* 我的探索和追求 (My Explorations and Pursuits). Beijing: China Film Press, 1986.

Xavier, Ismail. "Historical Allegory." In Toby Miller and Robert Stam, eds., *A Companion to Film Theory,* 333–362. Oxford: Blackwell Publishers, 1999.

Xia Yan 夏衍. *Lanxun jiumeng lu* 懒寻旧梦录 (Recollecting the Past in Leisure). Beijing: Sanlian shudian, 1985.

Xiang Lin 向霖. "Dianying de chulu: Yifeng gongkai xin" 电影的出路: 一封公开信

(The Future of Cinema: An Open Letter). *Dianying shibao* 电影时报 (Film Times), no. 80 (Aug. 1932): n.p.

"Xianggang chuanshuo: Hu Die jiang sui fu lai le" 香港传说：胡蝶将随夫来叻 (Rumor Says in Hong Kong: Hu Die to Come to Singapore with Husband). *Dianying quan* 电影圈 (Screen Voice), Sept. 1939: n.p.

Xianggang zaoqi dianying guiji 1896–1950 香港早期电影轨迹 (The Early Days of Hong Kong Cinema, 1896–1950). Hong Kong: The Urban Council, 1995.

Xiao Zhiwei. "Sanshi niandai 'zuoyi dianying' de shenhua" (The Myth of 1930s "Leftist Cinema"). *Ershiyi shiji shuangyuekan*二十一世纪双月刊 (Twenty-first Century Bimonthly), no. 103 (Oct. 2007): 42–52.

———. "Wu Yonggang and the Ambivalence in the Chinese Experience of Modernity: A Study of His Three Films of the Mid-1930s." *Asian Cinema* 9, no. 2 (1998): 3–15.

Xie Jin 谢晋 et al. "*Wutai jiemei*: Dianying wenxue juben" 舞台姐妹：电影文学剧本 (*Stage Sisters:* A Literary Script). In "*Wutai jiemei*": *Cong tigang dao yingpian* 舞台姐妹：从提纲到影片 (*Stage Sisters:* From an Outline to a Film), 65–148. Shanghai: Shanghai wenyi chubanshe, 1982.

Xin Xie 莘薤. "Ping *Yeban gesheng xuji*" 评夜半歌声续集 (Thoughts on *Song at Midnight II*) (1941). In Zhao Shihui 赵士荟, *Yingzi fuchen: Liu Qiong de yingju shengya* 影自浮沉：刘琼的影剧生涯 (A Life of Acting: Liu Qiong's Cinema and Theater Work), 148–149. Shanghai: Xuelin chubanshe, 2002.

"*Xin zimei hua*, huahua xuxu" 新姊妹花花花絮絮 (Anecdotes during the Shooting of *The Happy Reunion*). Hong Kong Film Archive clip file, n.d.

Xu, Gary G. "Remaking East Asia, Outsourcing Hollywood." In Leon Hunt and Leung Wing-Fai, eds., *East Asian Cinemas*, 191–202.

"Xu Hao laigang zhengchi yueyupian teji" 许浩来港整饬粤语片特辑 (A Special Column on Xu Hao's Investigation and Regulation of Cantonese Films in Hong Kong). In Huang Sumin and Zhang Zuokang, eds., *Yijiusanba zhi Zhongguo dianying: minguo nianqi nian dianying nianjian 1938*, 22–25.

Xu Xu 徐徐. "Dui *Zimei hua* maizuo dapo jilu de ganxiang 对姊妹花卖座打破纪录的感想 (Thoughts on the Box-Office Record of *Sister Flowers*)." *Dianying xiju* 电影戏剧 (Film Drama), Aug. 1934: 12.

Xuan Ren 宣人. "Yinian lai de Zhongguo dianying jie" 一年来的中国电影界 (China's Film Scene within the Last Year). In Huang Sumin and Zhang Zuokang, eds., *Yijiusanba zhi Zhongguo dianying: Minguo nianqi nian dianying nianjian 1938*, 7–8.

"*Xuangong yanshi* yu liangfei" 璇宫艳史与两肥 (*My Kingdom for a Husband* and the Two Fatty Comedians). *Yin deng* 银灯 (Spotlight), no. 103 (n.d.): 38–39.

Xue Juexian 薛觉先. "Nanyou zhiqu" 南游旨趣 (My Mission of the Southeast Asian Tour). *Nanguo hongdou* 南国红豆 (Red Bean of Southern China), no. 4 (2009): 36. Originally published in Mai Xiaoxia 麦啸霞 and Lu Juefei 卢觉非, eds., *Juexian ji* 觉先集 (Collected Writings by Xue Juexian). Hong Kong: Zhongguo Juexian lüxing jutuan, 1930.

Ya Fu 亚夫. "*Zimei hua:* ping yi" 姊妹花：评一 (*Sister Flowers:* Review One). In Chen Bo, ed., *Sanshi niandai Zhongguo dianying pinglun wenxuan*,. 34–35. Originally published in *Chen bao* 晨报 (Morning Newspaper), Feb. 24, 1934.

Yang Yuanying 杨远婴 and Ding Ning 丁宁. "Xianggang dianying de beijin xiangxiang: Guankan 2007 niandu gangchan hepai pian" 香港电影的北进想象：观看2007年度港产合拍片 (The Northward Advance Imaginary of Hong Kong

Cinema: On Sino-Hong Kong Coproductions in 2007). *Dangdai dianying* 当代电影 (Contemporary Cinema), 3 (2008): 48–53.

Ye, Fuqiang. "The Cantonese Cinema in the 1960s Hong Kong and Social Change." In *Liushi niandai Yueyu dianying hui* gu 六十年代粤语电影回顾 (Cantonese Cinema Retrospective: 1960–1969). Hong Kong: The Urban Council, 1982.

Yin xing 银星 (The Movie Guide), no. 10 (July 1927).

Ying Hong 尹鸿 and He Mei 何美. "Gongzao hou hepai shidai de Huayu dianying: Zhongguo neidi yu Xianggang dianying de sanshi nian hezuo/hepai licheng" 共造后合拍时代的华语电影：中国内地与香港电影的三十年合作/合拍历程 (Cobuilding Chinese-language Cinema in the Age of Post-Coproduction: The Thirty-Year History of Film Collaboration." *Jiefangjun yishu xueyuan xuebao* 解放军艺术学院学报 (Journal of the People's Liberation Army Art Academy), no. 3 (2008): 30–35.

"Yingju xinwen" 影剧新闻 (Film and Theater News). *Yin deng* (Spotlight), no. 107 (n.d.): n.p.

Yu Muyun 余慕云. *Xianggang dianying bashinian* 香港电影八十年 (The Eighty Years of Hong Kong Cinema). Hong Kong: Xianggang quyu shizhengju, 1994.

"Yuanban *Wujian dao* daoyan Liu Weiqiang: Gangpian you Aosika shuizhun" 原版无间道导演刘伟强: 港片有奥斯卡水准 (Andrew Lau, Director of *Infernal Affairs:* "Hong Kong Offers Oscar Quality Films). *Xinxi shibao* 信息时报 (Information Times), Feb. 27, 2007. http://ent.mop.com/movie/2011776.shtml (accessed May 12, 2010).

Yung Sai-shing 容世诚. "Cong *Xuangong yanshi* dao *Xuangong yanshi:* Helihuo dianying yu wushi niandai yueyu xiqupian" 从璇宫艳史到璇宫艳史：荷里活电影与五十年代粤语戏曲片 (From *The Love Parade* to *My Kingdom for a Husband:* Hollywood Musicals and Cantonese Opera Films of the 1950s). In Ain-ling Wong, ed., *Guotai gushi,* 190–289.

Zaodong de yidai: Liushi niandai Yuepian xinxing 躁動的一代：六十年代粵片新星 (The Restless Breed: Cantonese Stars of the Sixties). Hong Kong: The Urban Council, 1996.

Zhang Fangwei 张方卫. "Sanshi niandai Guangzhou yueju shengshuai ji" 三十年代广州粤剧盛衰记 (The Rise and Fall of Cantonese Opera in Guangzhou in the 1930s). *Yueju chunqiu* 粤剧春秋 (Chronicle of Cantonese Opera), Sept. 2008. http://www.gzzxws.gov.cn/gzws/gzws/ml/42/200809/t20080916_7587.htm (accessed Feb. 15, 2010).

Zhang, Xudong. *Chinese Modernism in the Era of Reforms: Cultural Fever, Avant-Garde Fiction, and the New Chinese Cinema.* Durham, NC: Duke University Press, 1997.

Zhang, Yingjin. "Beyond Binary Imagination: Progress and Problems in Chinese Film Historiography." *Chinese Historical Review* 15, no. 1 (Spring 2008): 65–87.

———, ed. *Cinema and Urban Culture in Shanghai, 1922–1943.* Stanford, CA: Stanford University Press, 1999.

———. *Cinema, Space, and Polylocality in a Globalizing China.* Honolulu: University of Hawai'i Press, 2010.

———. "Fandui xiuzheng: Zhanzheng shiqi de Xianggang dianying yu diyu zhengzhi" 反对修正：战争时期的香港电影与地域政治 (Against Revisionism: Wartime Hong Kong Cinema and Geopolitics). *Ershiyi shiji shuangyue kan* 二十一世纪双月刊 (Twenty-first Century Bimonthly), June 2007: 104–114.

———. "Prostitution and Urban Imagination: Negotiating the Public and Private in Chinese Films of the 1930s." In Zhang, ed., *Cinema and Urban Culture in Shanghai, 1922–1943,* 160–180.

———. "Transnationalism and Translocality in Chinese Cinema." *Cinema Journal* 49, no. 3 (2010): 135–139.

Zhang, Zhen. *An Amorous History of the Silver Screen: Shanghai Cinema, 1896–1937.* Chicago: University of Chicago Press, 2006.

Zhao Weifang 赵卫防. "Wuliushi niandai jingzheng geju zhong de Xianggang Guoyu dianying gongye—jianlun Shao Yifu yu Lu Yundao zhijian de jingzheng" 五六十年代竞争割据中的香港国语电影工业一简论邵逸夫与陆运涛之间的竞争 (Hong Kong Mandarin Film Industry in the Competitive 1950s to the 1960s). *Dangdai dianying* 当代电影 (Contemporary Film), no. 4 (2006): 71–75.

Zhao Zhongyu 赵仲瑜. "Zhongguo dianying shiye de mianmian guan" 中国电影事业的面面观 (A Comprehensive Picture of Chinese Cinema), part 2. *Huabei yinghua* 华北影画 (Hua Pei Movie), no. 28 (Feb. 1943): 11.

Zheng Junli 郑君里. "Xiandai Zhongguo dianying shi lue" 现代中国电影史略 (A Synoptic History of Modern Chinese Cinema). In Dai Xiaolan 戴小兰, ed., *Zhongguo wusheng dianying* 中国无声电影 (Chinese Silent Cinema), 1385–1432. Beijing: China Film Press, 1996.

Zheng Zhengqiu 郑正秋. "Ruhe zoushang qianjin zhi lu" 如何走上前进之路 (How I Found the Progressive Road) (1933). In Chen Bo, ed., *Zhongguo zuoyi dianying yundong,* 84–86.

———. "*Zimei hua* de ziwo pipan" 姊妹花的自我批判 (Self-Criticism of My *Sister Flowers*). *Shehui yuebao* 社会月报 (Society Monthly), 1934: 39–41.

Zhong, Dafeng, Zhen Zhang, and Yingjin Zhang. "From Wenmingxi (Civilized Play) to Yingxi (Shadowplay): The Foundation of Shanghai Film Industry in the 1920s." *Asian Cinema* 9, no. 1 (1997): 45–64.

Zhou Chengren 周承人 and Li Yizhuang 李以庄. *Zaoqi Xianggang dianyingshi (1897–1945)* 早期香港电影史 1897–1945 (History of Early Hong Kong Cinema [1897–1945]). Hong Kong: Joint Publishing (Sanlian shudian), 2005.

Zhu Jidong 朱继东. "*Gongfu xiongmao* weihe mofang Zhongguo gongfu ye rang Zhongguo yingren wangchen moji?" 功夫熊猫为何模仿中国功夫也让中国影人望尘莫及? (How Does *Kung Fu Panda* Awe and Shame Chinese Filmmakers by Imitating Chinese Kung Fu?). *Zhu Jidong blog,* 2008. http://xinhuashe2007.home.news.cn/blog/a/0101000029400355D310FDBB.html (accessed July 11, 2008).

Žižek, Slavoj. "I Hear You with My Eyes; or, The Invisible Master." In Renata Salecl and Slavoj Žižek, eds., *Gaze and Voice as Love Objects,* 90–126. Durham, NC: Duke University Press, 1996.

Filmography

Alice in Wonderland (dir. Tim Burton, 2010)
Back Door (*Hou men* 后门) (dir. Li Hanxiang 李翰祥, 1960)
Berlin, Symphony of a Great City (dir. Walter Ruttmann, 1927)
The Big Road (*Da lu* 大路) (dir. Sun Yu 孙瑜, 1934)
Blood-Bathed Baoshan City (*Xuejian Baoshan cheng* 血溅宝山城) (dir. Situ Huimin 司徒慧敏, 1938)
Bride of Chucky (dir. Ronny Yu 于仁泰, 1998)
Bride of Frankenstein (dir. James Whales, 1935)
The Broadway Melody (dir. Harry Beaumont, 1929)
Calendar Girl (*Longxiang fengwu* 龙翔凤舞) (dir. Tao Qin 陶秦, 1959)
Centre Stage 阮玲玉 (dir. Stanley Kwan 关锦鹏, 1992)
Chasing Rainbows (dir. Charles Reisner, 1930)
Children of Troubled Times (*Fengyun ernü* 风云儿女) (dir. Xu Xingzhi 许幸之, 1935)
The Critical Moment (*Zuihou guantou* 最后关头) (Hong Kong Film Studios, 1938)
Crouching Tiger, Hidden Dragon (dir. Ang Lee, 2000)
The Cry of the Apes in a Deserted Valley (*Konggu yuansheng* 空谷猿声) (dir. Maxu Weibang 马徐维邦, 1930)
Dancer in the Dark (dir. Lars von Trier, 2000)
Dark Matter (dir. Shi-zheng Chen 陈士争, 2007)
Dark Water (dir. Hideo Nakata, 2002)
The Departed (dir. Martin Scorsese, 2006)
Disney High School Musical: China (*Gewu qingchun* 歌舞青春) (dir. Shi-zheng Chen, 陈士争, 2010)
Eastern Condors (*Dongfang tuying* 东方秃鹰) (dir. Sammo Hung 洪金宝, 1986)
Everlasting Regret (*Changhen ge* 长恨歌) (dir. Stanley Kwan 关锦鹏, 2005)
The Eye (*Jiangui* 见鬼) (dir. Oxide Pang, Danny Pang, 2002)
Farewell My Concubine (*Bawang jieji* 霸王别姬) (dir. Chen Kaige 陈凯歌, 1993)
A Flower Reborn (*Zaisheng hua* 再生花) (dir. Zheng Zhengqiu 郑正秋, 1934)
Frankenstein (dir. James Whales, 1931)
The Goddess (*Shennü* 神女) (dir. Wu Yonggang 吴永刚, 1934)
The Golden Dragon (*Baijin long* 白金龙) (dir. Tang Xiaodan 汤晓丹, 1933)
The Grand Duchess and the Waiter (dir. Malcolm St. Clair, 1926)
The Happy Reunion (*Xin zimei hua* 新姊妹花) (dir. Hu Peng 胡鹏, 1962)
Hard Boiled (*Lashou shentan* 辣手神探) (dir. John Woo, 1992)

Hard Target (dir. John Woo, 1993)
Hong Kong Nocturne (*Xiangjiang huayue ye* 香江花月夜) (dir. Inoue Umetsugu, 1967)
Infernal Affairs (*Wujian dao* 无间道) (dir. Wai-keung Lau 刘伟强, Siu Fai Mak 麦兆辉, 2002)
The Joyless Street (*Die Freudlose Gasse*) (dir. G. W. Pabst, 1925)
Ju-on (dir. Takashi Shimizu, 2002)
Ju-on: The Grudge (dir. Takashi Shimizu, 2004)
The Karate Kid (dir. Harald Zwart, 2010)
Kill Bill I, II (dir. Quentin Tarantino 2003, 2004)
The Kite Runner (dir. Marc Forster, 2007)
Kung Fu Panda (dir. Mark Osborne, John Stevenson, 2008)
Kung Fu Panda 2 (dir. Jennifer Yuh Nelson, 2011)
Lan Yu 蓝宇 (dir. Stanley Kwan 关锦鹏, 2001)
The Legend of the 7 Golden Vampires (dir. Roy Ward Baker, Chang Cheh, 1974).
Lord Byron of Broadway (dir. Harry Beaumont, 1930)
Love Me or Leave Me (dir. Charles Vidor, 1955)
The Love Parade (dir. Ernst Lubitsch, 1929)
Mambo Girl (Manbo nülang 曼波女郎) (dir. Yi Wen 易文, 1957)
The Marriage Circle (dir. Ernst Lubitsch, 1924)
Maternal Love (*Mu ai* 母爱) (dir. Zhu Ji 珠玑, 1961)
The Matrix trilogy (Wachowski brothers, 1999–2003)
Mid-Nightmare (*Yeban gesheng* 夜半歌声) (dir. Yuan Qiufeng 袁秋枫, 1962)
Mid-Nightmare II (*Yeban gesheng 2* 夜半歌声2) (dir. Yuan Qiufeng, 袁秋枫1963)
Mulan (dir. Tony Bancroft, Barry Cook, 1998)
The Mummy: Tomb of the Dragon Emperor (dir. Rob Cohen, 2008)
My Kingdom for a Honeymoon (*Xuangong yanshi xuji* 璇宫艳史续集) (dir. Zuo Ji 左几, 1958)
My Kingdom for a Husband (*Xuangong yanshi* 璇宫艳史) (dir. Zuo Ji 左几, 1957)
My Sassy Girl (dir. Jae-young Kwak, 2001)
My Wife, My Wife (*Yu zhi qi* 余之妻) (dir. Zuo Ji 左几, 1955)
New Movietone Follies of 1930 (dir. Benjamin Stoloff, 1930)
The New Peach Blossom Fan (*Xin taohua shan* 新桃花扇) (dir. Ouyang Yuqian 欧阳予倩, 1935)
One Hour with You (dir. Ernest Lubitsch, 1932)
Orphan Island Paradise (*Gudao tiantang* 孤岛天堂) (dir. Cai Chusheng 蔡楚生, 1939)
Our Sister Hedy (*Si qianjin* 四千金) (dir. Tao Qin 陶秦, 1957)
The Phantom Lover (*Xin yeban gesheng* 新夜半歌声) (dir. Ronny Yu 于仁泰, 1995)
The Phantom of the Opera (dir. Rupert Julian, 1925)
The Plunder of Peach and Plum (*Taoli jie* 桃李劫) (dir. Ying Yunwei 应云卫, 1934)
Rashomon (dir. Akira Kurosawa, 1950)
Red Dawn (dir. Dan Bradley, 2012)
Ringu (dir. Hideo Nakata, 1998)
Romance of a Teenage Girl (*Shaonü xin* 少女心) (dir. Chen Yun 陈云, 1966)
Romance of the Songsters (*Gelü qingchao* 歌侣情潮) (dir. Joseph Sunn 赵树燊, 1933)
Rouge (*Yanzhi kou* 胭脂扣) (dir. Stanley Kwan 关锦鹏, 1987)
Rouge Tears (*Yanzhi lei* 胭脂泪) (dir. Wu Yonggang 吴永刚, Chen Pi 陈皮, 1938)
The Sable Cicada (*Diao chan* 貂蝉) (dir. Bu Wancang 卜万苍, 1938)

Scaramouche (dir. George Sidney, 1952)
Scarface (dir. Brian De Palma, 1983)
Seven Samurai (dir. Akira Kurosawa, 1954)
Showboat (dir. Harry Pollard, 1929)
Singsong Girl Red Peony (Genü Hong Mudan 歌女红牡丹) (dir. Zhang Shichuang 张石川, 1931)
Sister Flowers (*Zimei hua* 姊妹花) (dir. Zheng Zhengqiu 郑正秋, 1933)
Sister Flowers (*Zimei hua* 姊妹花) (dir. Yang Hongguan 杨弘冠, 1940)
Sister Flowers (*Zimei hua* 姊妹花) (dir. Chen Huanwen 陈焕文, 1958)
The Sister Flowers from the South (*Nanguo zimei hua* 南国姊妹花) (dir. Li Bin 黎斌, Liang Chen 梁琛, 1939)
Small Toys (*Xiao wanyi* 小玩意) (dir. Sun Yu 孙瑜, 1933)
The Sorrowful Lute (*Pipa yuan* 琵琶怨) (dir. Zuo Ji 左几 1957)
Song at Midnight (*Yeban gesheng* 夜半歌声) (dir. Maxu Weibang 马徐维邦, 1937)
Song at Midnight (*Yeban gesheng* 夜半歌声) (dir. Yang Yanjin 杨延晋, 1985)
Song at Midnight II (*Yeban gesheng 2* 夜半歌声2) (dir. Maxu Weibang 马徐维邦, 1941)
So This Is Paris (dir. Ernst Lubitsch, 1926)
Spring Silkworms (*Chuncan* 春蚕) (dir. Cheng Bugao 程步高, 1933)
Stage Sisters (*Wutai jiemei* 舞台姐妹) (dir. Xie Jin 谢晋, 1964)
Stella Dallas (dir. Henry King, 1925)
The Stranger on the Love Scene (*Qingchang guairen* 情场怪人) (dir. Maxu Weibang 马徐维邦, 1926)
Street Angel (dir. Frank Borzage, 1928)
Street Angel (*Malu tianshi* 马路天使) (dir. Yuan Muzhi 袁牧之, 1937)
Tears of Pearl (*Zhenzhu lei* 珍珠泪) (dir. Zuo Ji 左几, 1965)
The Testament of Dr. Mabuse (dir. Fritz Lang, 1933)
Thief of Bagdad (dir. Raoul Walsh, 1925)
The Thief Prince (*Zei wangzi* 贼王子) (dir. Huo Ran 霍然, 1939)
The Third Man (dir. Carol Reed, 1949)
Three Women (dir. Ernst Lubitsch, 1924)
Tragedy of the Street (*Dirnentragödie*) (dir. Bruno Rahn, 1927)
True Love (*Lijin cangsang yi meiren* 历尽沧桑一美人) (dir. Zuo Ji 左几, 1958)
The Unholy Three (dir. Jack Conway, 1930)
The Vagabond King (dir. Ludwig Berger, 1930)
We Moderns (dir. John Francis Dillon, 1925)
White Christmas (dir. Irving Berlin, 1954)
White Heat (dir. Raoul Walsh, 1949)
Young Lovers (*Qingchun zhi lian* 青春之恋) (dir. Chen Yun 陈云, 1967)

Index

Bold page references refer to figures.

Production Notes for Wang / *Remaking Chinese Cinema: Through the Prism of Shanghai, Hong Kong, and Hollywood*

Interior designed by University of Hawaiʻi Press production staff with text in Minion Pro and display in Seria Sans LF.

Composition by Mardee Melton

Printing and binding by Sheridan Books, Inc.